CONTENTS

EDITOR
Jim Charlton

DESIGNER
Glenn LeDoux

FRONT COVER PHOTO
Zach Bahill

Back cover photo
courtesy of the
Houston Astros

Our thanks to these
peer reviewers and
designated readers:

Phil Birnbaum
Paul Wendt
Pete Palmer
Lawrence Boes
Scott Flatow
Rod Nelson
Jim Riley
Lyle Spatz

ISBN 1-933599-04-9

EDITOR'S NOTE

ANY JOURNAL that includes one article by the estimable Pete Palmer is a worthy publication. *BRJ 35* serves up two offerings by Pete. He and Gary Gillette discuss the (mostly) mirage of the attendance boost provided by interleague games. This should give satisfaction to those who (mostly) dislike the practice instituted by MLB in 1997, including your editor. Palmer also teams up with Bill Deane, who updates Pete's 1985 article, which asked the question "Does Clutch Pitching Exist?"

Also weighing in with two articles apiece are David Smith, David Vincent, and Trent McCotter. Smith answers the question "Does walking the leadoff batter lead to big innings?" as Tim McCarver contends. McCotter, in his articles on consecutive times reaching base, takes the title away from Ted Williams and gives it to . . . I will leave it the reader to find out the surprise recipient. And Vincent, the guru of the home run, explains why rule changes in 1920 affected home run production. David also takes us behind the scenes at Fenway to show us a different view of the game.

There are two beautifully researched articles both written by SABR-Yoseloff grant winners. One is by Thomas Aiello on the 1932 Negro Southern League team, the Monroe Monarchs. The other is a riveting account by Gene Carney, who revisits the Black Sox, this time investigating the trial of Joe Jackson that took placed in Milwaukee in 1924.

In 1998 *The National Pastime* published a cover article by three of SABR's most respected historians that debunked the story that Bill Veeck had planned to buy the Phillies in 1943 and integrate the team. They contended that the colorful Veeck had mostly spun this tale in later years and that, at best, he had thought of the idea at the time but never acted on it. In this issue of *BRJ* another respected historian, Jules Tygiel, answers with a balanced rejoinder that says there may be truth to Veeck's story. It is well worth reading.

There are many other fine articles to enjoy, including George Michael's thank-you for mystery photos solved, Stew Thornley showing some reserve, and Steve Steinberg on the Curse of the Bambino. Or, rather, not the Bambino.

Lastly, the cover shot, dubbed the "Venus" photo, stumped everyone I showed it to until we titled it. Physicists Dave Baldwin (whose resume includes a bit of pitching), Terry Bahill, and Alan Nathan explain the nickel and dime pitch with a series of illuminating photos and readable text than even I could understand. And I for one did not know that the shape of the two pieces of leather that cover a baseball are known as the "ovals of Cassini" until the three explained that as well. The back cover photo, illustrating Bill Carle's article on one-team players, needs no explanation.

Jim Charlton

THOMAS AIELLO

The Composition of Kings
The Monroe Monarchs and the Negro Southern League, 1932

When Negro National League officials agreed to close operations for 1932 due to the hard realities of the Great Depression, the usually minor Negro Southern League and the newly created East-West Colored League became black baseball's "major leagues." Low attendance figures, disillusionment with the National League collapse, doubts about the ability of the leagues to complete a season, and the complications of player trade disputes led to a muddled portrait of black baseball in 1932. The collapse of the East-West in early July didn't help. The cumulative result was an historiographical lapse in coverage of black baseball in 1932. But baseball happened in the black communities that year—baseball with important consequences for the development of the Negro Leagues—and one of the year's most relevant teams was the Monroe Monarchs.

Monroe was in the northeast corner of Louisiana, the hub of a poor cotton-farming region in the Mississippi Delta approximately 70 miles from the river and 40 from the Arkansas border.[1] Its 10,112 African Americans constituted 38.9% of the city's 26,028 residents. Almost 43% of the black population was out of work, and almost 17% were unable to read. 19,041 of Ouachita Parish's 54,337 were black. Of those, close to 10,000 were gainfully employed and slightly more than 3,000 were illiterate.[2] In 1919, Monroe earned the moniker "lynch law center of Louisiana," and from the turn of the century to the close of 1918, the region witnessed 30 lynchings.[3] As Michael Lomax demonstrated in his study of 19th-century black baseball entrepreneurship, the Negro Leagues as a "unifying element" of a community is so common and self-evident a conclusion that it lacks any tangible edifying power.[4] Monroe's situation, however, served as a paradigmatic example of the need for this "unifying element." And unlike many small town baseball teams, the Monarchs' impact extended far beyond Monroe's city limits.

Fred Stovall wanted his Monarchs to be part of a new league in 1932 rather than the 1931 Texas League, which his team won. A white Dallas native, Stovall came to Monroe in 1917, and by 1932 owned both the Stovall Drilling Company and the J. M. Supply Company, among other enterprises, allowing him to found his black baseball team in 1930 with drilling employees. He never incorporated the team, even after its success led him to hire veteran professionals. Even before the pros arrived, however, Stovall built his team—and the larger black community, many of whom he employed at his various businesses—Casino Park, which included not only a ball field but a swim-

ming pool and dance pavilion. Historian Robert Peterson echoes contemporary reports that the erection of the stadium was largely the product of generosity. (Of course, Stovall was a businessman, and the entry fees of 25 and 50 cents demonstrated that profit was also a motive.[5])

Through a series of negotiations, Stovall maneuvered his team into the newly formed Negro Southern League for 1932, with a far more prestigious roster of teams than Monroe had ever faced. The Atlanta Black Crackers, Birmingham Black Barons, Memphis Red Sox, Montgomery Grey Sox, Little Rock Greys, and Nashville Elite Giants were joined by newcomers the Indianapolis ABCs, Louisville Black Caps, and Chicago American Giants (under the new ownership of Robert A. Cole), along with the Monarchs.[6]

The Monarchs acquitted themselves well the first half of the season. They were 33–7 on the Fourth of July. Chicago's 30–9 record kept them slightly behind the Monarchs. "All is not well in the Southern League," the *Chicago Defender* reported. League President Reuben B. Jackson issued a ruling at the close of the first-half schedule that, due to its use of players claimed by other teams, two Memphis Red Sox games against Cole's American Giants would be forfeited. Rather than nullifying the outcomes, however, Jackson ruled the games to be Chicago wins. The controversial decision gave Chicago the first-half pennant.[7]

The *Louisiana Weekly* acknowledged the league ruling on the games, but declared Monroe the victor anyway. The paper's coverage noted the protests mailed to the league office by Monroe fans, arguing that the NSL attempted "to give the Chicago nine something they have not rightfully won. All the southern papers as well as some of the northern and eastern papers carry the standing just as it is with Monroe leading and naturally, the fans are not fooled."[8]

Various reports of the first-half standings led to uncertainty. The *Defender*'s first half standings gave Chicago first place with a 34–7 record, while Monroe was 33–7.[9] The *Morning World* reported that the Monarchs' record trumped Chicago's 28–9.[10] As of mid-August, the remainder of the Southern League season seemed in doubt, with Monroe (according to the *Defender*) not playing any league games, and Chicago canceling a scheduled trip to Memphis. Montgomery, Atlanta, Little Rock, and Birmingham had already abandoned league play.[11]

In this confused state, Nashville took the second-half pennant. Although Chicago and Nashville began referring to the NSL championship as the only championship, the Pittsburgh Crawfords (who played games against the East-West and the Southern, not officially joining either in 1932) scheduled a series with the Monroe Monarchs billed in most black weeklies as the "World Series."[12] The season had been as beneficial for the Crawfords as it had for the Monarchs. Gus Greenlee, the team's owner, took the opportunity created by the financial destitution of the leagues to lure the best players from its Pittsburgh rival, the Homestead Grays. The Crawfords moved from beneath the shadow of Cumberland Posey's Grays to become a premier team in their own right. When playing at home, the Crawfords played in the newly opened Greenlee Park, which held 6,000 fans.[13]

The Monarchs opened their World Series in front of a capacity crowd on September 3. "Returns of the games at Pittsburgh will be given at Tenth and Desiard Streets every day starting about 2 o'clock," announced the *Morning World*. "This is the first time a Negro southern team has won the right to take part in the Negro World Series and the entire south is pulling for the Monarchs to win the series." The first game in front of that crowd was unsuccessful for the Monarchs, while the second was a win. The Monarchs broke a 1–1 tie in the 10th inning for what would be their only World Series victory. The following day was Labor Day, and the Pittsburgh fans celebrated "Louisiana Day" in honor of the visiting Monarchs as the team from Monroe lost a doubleheader. "The hustling, whole-hearted assault of the Monarchs, even though behind, made a hit with Greenlee field fans," reported the *Courier*. "Rounds of applause greeted their determined efforts to stage a batting rally at two or three different points." One of the Labor Day doubleheader losses served as an exhibition game, "with gate receipts going to charity," so the Monarchs returned home down two games to one.[14]

For the first home game, Stovall made arrangements with area railroads, both the Missouri Pacific and Illinois Central, "for the purpose of bringing spectators from Little Rock, New Orleans, Alexandria, Shreveport and intervening points." Though Chicago defeated Nashville four games to three to take the "Dixie World Series," the Monarchs held a Negro Southern League pennant-raising ceremony prior to the opening inning of the first home game against Pittsburgh. The game that followed served as something of an anticlimax as the teams played to a 6–6 tie before darkness halted the contest. The following day, a September 11 Crawfords win made them one short of series victory. On September 12, the Monarchs lost once and for all.[15]

The Crawfords' 1932 squad was managed by Oscar Charleston, who also played first base. Josh Gibson, Judy Johnson, Satchel Paige, and Ted Radcliffe were also on the team. Those players are now in the pantheon of Negro Leagues immortals. The Crawfords, too, continued to be a successful franchise even after its stars moved to other teams. Monroe, however, quickly faded away. The team resumed play in a reformulated "minor" Dixie League the following season and dissolved by 1936. But many of its players—who contributed to such a successful season and brought a small Southern town, "the lynch law center of Louisiana," to the precipice of a national championship (however makeshift it may have been)—went on to successful careers in larger markets.

Indeed, their talent was prolific. Homer "Blue Goose" Curry (a late-season addition from Memphis) played left field and pitched for the team, later enjoying a long and distinguished career with the Baltimore Elite Giants, Philadelphia Stars, and (again) Memphis Red Sox. Catcher Harry Else went on to play in the mid-1930s with the Kansas City Monarchs, making the East-West All-Star game in 1936. Monroe's shortstop, Leroy Morney, had a well-traveled but substantial all-star career for a variety of Negro National League teams through 1944. Pitchers Barney Morris and Samuel Thompson enjoyed success after leaving Monroe, Morris with the New York Cubans and Thompson with the Philadelphia Stars and Chicago American Giants. Right fielder Zollie Wright was another former Monarch to become an East-West All-Star, playing for Baltimore, New York, and Philadelphia. Roy Parnell played center field and pitched for the Monarchs. He played on a variety of minor Southern teams before coming to Monroe. His most productive years came with the Philadelphia Stars in the 1940s, and his success earned him candidacy for a special 2006 Negro and Pre-Negro Leagues election to the National Baseball Hall of Fame. Though Parnell was ultimately not included in the final group of enshrined players, his candidacy validates his talent. But the player who would become the most famous on the team did not join it until late August, when he came to Monroe from the Austin Black Senators. Hilton Smith's impressive showing against the Monarchs convinced the team to purchase his rights for the remainder of the season, and he would stay in Monroe for two more years. Smith would become a powerful pitcher for the Kansas City Monarchs in the 1930s and 1940s, though his career was often overshadowed by fellow Kansas City pitcher (and former 1932 World Series foe) Satchel Paige. He is now a member of the National Baseball Hall of Fame.[16]

The statistics of these players and the rest of the 1932 Monarchs that follow are necessarily incomplete. The statistical inconsistencies of the Negro Leagues were only exacerbated in the Monarchs' situation by (1) a newly created league struggling to stay afloat in the face of the Depression and (2) the realities of a small-town Southern team two years from its inception and four from its eventual demise. Monroe had a viable black press in 1932, though its *Southern Broadcast* did not begin until the middle of the year. Sherman Briscoe founded the *Broadcast*, which remained a solvent publication until 1939. Though Briscoe went on to serve as a press officer for the U.S. Department of Agriculture and Executive Director of the National Newspaper Publishers Association, his paper's longevity did not match his own. Only scattered editions of the *Southern Broadcast* from 1936 and 1937 now exist.[17]

Many of the surviving box scores of the Monarchs' 1932 season come from the town's white newspapers, the *Monroe Morning World* and the *Monroe News Star*, which, when compared with far larger mainstream newspapers in far larger markets, gave a significant amount of coverage to the local black team. Though many African-American papers throughout the nation published reports of the Monarchs' games, fewer carried box scores. The *Louisiana Weekly*, *Memphis World*, *Atlanta Daily World*, *Chicago Defender*, and *Pittsburgh Courier* were among those who did. What follows is an attempt to take some of the raw data from those papers and from other sources to create a statistical archive of the 1932 season—a measured documentation of a team whose prior appearances in scholarly work has been scarce and woefully unmeasured.

Part 2 of this study provides the Monarchs' schedule and results, along with win and loss totals divided by month and by team played. It compares Monroe's played schedule with the printed schedule as announced by the Negro Southern League. Finally, the section compares the author's results to other statistical tallies from encyclopedic accounts that are incomplete and incorrect. Part 3 provides a timeline of player and personnel acquisitions prior to and during the season. Part 4 catalogues the Monarchs' 1932 roster and compares the complete roster to the accounts of other encyclopedic treatments that are incomplete and incorrect. The fifth and final part provides a statistical analysis of the available data for the Monarchs' 1932 season. It includes an evaluation of the statistics of Monarchs' opponents and leaders from other leagues to gauge the comparative success of the team.

Throughout most of the 1930s, the Monroe Monarchs remained on the periphery of Negro Leagues baseball. But the 1932 team proved a success. A questionable midseason decision by the president of the Negro Southern League kept the Monarchs from a pennant, but their participation in what most of the nation considered the black baseball championship for 1932 gave the team its proverbial 15 minutes of fame. What follows is an attempt to document those 15 minutes of fame, to return them to black baseball's historical memory.

Part 2
1932 Monroe Monarchs Schedule and Results

EXG: Exhibition Game   NR: No Report   NBX: No Box Score Available   NPT: No Pitcher Tally Available

Date	Opponent		Score	Note
3/25	v. Pittsburgh (EXG)	L	2-11	NBX
3/27	v. Pittsburgh (EXG)	W	6-3	
4/3	v. Chicago (EXG)[18]	W	7-0	
4/4	v. Chicago (EXG)	W	8-5	
4/10	v. Houston (EXG)	W	1-0	
4/11	v. Houston (EXG)	W	5-2	
4/17	@ Houston (EXG)	L	3-4	
4/18[a]	@ Houston (EXG)	L	5-10	NBX
4/22	@ Little Rock	W	6-1	NBX
4/23	@ Little Rock	W	6-3	NBX
4/24	@ Little Rock	W	15-6	NBX, NPT
	@ Little Rock	W	8-3	NBX, NPT
4/30	@ Memphis	W	6-1	
5/1	@ Memphis	L	2-3	
	@ Memphis	L	2-3	
5/2	@ Memphis	W	9-1	
5/6	v. Cleveland	W	4-3	
5/7	v. Cleveland	W	5-2	
5/8	v. Cleveland	W	6-0	
	v. Cleveland	W	4-0	
5/12	v. Rayville (EXG)	W	27-3	NBX
5/14	v. Little Rock	W	7-1	
5/15	v. Little Rock	W	6-1	
	v. Little Rock	W	8-2	
5/16	v. Little Rock	W	4-3	
5/21	v. Birmingham	L	1-5	
5/22	v. Birmingham	W	2-0	
	v. Birmingham	W	1-0	
5/28	@ Montgomery	W	12-2	NBX
5/29	@ Montgomery	W	10-6	NBX
	@ Montgomery	W	4-2	NBX
5/30	@ Montgomery	W	8-1	NBX
6/5				
6/6	@ Nashville	W	4-2	
	@ Nashville	L	7-8	
6/7[b]				
6/11	v. Montgomery	W	3-0	
6/12	v. Montgomery	W	4-2	
	v. Montgomery	W	3-2	
6/13	v. Montgomery	W	7-2	
6/18	v. Nashville	W	16-5	
6/19	v. Nashville	W	2-3	
	v. Nashville	L	5-0	
6/20	v. Nashville	W	6-4	
6/25	@ Montgomery	W	6-3	
6/26	@ Montgomery	L	1-7	
	@ Montgomery	W	8-1	
6/27	@ Montgomery	W	2-0	

Date	Opponent		Score	Note
7/2	v. Memphis	W	6-5	
7/3	v. Memphis	W	5-3	
7/4	v. Memphis	W	6-1	
	v. Memphis[19]	W	8-2	
7/9	@ Memphis	L	6-7	
7/10	@ Memphis	W	15-2	
	@ Memphis	L	7-13	
7/11	@ Memphis	L	7-8	
7/16	@ Chicago	L	1-2	
7/17	@ Chicago	W	9-4	
	@ Chicago	L	2-4	
7/18	@ Chicago	L	6-1	NBX
7/19	@ Chicago	L	1-2	NBX
7/24	@ Louisville	W	4-1	NBX
	@ Louisville	L	3-4	NBX
7/31	v. Memphis	W	2-0	
	v. Memphis	L	0-1	
8/1	v. Memphis	W	10-0	
	v. Memphis	W	5-4	
8/7	v. Algiers[d]	W	4-2	
	v. Algiers	L	2-3	
8/8	v. Algiers	W	10-1	
8/11	@ Lincoln Giants[e]	W	7-3	NBX
8/12	@ Lincoln Giants	L	1-3	NBX, NPT
8/13	@ Algiers	W	5-0	NBX, NPT
8/14	@ Algiers	W	17-2	NBX
8/15	@ Algiers	L	2-6	NBX
8/16	@ Algiers	W	NR	NBX, NPT
8/20	@ Austin	W	5-2	NBX
8/21	@ Austin	L	2-3	NBX
8/22	@ Austin	W	5-4	NBX
8/28	v. Austin	L	2-4	
8/29	v. Austin	W	3-2	
8/30	v. Austin	W	10-0	
9/3	@ Pittsburgh	L	3-7	NBX, NPT
9/4	@ Pittsburgh	W	2-1	
9/5	@ Pittsburgh	L	2-7	
	@ Pittsburgh	L	2-9	NBX
9/10	v. Pittsburgh	T	6-6	
9/11[20]	v. Pittsburgh	L	4-11	
9/12	v. Pittsburgh	L	6-9	NBX
9/13	v. Pittsburgh[g] (EXG)	L	17-5	NBX, NPT
9/17	@ Lincoln Giants (EXG)	L	10-26	NBX
9/18	@ Lincoln Giants (EXG)	W	9-6	NBX
9/25	@ Lincoln Giants (EXG)	W	4-3	NBX
	@ Lincoln Giants (EXG)	L	1-2	NBX
10/6	v. Little Rock (EXG)	?	?-?	NBX, NPT
	v. Little Rock (EXG)	?	?-?	NBX, NPT
10/7	v. Little Rock (EXG)	?	?-?	NBX, NPT

NOTES

(a) Season begins. (b) MMW has them at 22–5, meaning they have assumed four games versus Nashville. (c) First half ends. (d) Played in New Orleans. (e) Played in Alexandria. (f) Available box scores come from the following 1932 sources: *Monroe Morning World* (March 27, April 4, 5, 11, 12, May 7–9, 15, 22, June 12–14, 19–21, July 3–5, August 1, 2, 8, 9, 29, 30, 31, September 5, 11, 12); *Monroe News Star* (May 16, 17, 23); *Memphis Commercial Appeal* (May 1–3, July 10–12); *Pittsburgh Courier* (September 10); *Kansas City Call* (April 22); *Chicago Defender* (June 11, July 2, 16, 23); *Atlanta Daily World* (June 30); *Afro-American*, (July 23); and *Louisiana Weekly* (September 17). (g) Played in New Orleans.

Win–Loss Totals

	W	L	T	Win%
Exhibition[21]	8	5	0	.615
Regular Season	51	20	0	.718
(Month-by-Month)				
(April)	(5)	(0)	(0)	(1.00)
(May)	(15)	(3)	(0)	(.833)
(June)	(11)	(3)	(0)	(.786)
(July)	(8)	(9)	(0)	(.471)
(August)	(12)	(5)	(0)	(.706)
World Series	1	5	1	.143
TOTAL	60	30	1	.659

Win/Loss Breakdown by Team

	W	L	T	Win%
Algiers Giants	5	2	0	.714
Austin Black Senators	4	2	0	.667
Birmingham Black Barons	2	1	0	.667
Chicago American Giants	3	4	0	.429
Cleveland Cubs	4	0	0	1.00
Houston Black Buffaloes	2	2	0	.500
Lincoln Giants (Alexandria)	3	3	0	.500
Little Rock Greys	8	0	0	1.00
Louisville Black Caps	1	1	0	.500
Memphis Red Sox	10	6	0	.625
Montgomery Grey Sox	11	1	0	.917
Nashville Elite Giants	4	2	0	.667
Pittsburgh Crawfords	2	6	1	.222
Rayville Sluggers	1	0	0	1.00
TOTAL	60	30	1	.659

Monroe's Original First-Half Schedule
(As Announced by the Negro Southern League in March 1932[22])

April	@ Little Rock (23, 24, 25)
	@ Memphis (30)
May	@ Memphis (1, 2)
	v. Cleveland (6, 7, 8)
	v. Little Rock (14, 15, 16)
	v. Birmingham (20, 21, 22)
	@ Montgomery (28, 29, 30)
June	@ Nashville (5, 6, 7)
	@ Little Rock (10, 11, 12)
	v. Nashville (18, 19, 20)
	v. Little Rock (25, 26, 27)
July	v. Memphis (2, 3, 4)

Monroe's Original Second-Half Schedule
(As Announced by the Negro Southern League in March 1932[23])

July	@ Memphis (9, 10, 11)
	@ Chicago (16, 17, 18)
	@ Louisville (23, 24, 25)
	@ Memphis (30, 31)
August	@ Memphis (1)
	v. Knoxville (6, 7, 8)
	OPEN (13-16)
	v. Memphis (21, 22, 23)
	@ Nashville (28, 29, 30)
September	v. Louisville (3, 4, 5)
	@ Montgomery (10, 11, 12)

Comparative Tallies of Other Sources

Robert Peterson's *Only the Ball Was White* and Dick Clark and Larry Lester's *The Negro Leagues Book* both give Monroe's first-half total as follows: 33 wins, 7 losses, a percentage of .825.[24]

John Holway's *The Complete Book of Baseball's Negro Leagues* offered a season total for the Southern League teams, and seems incredibly mistaken with his tally of 26 wins, 22 losses, a percentage of .542.[25]

The Monroe *Morning World*'s first-half standings were 33 wins, 7 losses, a percentage of .825.[26]

The *Pittsburgh Courier* did not print any final first half standings, but their standings as of (and including) July 3 seem to match my count: 31 wins, 7 losses, a percentage of .816.[27]

As part of its pre-World Series coverage, the *Courier* printed its breakdown of all of Monroe's games:[28]

Opponent	# Games	W	L
Memphis	13	8	5
Little Rock	12	12	0
Montgomery	12	11	1
Nashville	8	5	3
Louisville	2	1	1
Birmingham	3	2	1
J. Brown's Chicago	5	1	4
New Orleans	7	5	2
Austin	3	2	1
Cleveland	4	4	0
Cole's Chi. Giants	3	3	0
Houston	5	3	2
Crawfords	2	1	1
Alexandria	3	2	1
TOTAL	82	60	22

Part 3

Timeline of 1932 Player/ Personnel Acquisitions

2/27	Monroe admitted to the newly-formed Negro Southern League at its Nashville meeting[29]
3/23	The Monarchs purchase "Red" Murray (P) from the New York Black Yankees[30]
3/27	The Monarchs purchase Dick Mathews (P) from the New Orleans Black Pelicans[31]
4/7	The Monarchs purchase Elbert Williams (P) from the Cuban House of David[32]
4/9	The Monarchs reduce the team to the required 14-player roster[33]
4/19	The Monarchs acquire Roy "Red" Parnell (P-OF) and Chuffie Alexander (OF-IF) from the Houston Black Buffaloes[34]
5/14-16	The Monarchs add Leland Foster to the pitching staff.[35]
7/9-19	The Monarchs acquire Samuel "Sad Sam" Thompson (P) from Indianapolis.[36]
8/11	The Monarchs acquire Homer "Blue Goose" Curry (P) and Bob Harvey (P) from the Memphis Red Sox[37]
8/20-22	The Monarchs acquire "Red" Murray (P) from the Memphis Red Sox[38]
8/31	The Monarchs acquire Hilton Smith (P) from the Austin Black Senators.[39]

Part 4

1932 Monroe Monarchs Roster Breakdown and Comparison

The roster compiled by the author precedes rosters presented by three other sources. When considered with the acquisition list from Part 3 and the statistical analysis from Part 5, the presentation of the following rosters constitutes an inherent argument for the author's version of the team's list of players. This should *not* be construed as an indictment of the other versions, however.

The rosters demonstrate the ease with which inconsistencies can develop. The confusion of the season has led to historiographical confusion. Additionally, the final three lists appear in reference books containing the rosters of hundreds of Negro League teams. The author has focused on one team in one season.

Discrepancies will never fully disappear. The author's compilation below is not (and *cannot be*) definitive, but seeks to provide a more accurate count of the contributing players.

The 1932 Monroe Monarchs as Compiled by the Author

Core Position Players

Morney, Leroy	SS
Saunders, Augustus	2B
Wright, Zollie	RF
Dallas, Porter	3B
Else, Harry	C
Walker, W.	LF
Alexander, Chuffie	1B
Parnell, Roy	CF-P (and reserve 3B)
Curry, Homer	LF-P (late addition)

Core Pitchers

Matthews, Dick	P
Murray, Red	P
Morris, Barney	P
Williams, Elbert	P
Harvey, Bob	P (late addition)

Reserves

Harris, Samuel	OF (all), 3B, PH
Walker, H.[40]	C, LF
Johnson, Frank	LF, MGR
Sheppard, Ray	IF (all), P, PH
Gillespie, Murray	P (first half, returning for World Series)[41]
Smith, Hilton	P (late addition)
Thompson, Samuel	P (acquired midseason)

Players of Brief Consequence

Heller, (name unknown)	preseason 1B
Burnham, Willie	preseason P
Markham, (Johnny?)	preseason P
Sias, (name unknown)	preseason 3B
Carter, Marlin	preseason 2B
Sanders, Samuel	preseason P
Foster, Leland	reserve P (appeared for 2/3 inning against Little Rock on May 16, and 2/3 of an inning against Birmingham on May 21)
Purvis, (name unknown)	P (appeared in the second game of a May 29 doubleheader against Montgomery, earning the win)

The 1932 Monroe Monarchs as Compiled by Dick Clark and Larry Lester

From Dick Clark and Larry Lester, eds. *The Negro Leagues Book* (Cleveland: Society for American Baseball Research, 1994), 109.

? Alexander (Chuffy)	1B
Homer Allen	P
Willie Burnham	P
Marlin Cater (Mel)	SS
Homer Curry (Goose)	OF
Porter Dallas (Big Boy)	3B
Harry Else	C
Leland Foster	P
Murray Gillespie	P
Samuel Harris	OF, P
Bill Harris	C
David Harvey (Bill)	P
Frank Johnson	OF
James Liggons	P
Dick Matthews	P
P.D. Moore	C
Leroy Morney	SS
Barney Morris	P
Harold Morris	P
? Murray	P
Roy Parnell (Red)	CF, P
? Pervis	P
Bob Saunders*	2B
Ray Sheppard	1B, 3B
Hilton Smith	P
Samuel Thompson (Sad Sam)	P
H. Walker	C, 1F
W. Walker	OF
Graham H. Williams	P
Zollie Wright	RF, LF

* In some of the printed box scores of the season, Saunders is listed as "Bob," thereby creating this discrepancy. But Saunders was the only team member to settle in Monroe after his playing days. He lived until 1993. In 1992 he was interviewed by Paul J. Letlow, sports editor of the *Monroe News Star*. In that interview Saunders acknowledged that some had called him "Bob," but that his name—and his preference—was Augustus.

The 1932 Monroe Monarchs as Compiled by John Holway

From John Holway, *The Complete Book of Baseball's Negro Leagues: The Other Half of Baseball History* (Fern Park, FL: Hastings House Publishers, 2001), 292–293. The Holway book includes batting averages and/or pitching wins and losses. These are included and can be compared with the compiled statistics from Part 5: Statistical Analysis of the Available Data for the 1932 Monroe Monarchs.

Chuff Alexander	.293	Graham Williams	10-5
Bob Saunders	.225	Dick Matthews	7-5
Leroy Morney	.313	Big Boy Morris	6-4
Big Boy Dallas	.342	Red Parnell	5-1
Zolley Wright	.289	Purvis	1-0
Red Parnell	.500	Sandy Thompson	0-1
Hoss Walker	.107	Rube Curry	0-1
Bill Harris	.200	Square Moore	0-1
		Bob Harvey	0-1
		Yellowhorse Morris	0-1
		Murray Gillespie	0-2

The 1932 Monroe Monarchs as Compiled by James A. Riley

From James A. Riley, *The Biographical Encyclopedia of the Negro Baseball Leagues* (New York: Carroll and Graf Publishers, Inc., 1994), 28, 30–31, 136, 157–158, 206–207, 209, 266, 267, 292, 319, 358–359, 363, 432, 482, 520, 565, 568–569, 569–570, 605, 621, 698, 711, 723–725, 746, 781–782, 809, 811, 835, 848, 850, 884–885.

Alexander, Chuffy, OF, IF
Allen, Homer, P
Burnham, Willie "Bee," P
Carter, Marlin "Mel" "Pee Wee" Theodore, 3B
Curry, Homer "Blue Goose" "Rube," P, OF
Dallas, Porter "Big Boy," 3B
Else, Harry, C
English, HD, officer
Foster, Leland, P
Gillespie, Murray "Lefty," P
Harris, Bill, C, OF
Harris, Samuel "Sam," OF
Johnson, Frank, OF, MGR
Liggons, James, OF
Matthews, Dick, P
Moore, P.D. "Square," C
Morney, Leroy, SS
Morris, Barney "Big Ad" "Big Boy," P
Morris, Harold "Yellowhorse," P
Parnell, Roy "Red," P
Pervis, P
Saunders, Bob, 2B
Sheppard, Ray, P
Smith, Hilton, P
Stovall, Fred, Owner
Thompson, Samuel, P
Walker, Hoss, C
Walker, W., LF
White, Clarence "Red," P
Williams, Elbert, P
Williams, Graham, P
Wright, Zollie, RF

Other Monarchs Players Listed in Riley's Biographical Encyclopedia for Years Other Than 1932

Willard Jesse Brown, CF, 1934
Lloyd "Ducky" "Bear Man" Davenport, OF, 1934
Otis Henry, IF, 1934
John Mathew "Johnny" Markham, P, date not listed
Zearlee "Jiggs" Maxwell, 3B, 1931
Eldridge "Chili" "Ed" Mayweather, 1B, 1934
B. Muse, 2B, SS, 1934
Willie "Bill" Simms, OF, 1934
Thomas "Tom" "Big Train" Parker, P, 1934
Ernest Smith, ?, mid-1930s

Part 5

Statistical Analysis of the Available Data for the 1932 Monroe Monarchs

Team and individual totals based on available box scores. Highlights or significant figures from games with accompanying newspaper descriptions, but lacking box scores, will be noted following the available box score data. (Pitching wins, however, are, where appropriate, included in the statistical data from newspaper reports as well as box scores.) Exhibition games with box scores are included in the aggregate. Since the only constant among the available box scores are "at-bats," "hits," and "runs," these are the categories used to derive player and team statistics. The players are listed in order of appearance.

Season Totals Listed in descending order by number of at-bats

HITTING	AB	H	R	E	2B	3B	HR	SB	RBI	SAC	BA[42]
Morney, Leroy, SS	230	81	55	21	11	10	2	14	5	2	.352
Wright, Zollie, RF	218	57	35	2	7	5	5	3	12	5	.261
Saunders, Augustus, 2B	205	54	22	14	6	0	0	4	13	2	.263
Parnell, Roy, CF(PH)(P)(3B)	198	67	40	5	13	10	1	8	30	2	.338
Alexander, Chuffie, 1B(PH)	194	52	31	10	7	2	1	8	6	7	.268
Dallas, Porter, 3B	196	59	29	15	9	0	4	5	6	4	.301
Walker, W., LF(CF)(PH)[43]	170	38	20	1	3	0	1	3	9	7	.224
Else, Harry, C	165	39	19	4	6	3	0	2	7	1	.236
Harris, Samuel, CF,LF,RF,3B,PH	99	18	10	1	2	0	0	2	4	3	.182
Morris, Barney, P	60	8	7	3	0	0	0	0	0	0	.133
Williams, Elbert, P(PH)	48	7	4	1	1	0	0	0	2	3	.146
Matthews, Dick, P	43	8	2	0	1	0	0	0	1	1	.186
Sheppard, Ray,2B,1B,SS,PH,P	24	8	2	0	2	0	0	0	0	0	.333
Curry, Homer, LF	22	9	4	0	2	0	0	1	1	0	.409
Heller, (name unknown), 1B	24	5	5	0	1	0	1	0	0	0	.208
Walker, Hoss, C(LF)[44]	14	5	6	0	0	0	0	0	0	0	.357
Johnson, Frank, LF(CF)(PH)(M)	14	1	2	0	0	0	0	2	1	0	.071
Carter, Marlin, 2B	6	2	1	0	0	1	0	0	0	0	.333
Sias, (name unknown), 3b	6	0	0	1	0	0	0	0	0	0	.000
Murray, Red, P(PH)	5	1	1	0	0	0	0	0	0	0	.200
Smith, Hilton, P(PH)	3	0	0	0	0	0	0	0	0	0	.000
Markham, (Johnny?), P	2	2	0	0	0	0	0	0	0	0	1.000
Burnham, Willie, p	1	1	0	0	0	0	0	0	0	0	1.000
Sanders, Samuel, P	1	1	0	0	0	0	0	0	0	0	1.000
Harvey, Bob, P	1	0	0	1	0	0	0	0	0	0	.000
Foster, Leland, P	0	0	0	0	0	0	0	0	0	0	.000

PITCHING	W	L
Matthews, Dick, P	14	6
Morris, Barney, P	14	6
Williams, Elbert, P	13	8
Parnell, Roy, P	8	0
Murray, Red, P	2	0
Gillespie, Murray, P	1	1
Harvey, Bob, P	0	2
Purvis, (name unknown), P	1	0
Thompson, Samuel	0	1
Curry, Homer	0	1

1932 Monroe Monarchs Team Statistics[45]

W	L	T	Win%	ShO	ShO Against	Runs Scored				Runs Allowed			
						H1	H2	WS	Season	H1	H2	WS	Season
60	30	1	.659[46]	13	1	302	153	25	480	141	88	50	279

AB	H	R[47]	E	2B	3B	HR	SB	RBI	SAC	BA[48]
1949	523	295	80	71	31	15	52	97	37	.268

Derivative Statistics

The given statistics are few, and only for offensive categories. While doubles, triples, and home runs were consistently provided in all formats, regardless of newspaper, stolen bases, RBI, and sacrifices were not. Therefore, in the interest of consistency and accurate representation, only statistics derivative of the consistent numbers are created below. A brief description of the meaning of each statistic appears in a corresponding footnote.

	BA[49]	SLG[50]	TB[51]	ISO[52]	HRR[53]
Morney, Leroy, ss	.352	.513	118	.161	.009
Wright, Zollie, rf	.261	.408	89	.146	.023
Saunders, Augustus, 2b	.263	.293	60	.029	.000
Parnell, Roy, cf(ph)(p)(3b)	.338	.520	103	.182	.005
Alexander, Chuffie, 1b(ph)	.268	.340	66	.072	.005
Dallas, Porter, 3b	.301	.408	80	.107	.020
Walker, W., lf(cf)(ph)	.224	.259	44	.035	.006
Else, Harry, c	.236	.309	51	.073	.000
Harris, Samuel, cf,lf,rf,3b,ph	.182	.202	20	.020	.000
Morris, Barney, p	.133	.133	8	.000	.000
Williams, Elbert, p(ph)	.146	.167	8	.021	.000
Matthews, Dick, p	.186	.209	9	.023	.000
Sheppard, Ray,2b,1b,ss,ph,p	.333	.417	10	.083	.000
Curry, Homer, lf	.409	.500	11	.227	.000
Heller, (name unknown), 1b	.208	.375	9	.167	.042
Walker, Hoss, c(lf)	.357	.357	5	.000	.000
Johnson, Frank, lf(cf)(ph)(m)	.071	.071	1	.000	.000
Carter, Marlin, 2b	.333	.667	4	.333	.000
Sias, (name unknown), 3b	.000	.000	0	.000	.000
Murray, Red, p(ph)	.200	.200	1	.000	.000
Smith, Hilton, p(ph)	.000	.000	0	.000	.000
Markham, (Johnny?), p	1.000	1.000	2	.000	.000
Burnham, Willie, p	1.000	1.000	1	.000	.000
Sanders, Samuel, p	1.000	1.000	1	.000	.000
Harvey, Bob, p	.000	.000	0	.000	.000
Foster, Leland, p	.000	.000	0	.000	.000

World Series (3 through 12 September)

The players are listed in order of appearance.

	AB	H	R	E	2B	3B	HR	SB	RBI	SAC	BA[54]
Alexander, Chuffie, 1b	12	2	1	0	0	0	0	0	0	0	.167
Morney, Leroy, ss	14	9	7	1	3	2	0	0	0	0	.642
Parnell, Roy, cf(3b)	14	4	0	0	2	1	0	1	4	0	.286
Dallas, Porter, 3b	8	2	0	0	1	0	0	0	0	0	.250
Wright, Zollie, rf	15	5	0	0	1	0	0	0	1	0	.333
Saunders, Augustus, 2b	13	3	0	3	0	0	0	0	0	0	.231
Curry, Homer, lf	12	3	1	0	1	0	0	0	1	0	.250
Else, Harry, c	5	0	0	1	0	0	0	0	0	0	.000
Walker, Hoss, c	3	0	0	0	0	0	0	0	0	0	.000
Morris, Barney, p	6	0	0	1	0	0	0	0	0	0	.000
Murray, Red, p(ph)	2	1	1	0	0	0	0	0	0	0	.500
Williams, Elbert, p	0	0	0	0	0	0	0	0	0	0	.000
Smith, Hilton, p(ph)	3	0	0	0	0	0	0	0	0	0	.000
Walker, W., cf (ph)	6	1	1	0	0	0	0	0	0	0	.167
Harvey, Bob, p	0	0	0	1	0	0	0	0	0	0	.000
Harris, Samuel, (ph)	1	0	0	0	0	0	0	0	0	0	.000
Johnson, Frank (ph)	0	0	1	0	0	0	0	0	0	0	.000

	W	L	Pct.[‡]
Williams, Elbert, p	1	0	1.000
Gillespie, Murray, p	0	1	.000
Harvey, Bob, p	0	2	.000

Untallied highlights from games not recorded with a box score

@ Pittsburgh (9–3): Nothing but the 3–7 score was reported

@ Pittsburgh (9–5, game 1): An abbreviated box score for this game exists, but does not include at-bats in its statistics. Inclusion, therefore, would skew the sample, as estimated numbers of AB would be required. In the interest of keeping the absolutely known facts absolutely accurate, giving the best possible representative picture of the success and failure rates of the players, what information exists about the game is not included above, but is as follows: Morney, Parnell, Wright, and Dallas each had 1 hit; Saunders had two hits; Dallas scored a run, as did Hoss Walker, though he never recorded a hit; Alexander, Curry, Else, Harris, and Gillespie played, but neither hit nor scored.

@ Pittsburgh (9–5, game 2): Parnell and Wright each had an RBI; Curry and Parnell scored the team's two runs. The team had 9 hits; Parnell had one double.

v. Pittsburgh (9–10): {Box score above} Future MLB Hall of Fame inductee Hilton Smith pitches his first innings for the Monarchs: 5 2/3 innings, 6 hits, 4 runs, 2 strikeouts in a game ended by dark as a 6–6 tie, leaving Smith with a no decision

v. Pittsburgh (9–12): Nothing but the 6–9 score was reported

The Walker Discrepancy

The two Walkers, W. and H., are, in the author's opinion, the same person: W.C. Walker. (For more, see the footnote number 44). If that is the case, his statistics would be as follows:

	AB	H	R	E	2B	3B	HR	RBI	BA[*]	SLG	TB	ISO	HRR
Walker, W.C., lf,cf,c,ph	180	42	26	1	3	0	1	9	.233	.267	48	.033	.006

The Monarchs as a Comparative Statistical Success

When making comparisons between groups with varying numbers of games, at-bats, etc., the derivative statistics measuring percentages are understandably the only measures that offer fair evaluations of comparative statistical success. Therefore, the derivative batting statistics (minus total bases) and pitcher's winning percentage are the only categories included. While the other individuals on other teams in other leagues have far more available data, only that comparative to existing data for the 1932 Monroe Monarchs is considered below.

Statistics Produced by 1932 Monarchs' Opponents[55]

	AB	H	R	E	2B	3B	HR	RBI	BA	SLG	TB	ISO	HRR
Algiers (New Orleans) (3)	97	19	6	12	6	0	0	5	.196	.258	25	.062	.000
Austin (3)	97	17	6	4	0	0	0	5	.175	.175	17	.000	.000
Birmingham (3)	87	15	5	3	2	1	0	4	.172	.218	19	.046	.000
Chicago (5)	169	25	15	8	5	0	0	0	.148	.178	30	.030	.000
Cleveland (4)	127	13	5	5	1	1	0	2	.102	.126	16	.024	.000
Houston (2)	51	10	2	1	1	1	0	2	.196	.255	13	.059	.000
Little Rock (4)	131	27	7	8	4	1	0	7	.206	.252	33	.046	.000
Memphis (16)	500	116	54	32	13	2	1	7	.232	.272	136	.040	.002
Montgomery (8)	240	48	17	22	4	3	0	13	.200	.242	58	.042	.000
Nashville (6)	191	49	22	5	7	2	0	3	.257	.314	60	.058	.000
Pittsburgh (4)[56]	141	38	21	3	6	1	1	10	.270	.348	49	.078	.007
Opponent totals (58)	1831	377	140	103	49	12	2	58	.184	.249	456	.043	.001

1932 Pittsburgh Crawfords World Series Statistics[57]

The players are listed in order of appearance.

	AB	H	R	E	2B	3B	HR	SB	RBI	SAC	BA
Page, Ted, rf,cf	12	4	4	0	0	0	0	1	4	0	.333
Crutchfield, Jimmie, cf	9	1	1	0	0	0	0	1	1	0	.111
Wilson, Jud, lf,3b[58]	13	5	2	0	0	0	0	1	2	0	.385
Gibson, Josh, c	14	4	4	0	2	0	1	0	2	0	.286
Johnson, Judy, 3b,rf	12	2	3	0	1	0	0	0	1	0	.167
Charleston, Oscar, 1b	11	5	0	0	0	1	0	0	0	0	.455
Russell, Johnny, 2b	10	3	0	1	1	0	0	0	0	1	.300
Stevens, Jake, ss	11	0	1	2	0	0	0	1	0	0	.000
Streeter, Sam, p	4	1	0	0	0	0	0	0	0	0	.250
Kincannon, Harry, p	3	0	1	0	0	0	0	1	0	0	.000
Radcliffe, Ted, p,c	5	2	1	0	1	0	0	0	0	0	.400
Paige, Satchel, p	1	0	0	0	0	0	0	0	0	0	.000
Bell, William, p	2	0	1	0	0	0	0	0	0	0	.000

	W	L	Win %
Streeter, Sam, p	0	1	.000
Bell, William, p	2	0	1.00
Paige, Satchel, p	1	0	1.00

1932 East-West League Individual Leaders[59]

	BA[60]	SLG	ISO	HRR	Win%
Wilson, Ernest "Jud" (Homestead)	.500	--	--	--	--
Finley, Thomas (Baltimore)	--	.724	--	--	--
Siki, Roque (Cuban Stars)	--	--	.307	--	--
Siki, Roque (Cuban Stars)	--	--	--	.055	--
Smith, Herb (Baltimore)	--	--	--	--	1.000[61]

1932 East-West League Team Leaders

	BA	SLG	ISO	HRR	Win%
Homestead Greys	.315	--	--	--	--
Cuban Stars	--	.451	--	--	--
Cuban Stars	--	--	.143	--	--
Cuban Stars	--	--	--	.018[62]	--
Balt. Black Sox	--	--	--	--	.690[63]

1932 Cotton States Individual Leaders[64]

	BA	SLG	ISO	HRR	Win%[65]
Glass, Clyde (El Dorado)	.393	.679	.286	--	--
Baker, Bill (Monroe)	--	--	--	.051	--
Danforth, C.B.[66] (Pine Bluff)	--	--	--	--	.857

1932 Cotton States Team Leaders

	BA	SLG	ISO	HRR	Win%
Monroe	.298	--	--	--	--
Baton Rouge	--	.422	--	--	--
El Dorado	--	--	.135	--	--
Baton Rouge	--	--	--	.020	--
Baton Rouge	--	--	--	--	.707

1932 Monroe Twins Individual Statistics

	BA	SLG	ISO	HRR
Bilgere, Joe, ss	.389	.545	.246	.024
Terrier, Phil, of	.327	.463	.136	.007
Crouch, Bill, p	.313	.333	.021	.000
Baker, Bill, of	.309	.515	.206	.051
Ezzell, Homer, 1b	.297	.365	.068	.005
West, Tommy, c	.297	.465	.159	.022
Moses, Wallace, of	.294	.411	.117	.013
Smith, Red, 2b	.280	.413	.133	.028
Hammack, Sterling, 3b	.275	.365	.090	.011
Kitchens, Frank, c	.212	.242	.030	.000

	Win%
Perez, Elisea, p	.416
Florrid, Dick, p	.400
Lanning, Johnny, p	.500
Erwin, Ben, p	.333
Crouch, Bill, p	.214
Bryant, Dobie, p	.000

1932 Monroe Twins Team Statistics

	BA	SLG	ISO	HRR	Win%
Monroe	.298	.421	.123	.015	.456

The 1932 Monroe Monarchs. The front row, from left to right, depicts Zollie Wright, Red Parnell, Chuffie Alexander, W. L. Walker, and Harry Else. The back row, from left to right, depicts Elbert Williams, Barney Morris, Porter Dallas, Dick Matthews, Frank Johnson, Sam Harris, Leroy Morney, and Augustus Saunders.

Special thanks to Paul J. Letlow of the *Monroe News Star* for help with player identification. Picture from the Ouachita Parish Digital Archive, part of the Special Collections of the Ouachita Parish Public Library, Monroe, Louisiana.

NOTES

1. Fifteenth Census of the United States: 1930, vol. III, part I, Alabama–Missouri (US Government Printing Office, Washington: 1932), 979.
2. Fifteenth Census, vol. III, 965, 982, 990, 999, 1003.
3. *New Orleans Item*, May 6, 1919; *New Orleans Times-Picayune*, May 12, 1919; "The Monroe Lynching," *Southwestern Christian Advocate*, June 12, 1919, 1–2; National Association for the Advancement of Colored People, *Thirty Years of Lynching in the United States, 1889–1918* (New York: Arno Press, 1969), 71–73, 104–105; and *Papers of the NAACP, Part 7: The Anti-Lynching Campaign, 1912–1955*, Series A, reel 12 of 30 (Bethesda, MD: University Publications of America, 1982), 348–352, 354, 356, 373–380, 383, 393.
4. Michael E. Lomax, *Black Baseball Entrepreneurs, 1860–1901: Operating by Any Means Necessary* (Syracuse, NY: Syracuse University Press, 2003), xv–xvi, xvii.
5. Robert Peterson, *Only the Ball Was White: A History of Legendary Black Players and All-Black Professional Teams* (New York: Oxford University Press, 1970), 122; DeMorris Smith, interview, September 2, 2004; "The Realty Investment Co. Inc.—J.M. Supply Co. Inc.—Mortgage Deed, Sale of Land," Record 79482, April 23, 1927, Conveyance Record, Ouachita Parish, Book 157, pp. 775–778, Ouachita Parish Clerk of Court; "J.M. Supply Co., Inc. to the Realty Investment Co., Ltd.—Mortgage Deed, Vendor's Lien," Record 79482, April 23, 1927, Mortgage Record, Ouachita Parish, Book 129, pp. 707–710, Ouachita Parish Clerk of Court; "J.M. Supply Co., Inc. to Fred Stovall—Cash Deed, Sale of Land," Record 139386, May 21, 1930, Conveyance Record, Ouachita Parish, Book 20, pp. 435–456, Ouachita Parish Clerk of Court; Philip J. Lowry, *Green Cathedrals: The Ultimate Celebration of All 271 Major League and Negro League Ballparks Past and Present* (Reading, MA: Addison-Wesley Publishing Co., 1992), 81; and *Who's Who in the Twin Cities* (West Monroe: H.H. Brinsmade, 1931), 167.
6. *Atlanta Daily World*, 20, March 22, 1932; *Pittsburgh Courier*, March 19, 1932; and *Birmingham Reporter*, 12, March 26, 1932, April 2, 1932.
7. *Chicago Defender*, 4, 11, June 25, 1932.
8. *Louisiana Weekly*, July 9, 1932.
9. This is the formula generally repeated in historical accounts. Peterson's *Only the Ball Was White* sets the standings as follows: Cole's American Giants, 34–7, .829 winning percentage; Monroe Monarchs, 33–7, .825 winning percentage. The account of Dick Clark and Larry Lester is the same for the two front-running teams. John Holway's *The Complete Book of Baseball's Negro Leagues* offered a season total for the Southern League teams, and wrongly noted "Nashville was awarded the first half, Chicago the second.": Chicago American Giants, 52–31, .627 winning percentage; Monroe Monarchs, 26–22, .542 winning percentage. *Chicago Defender*, July 23, 1932; Robert Peterson, *Only the Ball Was White*; Dick Clark and Larry Lester, eds., *The Negro Leagues Book* (Cleveland: Society for American Baseball Research, 1994), 164; and John Holway, *The Complete Book of Baseball's Negro Leagues: The Other Half of Baseball History* (Fern Park, FL: Hastings House, 2001), 288, 292–293. See Part 2 for further details.
10. According to the *Morning World*, the first-half standings looked like this: Monroe, 33–7, .825 winning percentage; Chicago, 28–9, .756 winning percentage. The *Pittsburgh Courier*'s first-half standings as of July 3 tallied *eight* losses for Chicago: Monroe, 31–7, .816 winning percentage; Chicago, 31–8, .795 winning percentage. In contrast to Holway's 26 wins and 22 losses for the season, the *Courier* tallied Monroe's total as *60* wins and 22 losses. *Monroe Morning World*, July 6, 1932; and *Pittsburgh Courier*, July 9, 1932, September 3, 1932.
11. *Monroe Morning World*, July 28, 1932; *Pittsburgh Courier*, July 16, 1932; and *Chicago Defender*, July 9, 1932, August 13, 1932.
12. For more on coverage of the series by the African-American press in 1932, see Thomas Aiello, "Black Newspapers' Presentation of Black Baseball, 1932: A Case of Cultural Forgetting," *NINE: A Journal of Baseball History and Culture* 15 (Fall 2006).
13. Jim Bankes, *The Pittsburgh Crawfords: The Lives and Times of Black Baseball's Most Exciting Team* (Dubuque, IA: William C. Brown Publishers, 1991), 23, 26–27; *Chicago Defender*, July 2, 1932; and *Pittsburgh Courier*, April 9, 1932, August 27, 1932.
14. Much of this brief treatment of the 1932 World Series comes from Thomas Aiello, "The Casino and Its Kings Are Gone: The Transient Relationship of Monroe, Louisiana with Major League Black Baseball, 1932," *North Louisiana History* 37 (Winter 2006): 15–38. Though one of the Pittsburgh games was scheduled to be played in Cleveland, all took place at Greenlee Park. *Pittsburgh Courier*, September 10, 1932; *Chicago Defender*, August 27, 1932; *Monroe Morning World*, August 31, 1932; September 10, 1932.
15. *Monroe Morning World*, September 13, 1932.
16. Two years later, another Hall of Fame player would come from Shreveport to start his career with the Monroe Monarchs. Willard Brown played shortstop for the team before being purchased by J.L. Wilkinson to play for the Kansas City Monarchs. The same special 2006 Hall of Fame election that failed to elect Roy Parnell did elect Brown for induction. Much of this brief account comes from Riley's *Biographical Encyclopedia*, 206–207, 209, 266–267, 568, 569–570, 605, 723–725, 781–782, 884–885. Additional information from "Hilton Smith Autobiographical Account," Player File: Smith, Hilton, A. Bartlett Giamatti Research Center, National Baseball Hall of Fame, Cooperstown, NY; *Tri-State Defender*, April 13, 1974; "Pre-Negro Leagues Candidate Profile: Roy A. 'Red' Parnell," National Baseball Hall of Fame, www.baseballhalloffame.org/hofers_and_honorees/parnell_red.htm, accessed February 21, 2006; "Pre-Negro Leagues Candidate Profile: Willard Jessie 'Home Run' Brown," National Baseball Hall of Fame, www.baseballhalloffame.org/hofers_and_honorees/brown_willard.htm, accessed February 21, 2006; and Steve Rock, "Former Monarchs Pitcher Hilton Smith Elected to Baseball Hall of Fame," *Kansas City Star*, March 7, 2001.
17. Jessie Parkhurst Guzman, ed., *1952 Negro Year Book: A Review of Events Affecting Negro Life* (New York: William H. Wise & Co., 1952), v; *Who's Who Among Black Americans, 1977–1978*, 2nd ed., vol. 1 (Northbrook, IL: Who's Who Among Black Americans Publishing Company, 1978), 98; and *Southern Broadcast*, July 11, 1936, February 6, 1937.
18. The exhibitions were against the Rube Foster Memorial Giants—often confused, even in contemporary press reports—as the Chicago American Giants. A series of articles in the *Kansas City Call* in early April report on both teams and make their differences clear. *Kansas City Call*, 1, April 8, 1932.
19. The game total by this count is 42, with 35 wins and six losses (minus the exhibitions). This differs from any other account, contemporary or historical, of the season's first half. I stand by this count. The selective presentation by newspapers and the overall confused state of Negro League Baseball in 1932 both argue for the necessity of a new count. The contemporary and historical controversy over the first half standings, if nothing else, discredits any consistency in former counts. See below for a catalog of other tallies and for the Monarchs' original schedule as announced by the Negro Southern League in March 1932.
20. Available box scores come from the following sources: *Monroe Morning World*, March 27, 1932, April 4, 5, 11, 12, 1932, May 7, 8, 9, 15, 22, 1932, June 12, 13, 14, 19, 20, 21, 1932, July 3, 4, 5, 1932, August 1, 2, 8, 9, 29, 30, 31, 1932, September 5, 11, 12, 1932; *Monroe News Star*, May 16, 17, 23, 1932; *Memphis Commercial Appeal*, May 1, 2, 3, 1932, July 10, 11, 12, 1932; *Pittsburgh Courier*, September 10, 1932; *Kansas City Call*, April 22, 1932; *Chicago Defender*, June 11, 1932, July 2, 16, 23, 1932; *Atlanta Daily World*, June 30, 1932; *Afro-American*, July 23, 1932; and *Louisiana Weekly*, September 17, 1932.
21. The four final games with the Lincoln Giants of Alexandria, Louisiana are considered exhibition games, as they take place after the close of the World Series.
22. *Pittsburgh Courier*, 19 March 1932; and *Atlanta Daily World*, March 22, 1932.
23. *Pittsburgh Courier*, July 16, 1932; and *Chicago Defender*, July 9, 1932.
24. Robert Peterson, *Only the Ball Was White: A History of Legendary Black Players and All-Black Professional Teams* (New York: Oxford University Press, 1970), 269; and Dick Clark and Larry Lester, eds., *The Negro Leagues Book* (Cleveland: Society for American Baseball Research, 1994), 164.
25. John Holway, *The Complete Book of Baseball's Negro Leagues: The Other Half of Baseball History* (Fern Park, FL: Hastings House Publishers, 2001), 288, 292–293.
26. *Monroe Morning World*, July 6, 1932.
27. *Pittsburgh Courier*, July 9, 1932, September 3, 1932.
28. *Pittsburgh Courier*, September 3, 1932.

29. *Louisiana Weekly*, March 5, 1932; and *Shreveport Sun*, March 19, 1932.

30. Murray never played for the Monarchs in the first half of the season. He somehow made his way to Memphis, before returning to the Monarchs in late August. See below. *Monroe News Star*, March 24, 1932.

31. *Chicago Defender*, April 2, 1932.

32. *Monroe Morning World*, April 8, 1932.

33. *Monroe Morning World*, April 9, 1932.

34. *Monroe Morning World*, April 21, 1932.

35. *Louisiana Weekly*, May 21, 1932.

36. Thompson was the losing pitcher on Tuesday, 19 July loss to Chicago, described by the *Chicago Defender* as the "former Indianapolis twirler." *Chicago Defender*, July 23, 1932.

37. Announced in the *Monroe Morning World*, August 26, 1932. But the players appeared in games versus the Lincoln Giants beginning on August 11.

38. His first appearance came at Austin, August 22, 1932. *Monroe Morning World*, August 23, 26, 1932.

39. *Monroe Morning World*, September 10, 1932.

40. See "The Walker Discrepancy" in Part 5.

41. Gillespie was suspended by the Southern League for the second half of the season. See *Pittsburgh Courier*, September 7, 1932 for his return.

42. Batting average is the only statistic in this section not physically provided by the actual box scores. Further derivative statistics follow under the heading "Derivative Statistics."

43. On June 12, the Monarchs played a doubleheader with the Montgomery Grey Sox, and the box score for the first game lists the left fielder as Maher—a name never mentioned before or after. The number of incorrect spellings and misinterpretations of names leads the observer to conclude that the handwritten box score submission that included Walker appeared to be Maher to the Monroe *Morning World*'s typesetter. Walker (Maher) was 1 for 4 with 0 runs.

44. There here exists a discrepancy that must be acknowledged. James Riley's *The Biographical Encyclopedia of the Negro Baseball Leagues* lists two Walkers as players for the 1932 Monarchs. Neither are very well known. W. Walker is listed as a left fielder. H. Walker is listed as a catcher. In a game against the Chicago American Giants, the box score of which appears in the *Chicago Defender*, 23 July 1932, Walker is listed as playing lf and c in the Saturday box score. The dearth of information available about these players (even accurate first names) leaves open the very real possibility that this is these two players are the same, particularly with the prevalence of box score typographical errors. Box scores generally list "Walker" and a position, so absolute accuracy is impossible. For the sake of the best possible sample, however, I have separated the catching Walker from the left fielding Walker. One newspaper account, however, describes W. Walker as W.C. Walker, "former Campbell College star." This information doesn't discount the possibility that H. and W. Walker were different players, but it seems to suggest that there was one known Walker on the team, making the possibility that W.C. Walker was the only member of the 1932 Monarchs more than plausible. *Atlanta Daily World*, 15 September 1932; and James Riley, *The Biographical Encyclopedia of the Negro Baseball Leagues* (New York: Carroll and Graf Publishers, Inc., 1994), 809, 811. Following the combined season totals below, the statistics of both possible Walkers are combined to demonstrate the totals of one player, W.C., (in the event that the Walkers were indeed one player) under the heading "The Walker Discrepancy," page 10.

45. All totals derived from the available data. Wins, losses, and scores are totals from Part 2: 1932 Monroe Monarchs Schedule and Results. Statistical performance numbers are totals from the "Season Totals" section of Part 5: Statistical Analysis of the Available Data for the 1932 Monroe Monarchs, page 8. As in the First and Second Half statistical breakdowns, exhibition games with available scores (with the exception of those taking place after the close of the World Series) are included in the total runs scored and allowed.

46. Winning percentage is the only pitching statistic not physically provided by the actual box scores. The lack of consistent details about specific pitching performance categories makes derivative pitching statistics virtually impossible to provide. The percentage is calculated by dividing the number of wins by the number of decisions.

47. The run totals for this section of the team statistics are derived from available box scores, and thus from fewer games than

are the run totals based solely on the reported wins and losses. Addition of runs not included in the box scores cannot be included in this section, as they would skew the representative sample the box score statistical analysis is supposed to provide.

48. Batting average is the only statistic in this section not physically provided by the actual box scores. Further derivative statistics follow under the heading "Derivative Statistics."

49. Batting average is simply the batter's number of hits divided by his number of at bats (AB above).

50. Slugging percentage follows this formula: [singles + (2 x doubles) + (3 x triples) + (4 x home runs)] / at bats.

51. The total bases statistic follows this formula: singles + (2 x doubles) + (3 x triples) + (4 x home runs).

52. The isolated power statistic follows this formula: total bases – hits / at bats. The original formula calculated the "total bases" by awarding a 0 for singles, 1 for doubles, 2 for triples, and 3 for home runs. Here, total bases is calculated as described in note 3 above.

53. Home run ratio is calculated by dividing the number of a batter's home runs by his number of at bats.

54. Batting average is the only statistic in this section not physically provided by the actual box scores. Further derivative statistics follow under the heading "Derivative Statistics," pages 26-27.

55. Note, as mentioned above, that hits, runs, errors, and at bats are the most consistently noted statistics. In this section, for example, though Chicago has scored 15 runs, they have no listed rbi's. The box scores for games with Chicago did not include rbi as a statistic, and so is not there. While the first four numbers are clearly the most complete, the numbers to the left of the rbi column are reasonably accurate. The same derivatives generated above are generated below the hard numbers section. The given numbers are for the games noted in Part 2, "1932 Monroe Monarchs Schedule and Results," as having an available box score. The total number of games used to derive each team's statistics against the Monarchs follows the team name in parentheses.

56. The Pittsburgh statistics presented here include the three World Series games with available box scores and the early exhibition game. Pittsburgh's individual and team World Series statistics are included below.

57. The statistics here correspond to the three box scores used to compile the Monarchs World Series statistics. See above.

58. This Jud Wilson, one in a litany of future Hall of Fame inductees from the 1932 Crawfords, is the same Jud Wilson who led the 1932 East-West League in batting average for 1932. Wilson moved to the Crawfords after the East-West collapse. See below.

59. The East-West League, the other major Negro Baseball League in 1932, folded early in June. The final statistical release by the league was published in the Baltimore *Afro American*, 11 June 1932. The statistics and derivative numbers for individual and team East-West sections come from that source.

60. Minimum of fifty at bats, for batting average and the rest of the East-West League statistical leaders.

61. Smith was 4 and 0 in six games, with thirty innings pitched.

62. The Cuban Stars' home run ratio just edges Baltimore's .017.

63. This statistic comes from the Baltimore *Afro American*, 25 June 1932. Soon after this standings release, the league folded.

64. The Cotton States League was a white minor league of teams from Louisiana, Arkansas, and Mississippi. It included, among other teams, the Monroe Twins, who played across town from the Monarchs in Desiard Park. The league, however, did not outlast the NSL. It folded early in July. The final statistical release by the league was published in the *Monroe Morning World*, 10 July 1932. The statistics and derivative numbers for individual and team Cotton States sections come from that source, as do the Monroe Twins statistics that follow.

65. Minimum of fifty innings pitched imposed by the author.

66. The Pine Bluff rookie came from Dallas, and though the local paper used first names in its reports on the Pine Bluff Judges, Danforth was always called C.B., often with the nickname "Tarzan" added. *Pine Bluff Daily Graphic*, 22, 24, 26 April 1932, 1, 15, 27 May 1932.

THOMAS AIELLO *is a doctoral candidate in the Department of History at the University of Arkansas.*

Base Ball to Base-Ball to Baseball

Baseball didn't just develop into the national pastime in the late 19th century. Baseball also developed into one word at that time from its roots as a two-word phrase. The one-word term "baseball" developed into its compound form from its previous spelling as two separate words, the adjective "base" preceding the noun "ball," and an intermediate hyphenated version as "base-ball."

Linguists refer to this process as word formation, or the creation of a new word by combining two older words. The formation of solid compound words such as baseball typically follows a pattern. As noted in the *American Heritage Book of English Usage*, "Many solid compounds begin as separate words, evolve into hyphenated compounds, and later become solid compounds."

Using the archives of the *New York Times*, we can easily discern the evolution of how the new word "baseball" developed during the last half of the 19th century. From its first references in 1855 through 1869, the game was spelled as two words, "base ball." For example, a headline on September 1, 1868, regarding the match between the Athletics and the Atlantics read:

BASE BALL
THE GRAND MATCH IN PHILADELPHIA—
THE DEFEAT OF THE ATHLETICS—AN
IMMENSE ASSEMBLAGE OF SPECTATORS

Beginning in 1870, the *Times* switched to hyphenating the two words as "base-ball" rather than treat them as separate terms. Illustrating this is a headline of February 7, 1876, about the formation of the National League, which read:

BASE-BALL
A MEETING OF THE MANAGERS OF THE
PROFESSIONAL NINES—THE PHILADELPHIA
CLUB EXCLUDED FROM THE CHAMPIONSHIP
CONTESTS—NEW RULES

Then in 1884, the *Times* eliminated the hyphen and converted the sport into one word, "baseball." For instance, a headline on October 24, 1884, about the World Series game between Providence of the National League and the Metropolitan club of the American Association read:

THE BASEBALL FIELD
THE PROVIDENCE BOYS PUT A DAMPER ON
THE METROPOLITANS

Many newspapers started to print the term "baseball" as one word in the mid-1880s, including the Washington Post and the Atlanta Constitution in addition to the New York Times. Other newspapers adopted the one-word convention in the early 1890s, including the Chicago Tribune in 1891 and the Boston Globe in 1893 (the latter newspaper going straight from two words to one word without the intervening hyphenated step).

Accompanying the change in written form was likely a subtle change in speech pattern in how the term was pronounced. Typically, when the adjective–noun combination is treated as one word, the emphasis is on the first syllable (denoted here by capital letters), i.e., BASEball. When the combination is treated as two distinct words, the stress is usually on the second word, i.e., baseBALL. The classic example here is the pronunciation of greenhouse, a place where plants grow, and green house, a building painted green.

The development of the one-word term "baseball" happened in much the same way as did the modern day terms "online" and "website." Both of these terms linguistically began as two words, rapidly converted into a hyphenated form, then morphed into a single-term compound. Reflecting the vagaries of word formation, some publications still print these two Internet-related terms in their hyphenated or original two-word format.

The term "baseball" was treated just as inconsistently in the late 19th century as "online" and "website" are today. While many publications had evolved to spelling baseball as one word, others printed the term in its hyphenated and two-word forms. Not until the early 20th century was there general uniformity in the spelling of "baseball."

# # #

CHARLIE BEVIS *is a graduate student in the Master of Arts in Writing and Literature program at Rivier College in Nashua, NH, in addition to being the author of the book* Sunday Baseball: The Major Leagues' Struggle to Play Baseball on the Lord's Day, 1876–1934. *He lives in Chelmsford, MA.*

Relative Team Strength in the World Series

This essay examines some statistical features of the major league baseball World Series. We show that, based upon actual historical data, we cannot reject at the .05 level the hypothesis that the two World Series teams are evenly matched, but we could reject it comfortably at the .10 level. Yet we can also calculate the relative strengths of the teams that would best match the actual outcomes, and we find that those relative strengths are not equal. Including the home field advantage in the calculations indicates that the differential in relative strength between the competing teams can be explained by this advantage.

We present the relative team strengths that would maximize the probability of four-, five-, six-, and seven-game series. We find that a six- or seven-game series is most likely when the two teams are evenly matched, a four-game series is most likely when the probability of the stronger team winning is one, while the probability of a five-game series is maximized if one team has a relative strength of 0.789.

We also show that, on average, the expected number of World Series games will be between 4 and 5.81, depending upon the relative strengths of the teams and the home field advantage. Contracts that don't consider the likelihood of less than seven-game series create windfall gains to MLB and marginal economic losses to broadcasters.

Relative team strength is a factor determining the number of games played in baseball's World Series. This paper examines some statistical aspects of expected outcomes using the binomial probability distribution and data from the initial World Series in 1903 to the 2005 White Sox–Astros series. By extending the analysis we can also determine the revealed relative strength of World Series teams based upon the actual outcome of the 97 World Series played as best-of-seven series. The four World Series played as best of nine (1903, 1919–1921) were not included in the results, and games played to ties (1907, 1912, 1922) were not considered, although the actual World Series results were included.

Data and Analysis

The formula:
$$P(r) = \frac{n!}{r!(n-r!)} p^r q^{n-r}$$
, where r is the number of successes (in this case, four), n the number of trials (games played), and p the probability of one team winning a game (q=1-p), describes the probabilities of all possible outcomes of a World Series except that there are only a total

of 70 possible outcomes, not $2^7 = 128$, as the last trial must be a success

Assuming each team has an equal probability of winning each World Series game (p=q), the probabilities of the duration series are calculated simply:

Table 1. Probabilities of
World Series Duration

Total Games	Probability
4	0.125
5	0.25
6	0.3125
7	0.3125

Examining the actual results from all the World Series that have been played we find that 19 series were decided in four games, 21 were decided in five games, 22 were decided in six games, and 35 went the full seven games.

The theoretical outcomes, based upon the probabilities in Table 1, are 12.125 for a four-game series, 24.25 for a five-game series, and 30.3125 for both six- and seven-game series. Using the null hypothesis that the World Series teams are evenly matched, the computed value of chi-square is routinely found to be 7.338. Using the chi-square Đtest, at 0.05 permissible type one error and three degrees of freedom, we don't reject this hypothesis since the table value is 7.81 (but we could comfortably reject the equally matched hypothesis at the 0.10 level, as the table value there is only 6.25).

An interesting aspect of this analysis emerges as we minimize the computed chi square in order to find the revealed relative strengths of the teams given the actual results. In this sense we are finding the expected probabilities that best match the actual outcome over all World Series played. We find that the probabilities that minimize chi-square at a value of 6.886 are approximately p=0.5138 and q=0.4862. Based on actual outcomes utilizing the chi-square, the two teams entering the series do not have the same probabilities of emerging victorious in terms of the revealed team strengths.

One of the most surprising aspects of the actual outcome data is that while it indicates that if the two teams are equally matched, six- and seven-game series are equally probable, there have been only 22 six-game series but 35 seven-game series. Under the assumption that the teams are evenly matched, we compute the probability that of the 57 series that lasted more than five games, 35 or more would last the full seven games to be only .0427. Here we used the normal distribution as an approximation to the binomial distribution. For a one-tail test we can reject the null hypothesis at the 95% confidence level. Clearly the probability of a series that is not decided in five games ending with the sixth game should increase if the teams are not evenly matched (i.e., if p is greater than .50). We offer a non-statistical explanation for this statistical anomaly. The team that is behind must play to win games at all costs; thus it may change its rotation to start its best pitcher, use its best reliever for more innings than usual, etc., while the team that is ahead will formulate its strategy so as to win one more game, not necessarily the sixth game.

Finally, we can use the theoretical outcomes to see what relative team strengths are most likely to bring about each possible outcome in terms of games played. In other words, for what value of p are the probabilities in Table 1 above maximized? Our results are summarized in Table 2 below. The derivation of these results is a simple exercise in differential calculus; the details are omitted.

Table 2

Series Games	Probability That Maximizes	Maximum Probability
4	p = 1 or p = 0	1.0000
5	p = .789 or p = .211	.3333
6	p = .50	.3125
7	p = .50	.3125

Home Field Advantage

Home field advantage may play an important part in this analysis. Here we define home field advantage as the advantage gained by the team playing at home for the first game of the Series. There are at least two alternative definitions of home field advantage. One is that there is only home field advantage if there is a final deciding seventh game (ninth game in those World Series that were best five out of nine). There have been 35 such series with the home team winning the final deciding game 18 times and the visiting team winning 17 times. Clearly, this is not statistically significant. Another definition of home field advantage is that it exists in any series with an odd number of games. The advantage belongs to the team with more home games. There has been a total of 57 such World Series with the home team winning only 27 of them (less than half) while the visiting team has won 30 times.

Home Field Determination

The current mechanism awards home field advantage, and the commensurate higher probability of winning the World Series, to the league that wins the All-Star game. The effect on all-star voting remains to be seen. Imagine fans from the National League voting for the strongest players in their league on their All-Star ballots, while voting for the weakest All-Stars on the American League ballot. All-Star managers have limited possibilities to correct fan voting of position players; their selection strength is in the choice of pitchers. It may well be the case that the league with the strongest individual players gains a long-run advantage in World Series outcomes through home field advantage. Many will argue that this is an untenable situation. After all, the American League has won the last nine All-Star games played to a conclusion, and won 14 of the first 18 games. Having a World Series home field advantage determined on the basis of All-Star game victories may leave one league out in the cold for many consecutive years. This does not seem equitable in view of the demonstrated advantages of home field advantage in World Series play.

Contracts and Outcomes

MLB has a long history of contractual relationships with the broadcast media. The first national broadcast of the World Series occurred in 1922 and no fees were paid for the rights. The first rights were given to the Ford Motor Company in 1934 for $100,000. The current contract calls for $2.5 billion payments by Fox to MLB for the rights to World Series, league and divisional championships, regular season and All-Star games for six years, an average of $417 million per year.

Clearly, the rights include an estimate of the value of each of the components, since past contracts between MLB and broadcasters have often divided the four components listed above among more than one broadcaster. In fact, since 1976 at least two networks have been broadcasting national baseball games. The World Series is the highlight of the season and carries with it the highest per game value in terms of advertising fees. Based upon past contracts, we estimate current fees for the World Series broadcast rights to be approximately $115 million for a per game average of approximately $15 million. The average assumes that the value of all games is equal, an assumption that is dubious at best. Certainly the seventh game of a World Series played on a Sunday night in prime time is worth considerably more than any others.

Table 3 shows the relationship between the strength of the stronger team and the expected number of games to be played in the World Series. If the relative team strengths are 1 and 0, then the stronger team will sweep the series. If the balance of strength narrows somewhat to 0.75 and 0.25, an average of 5.163 games will be played in the World Series. If the teams are of equal relative strength, 0.5 and 0.5, we would expect the greatest number of games, an average of 5.81, until one team won four. If the networks are estimating a value of $15 million per game and expect a seven-game World Series, the networks winning the bid would lose almost $20 million, on average, even if the teams were equally matched. A four-game sweep would cost the broadcaster $45 million unless some provision for lowered payments were to be included in the contract.

One example of the effect of a short series on earnings was reported in CNNSI.com. In the 1998 World Series, the Yankees swept the Padres in four games. "Fox never had the benefit of a drama-building long series and ended up losing an estimated $15 million because of the sweep. The network needed a five-game series to break even."[2] Since the contract between Fox and MLB was substantially lower in 1998, the estimated figures cited for the value of a World Series game are in line with the increased value of the new contract.

Conclusion

Using the binomial distribution and actual World Series outcomes, we have determined the revealed team strengths and the most likely relative strengths for each of the possible outcomes of a seven-game series. We have also shown that a typical World Series has an expected number of games (5.81). Since each game has economic value to the contractual broadcaster, contracts that do not consider the probability of less than seven-game series are likely to cause marginal economic losses to the networks and windfall gains to MLB.

Table 3. The Effect of Team Strength on World Series Duration

Expected # of Games	Relative Strength of Strongest Team, Including Home Advantage
4	1.00
4.21	0.95
4.439	0.90
4.68	0.85
4.927	0.80
5.163	0.75
5.378	0.70
5.56	0.65
5.7	0.60
5.78	0.55
5.81	0.50

Conclusion

Using the binomial distribution and actual World Series outcomes, we have determined the revealed team strengths and the most likely relative strengths for each of the possible outcomes of a seven-game series. We have also shown that a typical World Series has an expected number of games (5.81). Since each game has economic value to the contractual broadcaster, contracts that do not consider the probability of less than seven-game series are likely to cause marginal economic losses to the networks and windfall gains to MLB.

# # #

NOTES

1. CNNSI.com. "Fox Lands Exclusive TV Rights to Postseason Baseball," sportsillustrated.cnn.com/baseball/mlb/news/2000/09/26/postseason_coverage_ap/
2. CNNSI.com. "Fox Posts Lowest Rated Series Ever," sportsillustrated.cnn.com/baseball/mlb/1998/postseason/news/1998/10/22/series_ratings/
3. *The Sporting News*. The Vault, www.sportingnews.com/archives/almanac/baseball/
4. Staudohar, Paul D. "The Symbiosis Between Baseball and Broadcasting," in Alvin L. Hall. ed., *The Cooperstown Symposium on Baseball and American Culture*, 2001,(Jefferson, NC: McFarland, 2002).
5. "Summer 1997: 75 Years of National Baseball Broadcasts," roadsidephotos.com/baseball/nationalbroadcast.htm
6. "Out of Control Yet?" www.ezboard.com

ALEXANDER E. CASSUTO *received his Ph.D. in Economics from UCLA in 1973. He is a professor at CSU East Bay and the author of many journal articles and monographs.*

FRANKLIN LOWENTHAL *grew up in the shadow of Yankee Stadium in the era of Diamaggio and Mantle. He teaches at Cal State Eastbay.*

DAVID VINCENT

How Rules Changes in 1920 Affected Home Runs

The home run was not a major part of a batter's arsenal in the 19th century. In fact, at the end of the century Roger Connor was the career leader in home runs with 138, and only seven players had smashed 100 or more four-baggers. During the first two decades of the new century, an era commonly referred to as the Deadball Era, home run production by batters decreased from the general production rate of the 19th century.

In measuring how the four-bagger has become more prevalent in the game though the years, raw counting totals will not suffice. It is easy to state that 40 homers were hit in the initial year of the National League in 1876, and 238 were clouted in 1883 in the major leagues by batters in the National League and the American Association, which started as a major league in 1882. At first glance, this looks as if homers were being hit at six times the rate in 1883 as in 1876. However, these numbers do not take into account the fact that more games were played in 1883 than in 1876, and by adding some context to the raw counting totals, we can get a better idea of the real difference between these two seasons (and in fact any two years).

The method employed here is a "home run production rate." It is calculated not by dividing homers by at-bats, similar to batting average, but by calculating how many circuit drives were hit per 500 plate appearances. A straight calculation of homers divided by plate appearances would provide numbers not readily understandable by the reader. In 1876 the 40 homers were hit in over 20,400 plate appearances. As a percentage (.196%), this number is hard to understand and hard to quantify as good or bad. Similarly, the 238 home runs hit in 1883 were clouted in approximately 60,000 plate appearances. This result is 0.397%, which is also hard to quantify.

The 500 plate appearance standard was chosen because the official minimum performance standard for individual batting championships as listed in rule 10.23(a) is 3.1 plate appearances times the number of games scheduled for each team.[1] Thus, in the 162-game schedule, 502 plate appearances is the minimum, but that was rounded here to 500 for simplicity. The home run production rate will generate numbers that can be compared to other numbers that have some context for the reader, such as a 30-homer season by a batter.

Look at the rates in the two previously discussed years as home runs per 500 plate appear-ances. In 1876, batters hit one homer for every 500 plate appearances while in 1883, batters hit two four-baggers for every 500 plate appearances. Thus 1883 batters were not hitting circuit drives six times more frequently than their 1876 brethren, as might be inferred by the raw totals, but rather only twice as often.

Figure 1 shows the yearly production rate for each season from 1876 through 1919, the end of the Deadball Era. It is clear from the figure that the rate during the start of the 20th century was lower than the general rate in the previous century. This drop in home run production in the Deadball Era can be attributed to a number of factors, a discussion that is beyond the scope of this article.

Figure 1. Home Run Production Rate (1876–1919)

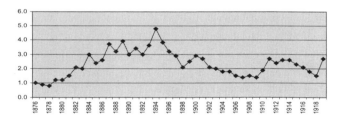

Before the start of the 1920 season, changes were made to the game that had a great effect on the balance between offense and defense. New playing rules were put into place that affected home runs and, in addition, the ball itself changed.

The *first of three rules changes* stated that fly balls hit over the fence along the left- and right-field lines would be judged fair or foul according to where the ball passed the fence rather than where it landed. The previous version of the rule had seemed reasonable and helpful to the umpires: they would call a fly ball fair or foul after watching it land, since judging the flight of the ball without a pole at the intersection of the line and the wall could be difficult, and there were no poles on the lines at this time.

This rule changed a few times during the 1920s. On June 25, 1920, with fewer than 60 games played by most teams under the new statute, the rule reverted to the 1919 version, which stated, "The umpire shall judge it fair or foul according to where it disappears from view." Before the 1928 season the rule again became "where the ball crosses the fence." National League president John Heydler stated that trying to determine where the ball actually landed was often very difficult. However, this applied only to balls crossing the barrier that indicated the edge of the playing field and that landed in the seating area. If a ball flew completely out of the park, it was to be judged not where it flew over the inner barrier but where it crossed the outer barrier. Therefore there were two different interpretations of the rule, which depended on how far the ball traveled before deciding the proper interpretation to use.

National League president Heydler held a meeting with all league umpires in his New York office on August 5, 1928. Part of the discussion regarded the double interpretation of judging a fly to be fair or foul. The umpires favored one rule for both situations, to call the ball fair if it crossed the inner barrier in fair territory regardless of the flight of the ball after that. Since most of the poles recently constructed to help umpires judge fly balls were not tall enough to allow a single interpretation of the rule as requested by the arbiters, Heydler decided not to change the rule interpretation during the 1928 season.

However, the league adopted a new rule for the 1929 season regarding those poles. It stated that a pole must be constructed at least 25 feet above the outer barrier to aid the umpires in calling balls fair or foul. The taller poles were constructed on either the top of the grandstand roof or the outer fence of the park, and the umpires got their wish for a single interpretation of the rule concerning calling flies fair or foul in 1929 to the "where the ball leaves the playing field" version. The American League continued to use the double interpretation of the rule through 1930.

The *second change in the playing rules* for 1920 concerned game-ending hits. Previously, if a batter hit a ball over the fence to end a game, he received credit only for enough bases on that hit to allow the winning run to score. In other words, if the game was tied and a runner was on second base, a ball hit out of the park became a double, since, when the runner on second scored, the game ended. The new rule allowed the batter and all runners to score on such game-ending hits, and the batter received credit for a home run.

There are 43 known instances of these game-ending hits before 1920. Since the rules of the day were clear about these hits not being home runs, it is incorrect to state that the players "lost" a homer. They were never home runs under the playing rules. Jimmy Collins of the Boston Beaneaters (later Braves) hit two of these game-ending blows, one in 1899 and one in 1900, and Sherry Magee of the Philadelphia Phillies hit two, in 1906 and 1914. Collins and Magee are the only batters who had two of these game-ending hits. The Boston Braves had the most as a team with nine, and the New York Giants hit eight of them.

Major League Baseball formed a special rules committee in 1968 to make decisions regarding record keeping in the early days of professional baseball. The committee attempted to make the old statistics consistent with modern scoring rules, and one of its rulings changed the known pre-1920 game-ending hits to home runs. Note that on July 8, 1918, Babe Ruth hit one of these game-enders and received credit for a triple at the time. Thus the committee's ill-advised ruling changed the record for most career home runs from 714 to 715. To make things worse, as part of this ruling the committee had to change the final score of the affected ball games and the pitching records of the hurlers who surrendered the hits.

When the committee announced this decision, many sports reporters wrote stories regarding the change in Ruth's record. Leonard Koppett, writing in the *New York Times* on April 27, 1969, stated: "For several years now, Willie Mays has been gradually closing in on Babe Ruth's career total of 714 home runs, one of the most hallowed statistics of all sports lore. Well, here's a shock for Willie and all his fans: the Babe just gained ground on him." Koppett discussed the entire computerization project which produced the first comprehensive baseball record book, published in 1969. He was generally complimentary about the project and the records committee; however, he ended his story with: "But it just lends support to those who believe that Ruth was the supreme slugger, the giant among giants. Here he is, after all, adding to his total 34 years after he played his last game."

Koppett's remarks helped focus attention on the ruling concerning game-ending hits. If the Babe had not been on the list, the ruling might have remained in place. However, changing the most recognizable statistic in all of sports generated a lot of negative feedback. Therefore, in May 1969 the special committee reversed itself on this one ruling, thus leaving the Babe's home run record intact at 714. It should be stated again that these batters did not lose home runs at this time because those hits were never homers according to the playing rules. The initial decision by the special committee granted something to the batters in conflict with the playing rules at the time of the event, and the reversal of this decision, although made for the wrong reason, achieved the correct status for these hits.

On July 11, 1920, the Boston Braves were tied with the Reds, 3–3, after eight innings in Cincinnati. In the bottom of the ninth, the Reds had Hod Eller running at second base and Morrie Rath at first when Jake Daubert came to the plate with two out. Daubert hit Hugh McQuillan's 1–1 pitch to center field, where it bounced once and hopped into the bleachers. Under the new rule on game-ending hits passed before this season, Daubert got credit for a three-run home run to win the game, 6–3, thus becoming the first batter to receive credit for a homer because of the rule change. (Through 1930, a ball which landed in fair territory and then bounced out of play was a home run.) Four days later, the St. Louis Browns and the New York Yankees were tied, 10–10, after 10 innings at the Polo Grounds in New York. In the bottom of the 11th inning, with Aaron Ward the runner at second base and Wally Pipp running at first base, Babe Ruth came to bat with no one out. Ruth hit the ball onto the right-field roof for a three-run, game-ending home run. This was the Babe's 29th of the season, tying his record set the previous year, and the first American League home run under the new rule. These were the only two game-ending home runs under the new rule in 1920. Ruth is the only batter on the list of game-ending hits under the old rules who hit a game-ending homer under the new rules that would not have qualified as a homer before 1920.

The *third playing rule that changed* for the 1920 season had a huge effect on hitting. It stated that the spitball and other unorthodox deliveries were outlawed. In other words, hurlers were no longer allowed to apply substances to the ball or scar its surface before pitching it, which included using rosin. Here is the wording agreed on at the meeting in February 1920:

At no time during the progress of the game shall the pitcher be allowed to (1) apply a foreign substance of any kind to the ball; (2) expectorate either on the ball or his glove; (3) to rub the ball on his glove, person or clothing; or (4) to deface the ball in any manner or to deliver what is called the "shine" ball, "spit ball," mud ball or emery ball. For a violation of any provision of this rule the pitcher shall be ordered from the game and be barred from participation in any championship contest for a period of ten days.

This change led to an increase in offense in 1920 and the following seasons because hurlers were no longer allowed to throw a "trick" or "freak" pitch to fool the batter. However, teams registered a group of pitchers already in the majors with the league presidents, and those hurlers could continue throwing the spitball (but not any other banned pitch) through the 1920 season only. After that year, all use of the spitball would be abolished. However, at a meeting the following December, the leagues extended the rule concerning these registered spitballers to allow them to continue throwing that pitch until they retired. Burleigh Grimes, who pitched until 1934, became the last of these grandfathered hurlers still in the major leagues.

These outlawed pitches were common during the Deadball Era. Applying a substance to the ball or scuffing it would cause it to curve, sometimes in an unusual way. Pitchers who did not have a good curveball liked these freak pitches because throwing one gave them a kind of breaking ball to use as a part of their arsenal. However, the unusual flight of these pitches meant that the hurler often had no control over where the pitch went, and sometimes that meant directly at the batter.

Because of the fear of a scuffed ball veering in toward a batter's head and causing serious injury, starting in 1920 umpires threw out any scuffed or discolored ball and placed a new ball into play immediately. Prior to this time, one baseball might be used for the entire contest regardless of its condition. With the elimination of the "freak" pitches and cleaner, easier-to-see balls in use, the batters had less fear of being injured by a baseball striking them. Therefore, they could stand in the batter's box with more confidence and have a better chance of hitting the ball long and hard.

The fact that balls hit into the stands were usually kept by the fans and not returned to the field became another consideration in ball replacement during a game. As the number of homers hit out of the park increased, so did the need to use a new baseball during the game, as each home run ball would be unavailable to the players, thus providing another situation in which a new, clean baseball replaced a used ball.

The *last change in 1920* involved the baseball itself. Historians generally refer to the baseball period starting in 1920 as the "Lively ball era," or a similar appellation. Starting that season, the baseball seemed to travel a lot farther off the bat, something that was discussed at great length and described with great negativity at the time.

Many older baseball men decried the "rabbit" ball and home run sluggers such as Babe Ruth. They were said to be not playing the game the way it was meant to be played and ruining the sport. Of course, the fact that fans were coming to the ballparks in record numbers was conveniently ignored by these detractors.

At the time, each league used a ball from a different manufacturer. The A.G. Spalding Company manufactured the National League baseball while Reach & Company made the sphere for the junior circuit. They were all made to the same specifications, the only difference being that the stitching on the cover of the National League ball had two colors, red and blue, while the American League ball had red yarn holding the outer cover on the ball.

The league presidents and representatives of the manufacturers all agreed during the 1921 season that no changes had been made to the specifications of the baseball. The primary theory discussed at the time as the cause of the "rabbit" ball was the fact that during World War I the government took the best quality wool for its own use, and commercial enterprises, such as Reach and Spalding, had to use wool of lower quality than they had previously used. With the end of the war, importers brought better quality wool from Australia into the United States. The yarn made from this wool was of better quality and was able to be wound tighter around the core of the baseball by the machines that completed that part of the process. The tighter winding was a result of the better-quality yarn, not a change to the machines, and created a slightly harder, more elastic ball—one that batters could hit farther than the old baseball.

The war had also depleted the ranks of workers in baseball factories, just as it had on the ball field. With new, inexperienced workers in the factories, the quality of the product was sure to deteriorate until the veteran laborers returned after the end of the war. Although machines performed the first part of the manufacturing process, workers hand-stitched the cover on the ball, and the post-war covers were probably more uniform in their quality than those used at the end of the Deadball Era.

What was the effect of these changes? The home run production rate soared in the 1920s, as shown in Figure 2. Whereas the highest rate before this time had been the 4.8 homers per 500 plate appearances in 1894, the production rate in eight of the 11 years in the chart was equal to or higher than the 1894 rate. Only 1920 (the start of the Lively ball era) and 1926 had lower rates than 1894.

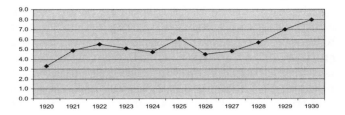

Figure 2. Home Run Production Rate (1920–1930)

There have been other rules changes that have affected offense and home runs in the history of baseball. However, none of the changes have had the impact of the set of modifications that took place before the 1920 season.

# # #

NOTES

1. Major League Baseball revised section 10 of the Official Rules before the 2007 season. Under the new organization of that section, rule 10.23 was renumbered as 10.22.

DAVID VINCENT, *called the "Sultan of Swat Stats" by ESPN, is the recognized authority on the history of the home run and was presented with the SABR's highest honor, the Bob Davids Award, in 1999. This article is excerpted from* Home Run: The Definitive History of Baseball's Ultimate Weapon, *published in March 2007 by Potomac Books.*

DAVID W. SMITH

Does Walking the Leadoff Batter Lead to Big Innings?

During a playoff broadcast in 2002, Tim McCarver made a comment to the effect that there are more multi-run innings that begin with a walk. McCarver also asserted, "The one thing I would tell a young pitcher is never walk the leadoff man. He always scores; he always scores." I examined the second of these comments in 1998 at the request of the San Diego Padres, although for the life of me I do not recall what use, if any, they made of what I gave them. I have expanded my data set since that 1998 study, and for this article I checked every game from 1974 through 2002. This 29-year period covered 61,365 games and 1,101,019 half innings. There were more than 4.5 million plate appearances in these games. Following is an analysis of the consequences of starting an inning with a walk. There are three tables of data which address the basic topic in different ways.

Table 1. Frequency of Methods by Which Leadoff Batters May Reach Base

	Reach	Score	Freq
1B	183,468	72,841	.397
2B	48,364	30,961	.640
3B	6,573	5,753	.875
HR	27,205	27,205	1.000
BB	82,637	33,002	.399
HP	6,217	2,543	.409
INT	81	22	.272
E	12,105	5,298	.438

Table 1 includes all the methods for leadoff batters to reach base, number of times each event occurred, the number of times that batters scored, and the frequency of each. Note that the "E" category includes all times the leadoff batters reached on an error, which includes those cases when he went past first base (e.g., a two-base error). The frequency for batters with leadoff walks scoring is insignificantly different from the frequency for leadoff singles; both are a tiny bit lower than the value for reaching via a hit-by-pitch.

My conclusion from this data is that a leadoff batter who walks does not "always score"; the walk has the same effect as any other way of reaching first base.

Table 2 lists all possible outcomes for leadoff batters (the eight categories from Table 1, plus making an out), the number of times the indicated number of runs were scored. For example, batters led off an inning with a single 183,468 times and in 104,074 of those innings his team did not score. One run was scored 35,868 times, two runs on 22,726 occasions, etc., with all innings of six or more runs combined.

These raw totals are not easy to compare. The various outcomes occur with very different frequencies. Therefore, I created Table 3. Table 3 contains data from Table 2 normalized per number of occurrences of each outcome. For example, a leadoff single led to no runs with a frequency of .567 (56.7%), one run was scored after the leadoff single with a frequency of .196, etc.

Table 2. Frequency of Possible Outcomes for Leadoff Batters

	Total	0	1	2	3	4	5	>5
1B	183468	104074	35868	22726	11329	5375	2415	1681
2B	48364	17671	17657	6772	3427	1632	683	522
3B	6573	984	3696	1019	467	228	101	78
HR	27205	0	19690	4130	1816	871	386	312
BB	82637	46794	15837	10481	5167	2503	1100	755
HP	6217	3453	1209	776	427	203	93	56
INT	81	56	9	7	6	1	0	2
E	12105	6427	2726	1580	744	355	159	114
OUT	734369	616379	70656	28839	11379	4441	1679	996
Total	1101019	795838	167348	76330	34762	15609	6616	4516

Table 3. Normalized Frequency of Possible Outcomes for Leadoff Batters

	0	1	2	3	4	5	>5
1B	.567	.196	.124	.061	.029	.013	.009
2B	.365	.365	.140	.070	.033	.014	.010
3B	.150	.562	.155	.071	.034	.015	.011
HR	0	.724	.152	.066	.032	.014	.011
BB	.566	.192	.127	.062	.030	.013	.009
HP	.555	.194	.125	.068	.032	.014	.009
INT	.691	.111	.086	.074	.012	0	.024
E	.531	.225	.131	.061	.029	.013	.009
OUT	.839	.096	.039	.015	.006	.002	.001

The values for leadoff singles and leadoff walks are virtually indistinguishable. The hit-by-pitch data are only slightly lower in the "no runs" category.

Conclusion

Both of McCarver's assertions are clearly contradicted by this huge body of evidence. Having the leadoff batter reach base is certainly an advantage for the offense (compare the values for the "out" row in Table 3). The data for reaching on interference are far too limited to be useful. When the leadoff man collects an extra-base hit or reaches on an error (with the occasional cases of going past first on the error included), it is even better than reaching first, as expected. However, if we look at just those instances when the leadoff batter reaches first, then *it does not matter how he got there*.

Even if we allow Tim some poetic license for his hyperbole—it is his job, after all—we do not need to accept his opinion as authoritative. I have great respect for anyone who played in the major leagues for 22 years, as McCarver did. However, anecdotal observations and gut feelings are just that and have no inherent credibility, no matter what the source. Since we can now check these opinions with evidence, and McCarver definitely has at his disposal the talents of people who can do such checking, then we should expect him and other announcers to get it right. Hunches and feelings may be fine places to start an investigation, but they are very poor substitutes for the substantiated conclusions that come from careful analysis based on appropriate evidence.

# # #

DAVE BALDWIN, TERRY BAHILL, & ALAN NATHAN

Nickel and Dime Pitches

The cover of a baseball comprises two strips of leather (identical dog bone–shaped geometrical figures called *ovals of Cassini*) stitched together with a single continuous red seam. The appearance of that seam during a pitch can provide information about the ball's spin characteristics, which in turn might make the behavior of the pitch predictable. Therefore batters, catchers, and pitching coaches look for the seam spin pattern in order to evaluate a pitch. A spinning pitch (i.e., one that is not a knuckleball) might display one of three patterns due to the rotation of the seam: a distinct dot, a circle of variable size and sharpness, or two fuzzy bands girding the ball (Bahill et al., 2005).

Pitching coaches often refer to the appearance of sliders and curves in terms of two U.S. coins—the dime and the nickel. The monetary designations allude to the dime-sized red dot (Fig. 1)[1] or nickel-sized red circle (Fig. 2) that is observable on some sliders and curveballs. When visible, these features can be seen on the face of the slider, from the side of the overhand curveball, or from above the sidearm curve.

Generally, coaches and players assume the dot indicates a fast-spinning pitch (sometimes called a "tight" spin) with a consequential large deflection; the circle or the pattern of indistinct bands is believed to signal a slower-spinning pitch with inferior deflection. Are those assumptions valid?

In this paper we will attempt to answer that question in a series of three steps. First, we present models that describe how the various orientations of spin axis and seam might result in the visible spin patterns of curveballs and sliders. Then for each of those two pitches, we describe how the grip and release of the ball could produce poor deflection. Finally, we speculate as to how these inadvisable grip and release features might have become associated with a circular or banded spin pattern.

Plausible Explanations of the Dot and Circle Features

The dot appears on the dime curve or slider if one of the ball's spin-axis poles is located on a seam. The farther the pole is shifted from the seam, the less distinct the dot becomes. We define the *manifest point* to be the point on the seam that is nearest the pole (Fig. 3). With a pole displacement of a few millimeters, a small, fuzzy, reddish circle can be discerned due to the manifest point rotating around the pole. Shifting the pole into the large *plain* of one of the Cassini ovals causes the circle to widen to an encompassing band. If the pole is located near the center of a plain, neither dot nor circle can be discerned.

A possible cause of a distinct nickel-sized circle on a pitch would be the location of the spin-axis pole near or at the midpoint of the narrow gap or *isthmus* between two of the plains (as shown in Fig. 4b). The distance across the seamless part of the isthmus is approximately 22 mm, nearly equal to the diameter of a nickel (~21 mm). The seam spinning rapidly around the mid-isthmian point would produce a reddish circle with an internal area about the size of a nickel. In contrast to the circles caused by a pole migrating into a plain, this circle would be quite distinct and invariable in size. Note that the circular pattern around a mid-isthmian pole would be reinforced by having two manifest points rotating about the axis.

Another possible cause of a circle on a nickel pitch would be a rotation of the dot, in a phenomenon called *precession*. This is a "wobble" or gyration of the spin axis about a secondary axis. If the dot at the end of the spin axis rotates, it circumscribes a small circle. The precession can rotate in the opposite direction or same direction as the spin.

Precession is a common feature of spinning objects. The term was first used by Hipparchus of Nicea in 130 B.C. when he described the effects of the wobble of the earth's spin axis. Precession is also the basis of the behavior of a toy top, a gyroscope, and a boomerang. In all cases, precession is caused by a secondary torque perturbing a spinning body.

Although the rotation of a manifest point or the precession of a pole might cause the appearance of the nickel-sized circle, this pattern does not necessarily indicate a reduced magnitude of spin or deflection. Note that the dot and circular patterns shown in Figs. 1 and 2 occur on balls spinning at the same rate. In addition, the spin axis has two poles—a dot pattern might appear at one pole, while the opposite pole displays a circle or

bands. Obviously, the ball would not have different spin and deflection rates at the two poles.

Precession could affect curveball quality by continuously shifting the angle of the spin axis during the ball's trajectory, thereby continuously redirecting instantaneous deflection and reducing total effective deflection. However, one of us (Bahill) has calculated that this reduction is insignificant.

Our approach to elucidating the assumed relationship between the circle and poor deflection, therefore, will be to present explanations coaches and pitchers have given us describing how grips and releases of pitches might have detrimental effects on deflection, and then to suggest how these manipulative flaws might yield the circular pattern.

Possible Pitch-Release Mechanics of the Nickel Curveball

As Sal Maglie has described the release of the curveball from an overhand delivery, it is "thrown with a strong downward snap of the wrist and released between the thumb and the forefinger" (Terrell, 1958). The torque action of the first and second fingers and the ball's forward linear momentum are translated into angular momentum as the ball rolls off the side of the forefinger, generating the curveball's spin (topspin for an overhand pitcher). If the pitcher uses the more common of two possible four-seam grips for the curve (see Fig. 4a and Bahill et al., 2005), then the spin axis is set so that one pole is located on or very near the

seam at a point directly distal to the fingertip of the index finger. With proper release, this might produce the visual effect of a dime curveball.

A slow spin (and consequent poor deflection) of a curve could be caused by a failure of the pitcher to snap the wrist hard just prior to release. Slow wrist action results in a weak torque applied to the ball by the fingers, producing insufficient angular momentum. This is probably one of the more common causes of poor deflection of the curve, but whether a reorientation of the spin axis occurs to create a nickel pattern must be the subject of further investigation.

A second possible cause of a poor curve is an overly active thumb. For the pitcher to get a rapid spin on the curve, the thumb should be directly behind the ball at the release. Most pitchers nudge the ball a bit with a little flick of the thumb—as long as the thumb stays behind the ball, it will not interfere with the spin.

Sometimes the flick is exaggerated, however, and the thumb pivots upward and to the right (for a right-handed pitcher), as shown in Fig. 5. When Sid Hudson was the pitching coach of the Washington Senators during the 1960s he invented a device that pitchers called the "Hudson Harness." It is a strap to be worn in practice as an aid in training pitchers to develop a faster spin and greater deflection of the curve. Hudson writes, "Most all pitchers coming out of high school will try to roll their thumbs over the top of the ball [as they release a curveball]. This is incorrect." An elastic band on Hudson's device holds the thumb behind the ball, preventing the thumb roll. He has made

Fig. 1	**Fig. 2**	**Fig. 3**
Dime-sized dot on a spinning ball. Spin axis pole was placed on the side of the seam. View is that of the batter of a right-handed pitcher's slider.	Nickel-sized circle on a spinning ball. Spin axis pole was placed in the center of an isthmus. View is that of the batter of a right-handed pitcher's slider.	Surface features of the ball.

this gadget for a large number of major league pitching coaches, so its use has been widespread in pro ball. After Hudson retired in 1986 from the Texas Rangers, where he had been pitching coach and then scout, he coached at Baylor University for six years and used the harness with great success.

According to Hudson, his device is designed to "keep the thumb from rolling over the top of the ball so that the ball will have more spin on it..." Although pitchers develop the thumb-rolling habit in their efforts to increase the ball's spin rate, the errant thumb's energy could be interfering with the spin somehow, thereby reducing deflection.

The rolling thumb applies torque to the right half of the spin axis at about a 15 to 20 degree angle to the direction of spin (see Fig. 5). Such a force applied asymmetrically to the axis of a spinning sphere might twist the axis into a wobble, or it might move an axis pole away from the seam. A nickel pattern could result in either case. Precession could produce poor deflection by redirecting spin momentum; alternatively, spin and deflection could be reduced by resistive friction of the thumb. In these models, the size of the circle on a nickel curveball and the quality of the pitch would be variable, depending upon the force applied by the thumb.

A third possible explanation for the nickel curveball is based on the position of the first and second fingers as they roll off the ball. If these fingers are on the side of the ball rather than the front at the moment of release, the pole could move far-ther from the fingertips—into the isthmus or the plain. The spin axis is not perpendicular to the trajectory of the pitch in this case, so the Magnus force (and, consequently, the magnitude of deflection) is reduced accordingly (see Adair, 2002, for an explanation of the Magnus force). This could result in the appearance of a nickel-sized circle and a poor curveball.

A fourth explanation for the nickel pattern on the curve involves the grip. The four-seam curveball can be gripped with either of two orientations. The grip shown in Fig. 4a seems to be the more common, but the ball could be rotated horizontally 180° (Fig. 4b), so that the index and second fingers are placed alongside the seam in such a way they point at an open end of an isthmus. The axis pole then occurs within the isthmus, creating the nickel aspect. This is true for several other possible curveball grips as well. The spin rate will be unaffected by the location of the axis pole, however, so a high-quality curve could result.

Possible Pitch-Release Mechanics of the Nickel Slider

Sometimes the slider is thrown with a four-seam fastball grip (Fig. 6), because pitchers consider the slider to be a modified fastball, and because they avoid changing their grips any more than necessary. With the ideal release from this grip, the slider's spin axis pole that is visible to the

Fig. 4a	Fig. 4b	Fig. 5
Side view of the most common four-seam curveball grip. Arrow indicates direction of spin; dot indicates a pole of the spin axis.	Side view of an alternative four-seam curveball grip. Arrow indicates direction of spin; dot indicates a pole of the spin axis.	Motion of the thumb rolling over the ball on a curve.

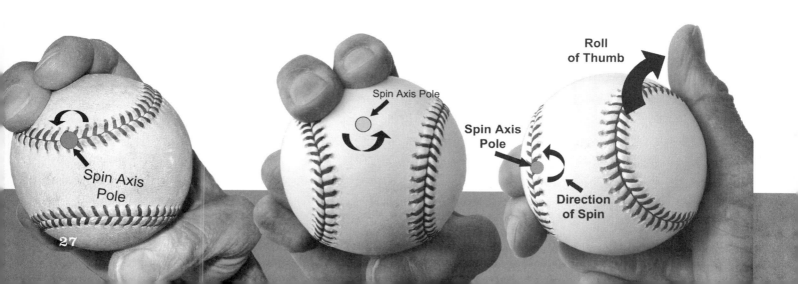

batter will be located on the ball's seam (Fig. 7). This point on the seam would form the dot that identifies a dime slider.

Hudson has specified that his device is not appropriate for training a pitcher to throw a slider; the nickel slider and nickel curve might be caused by different errors in the release of the ball. To determine the cause of a poor slider, we interviewed four former major league pitchers— Dick Bosman, Bob Humphreys, Jim Kaat, and Ken Sanders (Kaat is left-handed; the others are right-handed). No pitchers possessed better sliders during the 1960s and '70s.

All of these pitchers stressed that the ball must be thrown with good arm speed. The first and second fingers must be on top of the ball; the release point of the slider is slightly off-center, however. To ensure proper release, Humphreys (who learned to throw the slider from Frank Lary when they were teammates on the Tigers) says he concentrated on putting pressure on the right front corner of the ball. As a result of this pressure, the last part of his hand to touch the ball was the thumb-side edge of the index finger's tip. The ball left his hand with the spin axis assuming an oblique angle to the forward direction of the pitch (see Fig. 7). Three of our interviewees reported that throwing sliders caused blisters or calluses on the thumb side of the index finger's tip.

Pitchers often create a problem when they try to increase the spin rate of the slider—they have a tendency to throw a hybrid between the fastball and curve. On this point Sanders states, "When you break your wrist, it creates a bad slider," and Bosman explains, "If the hand rolls over on the ball, the slider will be lazy—the spin is too slow." Humphreys writes that a major problem occurs when the "hand gets around the side of the ball, instead of staying on top and throwing right-front corner." Kaat states, "Too many pitchers today throw the slider like they're 'turning a door knob'. . . bad for the elbow and doesn't have much 'bite' to it."

As in the curveball, the spin of the slider is created by the friction of the index and second fingers. If these fingers stay on top of the ball, as recommended by our interviewees, an effective slider is produced with its spin axis at an approximate 60 degree angle to trajectory to give the "sliding" effect. When the wrist rolls to the outside of the

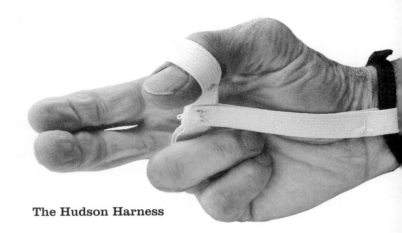

The Hudson Harness

Fig. 6

A batter's view of a four-seam (or cross-seam) fastball grip. This is also a common slider grip.

Fig. 7

Direction of spin imparted to a dime slider. Arrow indicates spin direction; dot indicates the axis pole visible to the batter. View is from above the hand as the ball is released.

Spin Axis Pole

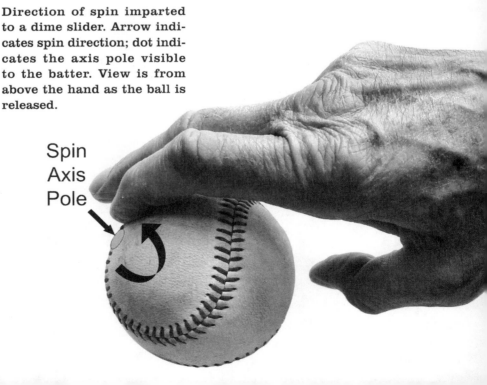

ball, the spin axis is shifted so that it is more nearly parallel to the trajectory. If the four-seam fastball grip is used, this shift moves the leading axis pole away from the seam, which might result in a nickel-sized circle. The Magnus force and deflection of the pitch are reduced because the hand rolling over the ball produces a slow spin with the axis shifted toward the direction in which the ball is moving.

As with the curveball, a number of different grips have been used for the slider. We do not know which grip is most popular. Some of these grips could produce a dot; some will not, no matter how well the pitch is released or how effective the pitch might be.

Summary

Coaches and players are in general agreement that spin rates and deflections of the nickel curve and nickel slider are considerably reduced compared to the dime versions of these pitches. As shown in our figures, the nickel pattern does not necessarily indicate a slow spin and poor deflection, however. The circular features that appear on nickel pitches might be caused by precession of the spin axis or by a shift of an axis pole to a position some distance from the seam, such as the midpoint of an isthmus. We have presented pitchers' and coaches' explanations of how the hand might create poor pitch quality, and we have suggested how the described pitch grips and release mechanics might create nickel patterns on pitches.

We conclude that the circular pattern seen on a nickel pitch results from certain orientations of the seam relative to the spin axis. Whether or not this pattern is associated with a pitch of poor quality depends on the pitcher's grip and release of the ball.

# # #

ACKNOWLEDGMENTS

We are grateful to Dick Bosman, Sid Hudson, Bob Humphreys, Jim Kaat, and Ken Sanders for providing their cooperation, advice, and valuable information to make this article possible. We thank Sid Hudson for sending us an example of his device. Also, we thank Zach Bahill for photographing the pitch simulations shown in Figs. 1 and 2; for all other figures the photographer was Burgundy Featherkile. Additional thanks go to Eric Sallee for his help with experimentation on spin axis angles.

REFERENCES

Adair, R. K. *The Physics of Baseball*, 3rd ed. New York: HarperCollins, 2002.

Bahill, A.T., D.G. Baldwin, and J. Venkateswaran. "Predicting a Baseball's Path," *American Scientist*, 93(3):218–225 (May–June 2005).

Terrell, R. Sal Maglie on the Art of Pitching, *Sports Illustrated*, 8(11): 34–45 (March 17, 1958).

NOTES

1. To create the simulations shown in Fig. 1 and Fig. 2 we drilled a hole in a regulation baseball and inserted a four inch bolt. The bolt was chucked in a drill and spun at a rate of 250 rpm. The bolt is the spin axis, which defines the pole. The shutter speed was 0.5 seconds and the f-stop was set at 5.6. We have shown the batter's view of a right-handed pitcher's slider.

DAVE BALDWIN *pitched for the Washington Senators, Milwaukee Brewers, and the Chicago White Sox in the 1960s and 70s. Later, he earned a Ph.D. in genetics and an M.S. in systems engineering from the University of Arizona.*

TERRY BAHILL *is a Professor of Systems Engineering at the University of Arizona in Tucson. He received the Sandia National Laboratories Gold President's Quality Award. He is a Fellow of the Institute of Electrical and Electronics Engineers (IEEE) and a Fellow of the International Council on Systems Engineering (INCOSE).*

ALAN NATHAN *is a professor of physics at the University of Illinois with research specialties that include the physics of baseball. He has done extensive research on the aerodynamics of a baseball in flight and the science of the collision between bat and ball. He is currently writing a book on the subject.*

Mystery Photos

Since 1947 I have been researching and collecting baseball photographs, writing captions and reassembling the facts that surround them. My specialty is action photos of players sliding. Over the years I have learned that when all research tools have been exhausted, it is time for fresh eyes to view the photo; there are none better than those of SABR members. Here are two tough new cases, and the status of the cases I presented last year ("Nine Mystery Photos" in *Baseball Research Journal* #34). I am happy to say that seven of those mysteries have been solved and thanks to the hundreds of members who helped unravel them.

1. The Braves Mystery

Who is this Braves runner? The Braves uniform is 1934 or 1935. The third baseman's stockings tell us it is the 1934 Dodgers. So we know it is the Dodgers versus the Braves in 1934, at Braves Field. With very few clues available, the runner needs to be identified before the mystery can be completely solved.

2. The Honus Mystery

This is a famous photo, but there are few clues to identify it. The runner is the Pirates Honus Wagner. His socks tell us it is either 1912, 1913, or 1914. Don Duran, author of the book *Boiling Out at the Springs*, identifies the ballpark as Whittington Park in Hot Springs, AK. But the identity of the catcher and the umpire remains a mystery.

If you have any information on either of these photos contact:

George Michael
1201 Sugarloaf Mountain Road
Comus, MD 20842
George.Michael@nbcuni.com

Solutions to Previous Mysteries

1. THE SENATORS MYSTERY —Many thought the Senators pitcher was Joe Martina. In fact, the Washington pitcher is Allan Russell. SABR member Edward Marly sent photos that helped solve this one.

   July 19, 1924: The Browns' Wally Gerber scored on Jack Tobin's base hit in the 10th inning. The Senators catcher is Bennie Tate, and the umpire is Dick Nallin. The Browns won, 10–9. The game lasted four hours and 45 minutes. CASE CLOSED.

2. THE DODGERS MYSTERY—Ray Bilbrough of Saline, MI, identifed the catcher as being Butch Henline of the Phillies. The runner, according to a photo in the *New York Daily News* on May 2, 1922, is Jimmy Johnston, who was tagged out in the first inning of the May 1 game won by the Dodgers, 2–0. CASE CLOSED.

3. THE HOOPER MYSTERY—Despite many letters, the identity of the third baseman and the year remain a mystery. UNSOLVED.

4. THE JACKIE ROBINSON MYSTERY—Bob Clobes of Chesterfield, MO, identified the Phillies runner as Granny Hamner. Dave Smith of Retrosheet determined that the play occurred on April 23, 1948, as the Phillies beat the Dodgers, 10–2. CASE CLOSED.

5. THE CUBS MYSTERY—I received a ton of mail on this photo, but no one could absolutely identify the Cubs player. The most popular guesses were Lou Stringer, Emil Verban, Bobby Sturgeon, Johnny Ostrowski, and Gene Mauch. If you are a serious Cubs fan, can you help with this one? UNSOLVED.

6. THE GIANTS MYSTERY—Richard Westin of San Anselmo, CA, solved this mystery with a photo of the same play taken from a different angle. The photo shows that on June 7, 1939, the Giants' Jo Jo Moore was forced out at second when the Cubs' Dick Bartell stepped on the bag. The Cubs won, 7–1. CASE CLOSED.

7. THE DiMAGGIO MYSTERY—Dave Jordan of Jenkintown, PA, gets the key assist on this mystery. He pointed out that the A's third baseman is *not* Hank Majeski but Mickey Rutner. Rutner played third base for just 11 games in 1947. One of those games took place on September 28, when Hal Weafer was the umpire at third. DiMaggio advanced to third base on George McQuinn's single in the sixth inning of New York's 5–3 win. It was the season's last day, and the last major league game for Weafer and Rutner. CASE CLOSED.

8. THE CARDINALS MYSTERY—It did not take long for a lot of Cardinal fans to identify the Cards' runner as Frankie Frisch. Researching a number of Boston newspapers revealed that the play took place in the first inning of the opener of a doubleheader in Boston on August 26, 1931. Frisch slid under the tag of catcher Al Spohrer as umpire Dolly Stark looked on. St. Louis won, 6–1. CASE CLOSED.

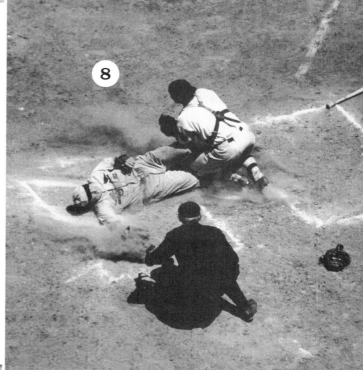

9. THE RED SOX MYSTERY—Many people swore that the Red Sox runner was Joe Vosmik. In all the mail I received, Charles Marsh of Allentown, PA, included a photo from a book showing this play taken from a different angle. It identified pitcher Monte Pearson tagging Lou Finney out at home. The umpire was George Moriarty. The play took place in the first inning of an April 26, 1940, game at Fenway Park when the Sox beat the Yankees, 8–1. CASE CLOSED.

33

ROY E. BROWNELL II

Was Ty Cobb a Power Hitter?

Ty Cobb is usually thought of as the very embodiment of the Deadball Era hitter; the "Punch and Judy" counterpoint to the post-1920 Ruthian power game.[1] This common misconception is underscored in a number of ways. First, it is supported by the types of players who have surpassed Cobb's career records. Lou Brock bested his lifetime stolen base record, Pete Rose his career hit mark and Rickey Henderson his modern record for total runs scored. Other recent players frequently compared to Cobb are high-average contact hitters such as Wade Boggs, Rod Carew, Tony Gwynn and Ichiro Suzuki. These players have been either speedsters, contact hitters or both and none is known for his power hitting (with the possible exception of Henderson). Because of the natural tendency to place players from a different era into a familiar, contemporary context, Cobb's ability to steal bases, collect base hits, score runs and hit for high average has led to some misleading comparisons; which contribute to the view that Cobb could not and did not hit for power.[2]

Second, Cobb's open contempt for the Ruthian power game has done little to dispel this modern misconception. Cobb much preferred baseball the way it was played during the Deadball Era. Cobb's approach to batting involved him choking up, holding the bat with his hands apart, and hitting to all fields, often just pecking at the ball.[3]

Third, Cobb's Deadball home run totals appear quaint compared to Lively ball era totals and seem to bespeak a contact hitter's batting style. By averaging less than five home runs a season—a good week's work for today's sluggers—Cobb's home run output on its face seems to confirm his lack of power.

The perception of Cobb as solely a contact hitter has long been in need of revision. Contrary to contemporary myth, Cobb could indeed hit for power and, while he might not be properly characterized as a power hitter during his prime, he could (and did) hit for power more effectively than the majority of his contemporaries. There are a number of factors that point to this conclusion. They include: (1) his actual home run hitting, which has long been overlooked; (2) his ability to collect extra-base hits; (3) his prolific slugging average and total base output; and (4) his ability to drive in runs.

Cobb's Home Run Hitting

Cobb spent the majority of his career playing in the Deadball Era, when home runs were a rarity and those that were hit were much more apt to be of the inside-the-park variety. Within the confines of the Deadball Era, Cobb displayed impressive power. He led the major leagues with nine home runs in 1909, establishing a team record unsur-

passed in the Deadball Era. Leading one league in home runs (let alone both) is a feat that certainly eluded purported modern-day "Cobb prototypes" such as Brock, Rose, Henderson, and the like. Moreover, to claim this honor, Cobb had to out-homer some distinguished sluggers. They included the likes of Harry Davis, "Home Run" Baker, and Sam Crawford, who won 10 league home run crowns between them.

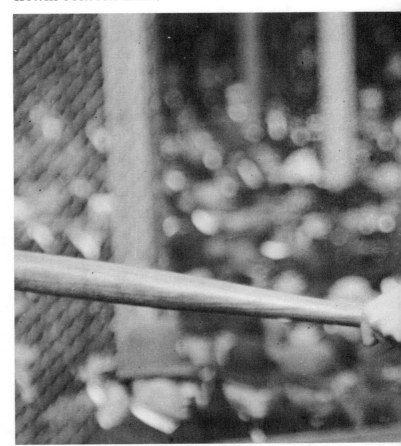

Nor was Cobb's 1909 home run total a fluke. He finished runner-up or tied for runner-up in the AL in home runs on three occasions (1907, 1910, and 1911), seven times in the top five, and 11 times in the top ten.[4] In fact, one of his top-ten finishes occurred in 1921, during the Lively ball era. Cobb even out-homered entire teams. For each of three straight years (1908–1910) Cobb hit more home runs than the Chicago White Sox, a feat he replicated in 1917 by out-homering the Washington Senators. Cobb also led his team in home runs six times—no small feat playing next to Crawford, Bobby Veach, and Harry Heilmann.

It could, of course, be argued that since 46 of Cobb's 117 career round-trippers were inside-the-park, his home run totals reflect more speed than power. Proponents of this outlook could point out, for example, that in 1909 all of Cobb's home runs were inside-the-park jobs (tying an AL record for most inside-the-park home runs in a season).[5] Since all his home runs were inside-the-park, the logic goes, Cobb must not have hit for power. There are, however, at least four reasons why such a position is fundamentally flawed.

First, Cobb hit a good number of out-of-the-park home runs. Excepting 1909, approximately one half of his career Deadball Era circuit clouts were out-of-the-park home runs. In fact, Cobb ranked among the league leaders in *out-of-the-park* home runs, thus belying the notion that his home run totals were solely the product of speed. Cobb finished tied for third in the league in 1907 and placed second outright in 1912. His six out-of-the-park home runs in 1912 set a team record at the time, and Cobb led or was second on his team in this category on seven occasions.

Second, if speed were the only factor involved in finishing among the league home run leaders during the Deadball Era, then why did Clyde "Deerfoot" Milan never have a top-ten finish? Why could neither Max Carey nor Eddie Collins muster more than one top-ten finish each? The answer is essentially that Milan, Carey, and Collins had the speed but not the power. Cobb had both.

Third, viewing Deadball inside-the-park home runs as solely a reflection of speed projects modern-day notions of inside-the-park home runs back to the Deadball Era. During that period the field of play was generally much larger than it is today. Cobb played 15 years in Detroit's Navin Field, which had its right-field fence 370 feet from home plate and its center-field fence 467 feet away (as opposed to 325 and 440 feet, respectively, when Tiger Stadium closed in 1999).[6] The extra 45 feet in

Cobb tied for second in the AL in out-of-the-park home runs in 1911 and placed second outright the next year.

(as opposed to 325 and 440 feet, respectively, when Tiger Stadium closed in 1999).[6] The extra 45 feet in right field and 27 feet in center field almost certainly cost Cobb a good share of out-of-the-park home runs. Because of these inhospitable dimensions, in 15 years playing in Navin Field, Cobb hit just 16 home runs.[7]

Not only was hitting out-of-the-park home runs rare during the Deadball Era, but hitting inside-the-park home runs could be difficult as well. If the crowd was large enough, fans were often permitted to view the game from standing-room-only sections placed on the outfield grass. Balls hit over the outfielders' heads into these sections, which might have been inside-the-park home runs without the crowd or out-of-the-park home runs in today's ballparks, were frequently ruled only ground-rule doubles or triples, thus costing the hitter home runs.

Fourth, Cobb's home run hitting during the Lively ball era reinforces the view that his home run totals were not merely the product of his speed. During the Lively ball era—when Cobb began to hit home runs more frequently—*only six* of his 50 home runs were of the inside-the-park variety. In 1925, Cobb finished 11th in the American League with 12 home runs, none of which was an inside-the-park job.[8] Clearly, during the Lively ball era, Cobb was not relying on speed for his home runs—he was hitting the ball out of the park.[9] Knowing Cobb's stubborn refusal to change his style of play, the most plausible explanation would seem to be that Cobb was hitting as he always had—often with punch but with the added benefit of liveball conditions.

Comparison of Cobb's Home Run Hitting Across Historical Eras

The number of times Cobb finished in the top ten in home runs is worthy of some elaboration. Consider the following chart.[10] The players listed in it are generally considered sluggers. Cobb's home run title and 11 top-ten finishes compare favorably against these Lively ball power hitters, even allowing for the fact that expansion has increased the number of players in the modern era.

Cobb, of course, was not a greater slugger than Eddie Murray or Ted Kluszewski. Nonetheless, this chart does reflect that Cobb did hit for power and, within the context of his time, he did so more effectively than many players traditionally viewed as power hitters.

More elaborate quantitative efforts have been undertaken to compare players across historical eras, and these studies confirm Cobb's home-run hitting. G. Scott Thomas, for example, has recali-

HR Titles, HR Finishes, and Career HR

	HR Titles	Top-10 Finishes	Career HR
Ty Cobb	1	11	117
Rafael Palmeiro	0	11	569
Eddie Murray	1	8	504
Frank Thomas	0	9	487
Dave Winfield	0	7	465
Jeff Bagwell	0	7	449
Andre Dawson	1	9	438
Billy Williams	0	9	426
Darrell Evans	1	6	414
Duke Snider	1	9	407
Al Kaline	0	8	399
Joe Carter	0	7	396
Tony Perez	0	6	379
Norm Cash	0	9	377
Rocky Colavito	1	9	374
Gil Hodges	0	10	370
Yogi Berra	0	9	358
Lee May	0	7	354
Boog Powell	0	7	339
Don Baylor	0	5	338
Greg Luzinski	0	7	307
Ted Kluszewski	1	5	279
Rudy York	1	11	277

brated player statistics as if they had played from 1996 to 2000. While one should not lose sight of the fact that projections are not hard numbers, and as such should not be relied upon unduly, it is worth noting that under Thomas' formula, Cobb's career adjusted home runs are 587, ranking him 25th on his list. Among those players who spent most of their career before 1920, Roger Connor is the only player ahead of Cobb.[11]

Michael Schell lays out his own statistical model that also permits comparison of player statistics across eras. Schell's model computes Cobb's adjusted home run total for an average season to be 22,[12] tying him with Don Baylor, Darrell Evans, Andre Thornton, and Jim Rice. Among players who spent the majority of their career before the Lively ball era, Cobb is tied with Honus Wagner, Tilly Walker, and Joe Jackson and finishes ahead of Harry Davis, Connor, Sam Thompson, and Dan Brouthers. By contrast, under Schell's model, other Deadball speedsters do not fare nearly as well as Cobb. Collins' home runs are recalculated at nine, Carey at 13, and Milan at five.[13]

Schell also projects Cobb's adjusted career home run total to be 418, 29th on his list, trailing only Crawford among players who completed most of their playing days before 1920.[14] These are all projections, to be sure, but they do reinforce the notion that Cobb could hit for power.

It is worth remembering that prior to 1920 the threshold for hitting a high number of career home runs was not 500 but 100. During this period only ten players reached the 100 home run plateau. Going into the 1920 season—not quite two-thirds of the way through his career—Cobb had 67 home runs, well on his way toward the 100 threshold.

As noted by Cobb's first full-length biographer, while his career home run total did

> not begin to equal Ruth's record . . . it must be remembered that in this respect Ruth stands in a class by himself. As compared with the home-run records of other great stars of the diamond in days gone by or with those of today's heroes, Ty's record looms large on baseball's horizon. He is one of the few players who have driven out more than 100 homers in a life time.[15]

After his final season, Cobb was tied for 16th on the all-time home run list.[16]

The Views of Cobb's Contemporaries

Deadball Era players and observers recognized Cobb's ability to hit for distance. Charles Comiskey, owner of the Chicago White Sox, wrote of Cobb in 1910 that he is "able to hit the ball further away than the majority of 'cleanup' hitters."[17] Rube Bressler observed, "Cobb could hit the long ball—when he wanted to. Of course, that dead ball . . . we didn't have a baseball to hit in those days. We had a squash. . . . Still, Cobb could hit them a distance when he wanted to."[18] Joe Sewell stated, "Ruth hit all those home runs, but Cobb could whack the ball as hard as anyone."[19] Tris Speaker noted that Cobb "can bunt, chop-hit, deliver long drives, or put balls out of sight."[20]

Heilmann said of Cobb: "Cobb was always, by preference, a place hitter. People never figured him as a slugger, but he could have been a dangerous slugger if he had set out to be. He is now, when he feels in the mood. But when he sets out to slug the ball, he takes a big stride forward and wades right in."[21] A prominent baseball writer observed in 1922, "Ty be it noted, is not primarily a slugger. . . . He does slug oftentimes and to some purpose. His doubles are many and his homers total up to impressive figures."[22]

Cobb himself stated in the early 1920s:

> [i]f I had set out to be a home run hitter, I am confident that in a good season I could have made between twenty and thirty home runs. True, I couldn't hope to challenge Babe Ruth in his specialty. But I do feel that I could have made an impressive number of homers if I had set out with that end in view. . . . My idea of a genuine hitter is a hitter who can bunt, who can place his hits and who, when the need arises, can slug.[23]

Anecdotal Evidence of Cobb's Power Hitting

Anecdotal evidence reinforces the view that Cobb could hit for power when he so desired. The most famous example occurred in May 1925 in St. Louis. Fed up with hearing about Babe Ruth's power game (and no doubt alert to a breeze blowing out to right field),[24] Cobb reportedly informed the press: "I'll show you something today. . . . I'm going for home runs for the first time in my career."[25] That day Cobb hit three home runs—tying an American League record at the time—and launched a double to the far reaches of right-center field.[26] Cobb hit two more home runs the following day, drove another ball to the wall, and came within a foot of yet another home run the next game, settling for a double.[27] Cobb's five home runs in consecutive games (all out-of-the-park home runs) tied a major league record, a mark subsequently equaled but never surpassed. As Cobb's premier biographer reflected,

> [this] home run outburst marked no new, power-oriented phase in Cobb's career. . . . He still loved the old game, still preferred most of the time just to 'nip' at the ball, as Walter Johnson had once described his hitting style. But he could also clout with the musclemen when he chose. It was a question of how the game *ought* to be played.[28]

On September 30, 1907, with the American League pennant going down to the wire, Cobb's Detroit Tigers faced off in a pivotal and long-remembered game in Philadelphia against the Athletics. The Tigers trailed 8–6 going into the top of the ninth. With a runner on first, Cobb stepped in against future Hall of Famer Rube Waddell. Cobb sent Waddell's second pitch over the right-field wall to send the game into extra innings.[29] Ultimately, the game was called for darkness after 17 innings, the Athletics were deprived of a key victory (there being no makeup games), and the Tigers went on to win their first of three consecutive American League crowns. Of the home run, one author wrote: "It was just another case of Cobb doing what he wanted when he wanted."[30] Incidentally, that home run was one of five Cobb hit that year, almost half of the Tigers' team total of 11.

He was also known to hit tape-measure blasts. In 1907, against another future Hall of Famer, Addie Joss, Cobb stroked one of the longest home runs hit up to that time at Cleveland's League Park.[32] Five years later, again at League Park, Cobb hit another shot that may have matched or even exceeded the length of his 1907 effort.[33] In 1917, in Boston, Cobb drilled a pitch into the center-field stands, a spot reached before only by Ruth.[34] That same year in St. Louis, Cobb drove a home run ball over 500 feet, thought to have exceeded prior tape-measure shots by Jackson and Ruth.[35]

Cobb's home-run hitting exploits should not be all that surprising considering that he matured to reach over six feet tall and weigh approximately 190 pounds, a good-sized player for the time.

Cobb's Ability to Hit for Extra Bases

During the Deadball Era, home runs were only one indication of power hitting. Extra-base hits help to provide a fuller picture of a player's slugging ability. At the time of his retirement, Cobb was the all-time leader with 1,136 extra-base hits. He still ranks tenth on the all-time list.

Cobb led the league in extra-base hits three times and finished either second or third on four other occasions. His 79 extra-base hits in 1911 were the highest of the Deadball Era, and his 74 extra-base hits in 1917 the fifth highest.

Cobb's output of doubles and triples was prolific. Cobb ranks fourth all-time in doubles, having led the league three times in this category. Cobb is second all-time in triples, a statistic he led the league in on four occasions. Triples, of course, were "the real power statistic of the dead-ball era."[36] Today, batters who hit large numbers of triples are generally speedsters who hit balls in the gaps and can turn doubles into three-base hits. In the Deadball Era, with its larger fields of play, triples (as with inside-the-park home runs) were more apt to come from batters, like Cobb, who could hit the ball far enough to get it past outfielders and mobile enough to get to third quickly.

Cobb's Slugging Average and Total Bases Output

Slugging average is traditionally viewed as a key indicator of power hitting (hence its name). Cobb led the league eight times in this category and finished second or third on six other occasions.[37] Only Ruth, Ted Williams, and Rogers Hornsby led the league in slugging average more often.

Despite playing most of his career in the Deadball Era, Cobb posted impressive slugging figures. Cobb's .621 slugging average in 1911 was the third highest mark of the Deadball period, and his .584 slugging average in 1912 the sixth highest.

Nor did Cobb's success in slugging average end with the advent of the Lively ball. Cobb racked up three top-ten finishes in slugging in the 1920s despite being at the end of his career. Furthermore, his career slugging average—despite 15 Deadball seasons—is higher than a number of liveball sluggers such as Harmon Killebrew, Jim Rice, Ernie Banks, Frank Howard, Eddie Mathews, Reggie Jackson, Dave Winfield, and Dave Kingman, to name just a few. Needless to say, Cobb's career slugging average exceeds those of Rose, Brock, Henderson, Carew, Boggs, Gwynn, and Suzuki (none of whom has *ever* led the league in this category). Finally, it bears mentioning that Thomas' statistical formula ranks Cobb 10th in adjusted career slugging average[38] and Schell's formula 14th.[39]

Cobb's total base output is also impressive. Cobb led the league in this category six times, an American League record he shares with Ruth and Williams. Only Hank Aaron and Hornsby led the league more often. Nine other times Cobb finished in the top ten in this category, including three times during the 1920s. His 367 total bases in 1911 were the second most ever prior to the Lively ball era. Even today, Cobb remains fourth all-time in career total bases.

Cobb's Ability to Drive in Runs

Runs batted in is another category typically viewed as an indicator of a slugger's prowess. Cobb was a prolific RBI man. He ranks sixth all-time in career RBI, led the league four times, and had 13 seasons in the top ten. In fact, four of those top-ten finishes occurred during the power-happy 1920s. Cobb's 127 RBI in 1911 set an American League record at the time and were the third highest of the Deadball Era.

It should hardly be surprising that a hitter of Cobb's caliber was so effective at driving in runs since Cobb batted third or clean-up throughout most of his career. That is noteworthy in and of itself since modern "Cobb prototypes" have typically not batted in the middle of the order but tended to hit first or second.

Conclusion

Ty Cobb was not a power hitter per se, any more than George Brett or Stan Musial were principally power hitters. Nonetheless, Cobb *could and did hit for power*, a point that should not be lost on students of baseball history.

#

ACKNOWLEDGMENTS

The author would like to thank the residents of Ty Cobb Avenue for their support and Jim Charlton, Ron Cobb, Scott Flatow, David Stephan, Tom Simon, and David Vincent for their invaluable critiques of this paper. Any errors remain the author's alone.

ROY BROWNELL II *is an attorney. He lives in Washington, D.C., with his wife Sandy.*

NOTES

1. Donald Honig. *Baseball America* 232 (1985) ("Ty did not hit with power").
2. William Curran. *Big Sticks* 203 (1990) ("During . . . Pete Rose's pursuit of Cobb's lifetime record for base hits . . . . [m]any young fans may have been left with the impression that the Georgian had been little more than an ill-tempered singles hitter").
3. Charles C. Alexander. *Ty Cobb* 90 (1984). Cobb denied that his approach to hitting cost him power. "'Loss of power' remains the criticism against spread hands hitting. The truth is that the mania for killing the ball has replaced common sense. 'Power' is not just producing home runs." Cobb continued: "Loss of power through choking up? The statement is laughable. . . . there was power aplenty in my style of holding a bat." Ty Cobb, *My Life in Baseball*, 148–49 (1993 ed.).
4. See www.Baseball-reference.com for all single-season and career rankings.
5. Inside-the-park and home/away home run statistics come from SABR's *The Home Run Encyclopedia*. See SABR, *The Home Run Encyclopedia*, 56 (1996). Inside-the-park home run totals are subject to periodic updating as ongoing research unearths new data.
6. www.baseball-almanac.com/stadium/tiger_stadium.shtml.
7. Bill James compared Cobb's home run hitting to that of the celebrated Deadball slugger Gavy Cravath, noting that Cravath played in homer-happy Baker Bowl while Cobb languished in Navin Field. James points out that Cobb more than tripled Cravath's career road home run output (82–26). *See The New Bill James Historical Baseball Abstract*, 102 (2001). One can only speculate as to how Cobb's home run statistics might have looked had he played in Baker Bowl with its right-field fence only 273 feet from home plate (97 feet closer than in Navin Field). Philip S. Lowry, *Green Cathedrals*, 173 (2006).
8. *Home Run Encyclopedia, supra* note 5, at 387.
9. The author thanks Tom Simon for raising this point.
10. The statistics in the table are taken from www.Baseball-reference.com.
11. G. Scott Thomas. *Leveling the Field*, 256 (2002).
12. Michael J. Schell. *Baseball's All-Time Best Sluggers*, 360 (2005).
13. *Ibid.* at Appendix N.
14. *Ibid.* at 334.
15. Sverre O. Braathen. *Ty Cobb: The Idol of Fandom*, 184 (1928).
16. The ranking is derived from Steve Nadel & Mike Caragliano's "All-Time Home Run List."
17. Marc Okkonen. *The Ty Cobb Scrapbook*, 227 (2001).
18. Lawrence S. Ritter. *The Glory of Their Times*, 204–05 (1984 ed.).
19. Robert Obojski. *Baseball's Strangest Moments*, 78 (1988).
20. Al Stump. *Cobb*, 363 (1996).
21. Harry Heilmann. "When you slug, step into the ball," 38 *Baseball Magazine*, 438 (March 1927).
22. F.C. Lane. "Natural Slugging vs. Scientific Batting," 29 *Baseball Magazine*, 388 (August 1922).
23. *Ibid.* at 388–89.
24. Okkonen, *supra* note 18, at 192.
25. Alexander, *supra* note 3, at 175.
26. Dan Holmes. *Ty Cobb: A Biography*, 103 (2004).
27. *See ibid.*
28. Alexander, *supra* note 3, at 176.
29. John Thorn. *Baseball's Ten Greatest Games*, 17–19 (1981).
30. Glenn Dickey. *The History of the American League*, 24 (1980).
31. Okkonen, *supra* note 17, at 8.
32. *Ibid.* at 78.
33. *Ibid.* at 118.
34. Stump, *supra* note 20, at 260; Okkonen, *supra* note 18, at 119.
35. Thomas Gilbert. *Dead Ball: Major League Baseball Before Babe Ruth*, 27 (1996).
36. Cobb's slugging titles were no mere reflection of his high batting average. Cobb led the league in Isolated Power five times. See *The Sabermetric Baseball Encyclopedia*. Isolated power is computed by subtracting batting average from slugging average, thus "isolating" extra-base hitting. Only Ruth, Williams, Mike Schmidt, and Barry Bonds have led the league more often in this category. The author wishes to thank Tom Simon for raising this issue.
37. Thomas, *supra* note 12, at 268.
38. Schell, *supra* note 13, at 348.
39. David Jones, ed. *Deadball Stars of the American League*. SABR, 2007. 529-530.

PHIL BIRNBAUM

Do Players Outperform in a Walk Season?

Do players perform better in their walk year? Conventional wisdom would say they do perform better in the year before they become free agents, at least according to the stereotype of the greedy player, who will put out extra effort only when he will be rewarded financially. Traditional economic theory agrees. Like all rational economic actors, baseball players should produce more of a product when the going price rises.

Take infielder Bret Boone, for example. From 1992 to 2000, the second baseman never hit more than 24 home runs or drove in more than 95 runs. In 2000, he hit only .251. But in 2001, the season before free agency, Boone set new highs in all three categories, going 37–141-.331 and finished third in the American League MVP voting.

It could be argued that Boone, realizing a good 2001 season could be worth millions of dollars on the free-agent market, decided to turn it on a bit and have a career year. That got him a raise of 146%, from $3.25 million to $8 million for 2002.

However, there's also the case of David Cone. Cone's last year as a Yankee was 2000, and you'd predict a good season ahead of his being shopped around for 2001. But Cone was horrible; he took a pay cut from $12,000,000 down to $1,000,000 and signed with the Red Sox for 2001, where he had a reasonable season. But, clearly, his off-year in 2000 cost him a great deal of money.

For every Bret Boone, who appears to turn it on his free-agent year, there's a David Cone, who collapses. To decide if there really is a free-agent effect, it's not enough to list specific cases—we need a systematic study.

Here's what I did. For every MLB free agent up to and including the end of 2001, I used an algorithm to predict how the player "should" have done based on historical trends. I then compared his actual performance to his prediction. If there is a tendency to outperform with free agency impending, the group of free agents should do better than their predictions overall, notwithstanding an occasional David Cone.

The Algorithm

The prediction algorithm is a modified version of the one I wrote about in the 2005 BRJ ("Which Great Teams Were Just Lucky?"); I tweaked it to be a bit more accurate for older players, since free agents tend to be from that group, and also to be more accurate for starting pitchers. The algorithm looks at the four years surrounding the given year, and tries to predict what the player should have done. It should be reasonably close to what you would guess just by eyeing the player's record.[1]

For instance, here's (non-free agent) random player X from 1976–1980. The statistic shown is "Runs Created per 27 outs," which estimates how many runs a team of nine of this same player would score in a game.

Player X	RC/27
1976	4.76
1977	6.27
1978	?
1979	8.95
1980	4.28

Table 1. Bret Boone's Batting Performance, 1999–2003

Year	G	AB	R	H	2B	3B	HR	RBI	SB	CS	BB	K	AVG	OBA	SLG	RC27
1999	152	608	102	153	38	1	20	63	14	9	47	112	.252	.310	.416	4.28
2000	127	463	61	116	18	2	19	74	8	4	50	97	.251	.326	.421	4.68
2001	158	623	118	206	37	3	37	141	5	5	40	110	.331	.372	.578	7.95
2002	155	608	88	169	34	3	24	107	12	5	53	102	.278	.339	.462	5.60
2003	159	622	111	183	35	5	35	117	16	3	68	125	.294	.366	.535	7.11

Table 2. David Cone's Pitching Performance, 1998–2003

Year	W	L	G	GS	CG	SO	GF	SV	IP	H	R	ER	HR	BB	K	ERA
1998	20	7	31	31	3	0	0	0	207.3	186	89	82	20	59	209	3.55
1999	12	9	31	31	1	1	0	0	193.2	164	84	74	21	90	177	3.44
2000	4	14	30	29	0	0	0	0	155.1	192	124	119	25	82	120	6.91
2001	9	7	25	25	0	0	0	0	135.3	148	74	65	17	57	115	4.31
2003	1	3	5	4	0	0	0	0	18.1	20	13	13	4	13	13	6.50

What would you expect for 1978? It looks like the average for the surrounding years is about 6.00, but the years closer to 1978 were a bit better . . . so the weighted average is maybe 6.75 or 7. A player is usually a bit closer to average than his stats suggest, so regressing that to the mean a bit gives maybe 6.25 or 6.5.

The algorithm comes up with 6.52. The player—Sixto Lezcano—was actually 6.57 for 1978, almost exactly what you would fill in. That is not all that common; players often surprise, as we saw with David Cone and Bret Boone. And Lezcano himself wasn't all that consistent in the surrounding years.

So Lezcano overachieved in 1978 by 0.05 runs per game. That works out to 0.4 runs for the season, which rounds down to zero. Zero is rare; a typical value for a full-time player would be ten runs or so, either way.

Using this algorithm, we calculate Bret Boone was +40 runs in 2001. David Cone was minus 39 runs in 2000. They're both extreme cases, and they pretty much cancel each other out.

The Results: Hitters

So what happens when we run the algorithm, not just for Cone and Boone, but for every free agent? We'll start with the hitters.

There were 399 free-agent hitters between 1977 and 2001 with at least 300 batting outs (AB-H) in the season before becoming a free agent. To put them on the same scale, I adjusted each player to exactly 400 batting outs, and checked their performance.

Overall, they exceeded their expectation by 2.3 runs. It looks like there may be an effect, albeit a small one. However, the algorithm isn't accurate enough to say for sure whether the 2.3 runs is significant.

So we have to do a comparison. Taking the 3,692 players who *weren't* free agents, they also exceeded their expectation, by 1.1 runs:

# of hitters performance vs. expected (runs)

Free agent hitters	399	+2.3
All other hitters	3692	+1.1

If there is a free-agent effect, it's only 1.2 runs per year—less the equivalent of turning one out into a triple. When pundits talk about greedy players putting out effort only when there's money on the line, they're certainly talking about more than one triple per year.

And the result is not statistically significant. The standard deviation of the difference between the two groups is about .75, so there is about an

11% probability that even if there were no effect, we would see a result this big (in either direction) by chance alone.

As stated, the estimate algorithm isn't perfect, so there could be some kind of bias causing these results. The most obvious is that it might overestimate older players and underestimate younger players. Since free agents tend to be older, that would cause the effect we're seeing here.

To check that, I checked only non-free agent hitters who were 29 or older (as of June 30 in their free-agent year):

Non-free-agent hitters age 29+: 1892 +0.8

So the difference rises from 1.2 runs to 1.4 runs—still not very much.

The Results: Pitchers

I took all free agents-to-be who started at least 20 games their free-agent season, and normalized them to 200 innings. The results were surprising:

Free Agent starters:	239	-4.1
All other starters:	2223	+0.5
All other starters age 29+:	1039	+0.7

There's a definite effect here, but it goes the wrong way; pitchers about to become free agents actually did *worse* than others! It could be that free agency makes pitchers less effective; perhaps they overthrow or something. But there are more plausible explanations, which I'll discuss below.

The difference between the two groups is about 4.5 runs per 200 innings, or a difference of about .19 in ERA. In one sense, that's not much. But over such a large group of pitchers, it's very unlikely to have occurred by chance. Further investigation into this group of players might be worthwhile.

Arbitration

Another common theory is that players who lose arbitration cases wind up underperforming, out of anger at perceived mistreatment by management. Under a version of this hypothesis, happy players who win arbitration cases should outperform those unhappy players who lose.

I checked these groups the same way as the free agents, up to 1996. Here are the results for batters:

No Arbitration	3877	+1.20
Won	46	-0.53
Lost	67	+0.34

And for starting pitchers:

No Arbitration	1917	+1.85
Won	32	-1.46
Lost	34	-1.02

There is no significant difference among any of the groups. The largest difference, 3.32 runs between the "no arbitration" pitchers and the losing pitchers, is not statistically significant.

Biases

There are a few possible biases to this study that may have affected the results.

The most important one, perhaps, is the "option year" problem. Often, a contract will provide for an option year, where the team has the choice of either keeping the player or letting him become a free agent. Since teams are more likely to keep a player who just had a good year, this would mean that players having off-years would be overrepresented in the free-agent pool, which would appear to have lowered their performance relative to expectations.

Theoretically, this bias could explain the findings for pitchers, in which free-agent pitchers retrospectively performed more poorly than expected. The good pitchers may have been removed from consideration by the exercise of the team's option, biasing the sample downward.

Of course, the same would apply to batters; if that is the case, then there might be a larger free-agent effect for batters than the study indicated. And so a good update to this study would be to include these option players along with the free agents, since the motivation issues affecting free-agent performance would apply equally to these players.

Another bias, one that goes the opposite way, is that players who have especially poor free-agent years are somewhat more likely to retire. Since this study didn't include retired players, that would bias the free-agent pool in the upward direction, which means that any positive free-agent effect would be increased by the retirement effect.

A third bias, which would also amplify any positive results, is that players having a bad free-agent year would likely be benched, and would therefore fail to meet the playing time requirements (20 starts or 300 batting outs) of this study.

Again, this means that players having good years are more likely to be considered, which would again bias the results in a positive direction.

So there is one source of bias that would tend to bring the observed free-agent effect down, and two others that would bring it up. More study would be worthwhile—but, in any case, there is no evidence so far for any "greed" effect motivating free agents.

#

PREVIOUS STUDIES

The most recent similar study on this question appeared in Baseball Prospectus's 2006 book *Baseball Between the Numbers*. There, Dayn Perry found a much larger effect—five runs instead of the one or two runs found here. However, Perry used a non-random sample of "prominent" free agents. Players who figure prominently may be those who were more likely to have had notable years, and this may have biased the sample upward.

An academic study by Evan C. Holden and Paul M. Sommers, "The Influence of Free-Agent Filing on MLB Player Performance," found no free-agent year effect. It did, however, find that performance declined the year after the contract was signed. However, since free agents tend to be older players more likely to be in their declining phase, this might simply be a case of the normal effects of player aging.

In "Shirking or Stochastic Productivity in Major League Baseball?" Anthony Krautmann checked all free agents signing five-year contracts between 1976 and 1983. He counted the number of players with outlying performances, and found only the expected number, which means no evidence of the free-agent year effect.

Benjamin Grad, in his study "A Test of Additional Effort Expenditure in the 'Walk Year' for Major League Baseball Players," regressed player performance on a group of variables, including one representing whether the player was in his free-agent year. He found no effect for that variable.

In a poster presentation at the 2006 SABR convention in Seattle, Allison Binns ran a regression on players' career performance vs. age, including a dummy variable to represent the season following an arbitration hearing. She found that in that season, a hitter's OPS dropped by an average .040. That's a very large difference, about seven runs for a player with 500 PA. Binns also found a similar effect for pitchers. Both effects were statistically significant.

NOTES

Statistics are from *Total Baseball* (8th ed.); data on free agency is from Retrosheet; data on arbitration is from SABR's Business of Baseball committee (http://businessofbaseball.com/data/arbitrationresults.pdf).

1. Details on the algorithm can be found at www.philbirnbaum.com/algorithm.txt

PHIL BIRNBAUM *is editor of* By the Numbers, *SABR's statistical analysis newsletter. A native of Toronto, he now lives in Ottawa, where he works as a software developer.*

Consecutive Times Reaching Base

Ted Williams Dethroned by an Unlikely Record Holder

When Frank Thomas reached base in 15 consecutive plate appearances in May 1997, all the record books were examined to see who was the all-time record holder of this obscure feat. The only book with this entry listed was *The Sporting News Complete Baseball Record Book*. To no one's surprise, Ted Williams was listed with the major league record, when (as a 39-year-old) he reached base in 16 straight plate appearances in late 1957.

However, not everyone was in agreement that Williams was the record holder. Seymour Siwoff of the Elias Sports Bureau, baseball's official statisticians, was contacted by Jerome Holtzman of the *Chicago Tribune* for Siwoff's opinion on the matter. "We can't verify [that Williams holds the record]," he was quoted. "We haven't put it in our record book because we've never been satisfied with the research." Craig Carter, *The Sporting News's* longtime and highly respected editor, said that "somebody had looked it up." But, like many records, it is difficult to establish the record holder because play-by-play accounts of old games, which would be necessary to find a record like this, can be so hard to find.[1]

Holtzman's gripe was how Williams could be the record holder when no one could say who previously held the record. The subject came up again when Barry Bonds and John Olerud each reached base 15 consecutive times in 1998.[1]

This is where my work on Frank Ward, who was occasionally called "Piggy," comes in. According to my research, Ward reached base safely in 17 consecutive plate appearances in 1893. Just for clarification, "reached base safely" can mean reaching base on a hit, walk, or hit by pitch, but reaching on force-outs or errors are not included. Of course, this doesn't necessarily mean that Ward is the all-time record holder for consecutive times on base (there may be a longer one out there waiting to be found), but it does mean he has supplanted Ted Williams's mark of 16. To be correct, Williams actually never held the record, since Ward's streak was first.

Frank "Piggy" Ward

Frank Ward's Streak

Ward's streak began on June 16, 1893, during a six-inning, rain-shortened game between Baltimore and Cincinnati. Baltimore, Ward's team, scored 19 runs in the final three innings of the game, including four by Ward. Ward went 2-for-3 with two walks. According to newspaper reports, Ward was put out in the first inning, singled in the fourth inning, tripled and walked in the fifth inning, and then walked again in the sixth inning. A drenching rain had been falling for some time now (probably the cause of Baltimore's sudden offensive output), and the game was called after six innings, with Frank Ward reaching base safely in his last four plate appearances.

Here's where the story becomes even more interesting. After that day's game, Ward was traded to the team in the other clubhouse, Cincinnati, for pitcher Tony Mullane. Ward would have a day off on the 17th, then continue one of the hottest hitting streaks in history.

On June 18, 1893, Ward, now playing for Cincinnati against Louisville, set a record that has yet been unmatched. In a nine-inning game, he came up to bat eight times and reached base safely in every single one of them. Although newspaper accounts of the specifics of the game are scant due to Cincinnati scoring 30 runs, all sources agree that Ward was 2-for-2 with five walks and was also hit by a pitch during the game. He started the day off with two walks in the first inning, and continued to reach in his next six times up to bat.

At the end of June 18, Ward had reached base in 12 consecutive plate appearances. He marched on against Louisville on June 19, when he began with a single in the first inning, then walked in the second. He then singled in the fifth, sixth, and seventh innings. For the day, the damage was 4-for-4 with a walk.

Frank Ward had now reached base safely in 17 consecutive plate appearances in a stretch spanning three games, two cities, and even two different teams. He was finally stopped by Louisville's

George Hemming in the first inning of the June 20 game vs. Louisville. He finished the day 0-for-3 with a walk.

Ward's streak, which ran from June 16 through June 19, included seven singles, no doubles, one triple, no home runs, eight walks, and one hit by pitch. He reached in his final four plate appearances with Baltimore before being traded, and started his Cincinnati career by reaching in his first 13 times up to bat.

So, let Frank Ward's feat be listed in the record books—with Williams being relegated to the American League record holder, and Bonds and Olerud limited to being the "modern" National League record holders—that is, until someone can find a streak even longer than Ward's, if such a feat has ever taken place.

The Longest Streaks

Ward's great achievement is made even more exciting when seen in the context of the other long streaks of reaching base safely—Williams at 16, and Thomas, Bonds, and Olerud at 15. As it stands, those are the only players besides Ward known to have reached base in 15 consecutive plate appearances.

Table 1 lists the details for each of the known streaks of 15 or more consecutive times on base safely; I've reduced down to a single batting line the games where the batter did not make an out, while showing the details for games where outs were made by the batter.

Other Long Streaks

Thanks to Pete Palmer and Retrosheet, I was able to compile a list of other long streaks of reaching base safely. Table 2 lists all occurrences of a player reaching base safely 12 or more consecutive times since 1960, plus several more streaks from before 1960 that I was able to find and verify.

Conclusion

I doubt anyone would have suspected a lifetime .286 hitter would have put together one of the top streaks in baseball history. Ward's streak did not get much press at the time, and it apparently didn't help him keep a job, either; he played only 42 games for Cincinnati that season and is reported to have played for at least 30 different baseball clubs in 20 leagues throughout his career. Also, although he is listed as "Piggy" in the encyclopedias, my research has shown that Frank Ward was very rarely called that, and, when it was used, was only done so mockingly. Interestingly, in an

Table 1. Streaks of 15 or More Consecutive Times of Reaching Base Safely

17: Frank Ward (Baltimore/Cincinnati)
June 16-June 19, 1893

1	06/16	1B; 4th inning
2		3B; 5th inning
3		BB; 5th inning
4		BB; 6th inning
5-12	06/18	2-for-2, 5 BB, 1 HBP
13-17	06/19	4-for-4, 1 BB
End	06/20	OUT; 1st inning
		v. George Hemming

16: Ted Williams (BOS-A)
September 17-23, 1957

1	09/17	1-for-1
2	09/18	0-for-0, 1 BB
3	09/20	1-for-1
4-7	09/21	1-for-1, 3 BB
8-11	09/22	2-for-2, 2 BB
12-16	09/23	1-for-1, 3 BB, 1 HBP
End	09/24	GO 4-3; 1st inning
		v. Hal Griggs

15: Frank Thomas (CHI-A)
May 16-20, 1997

1	05/16	HR; 7th inning
2		1B; 9th inning
3-7	05/17	3-for-3, 2 BB
8-12	05/18	4-for-4, 1 BB
13	05/20	2B; 1st inning
14		BB; 3rd inning
15		BB; 4th inning
End		F8; 5th inning
		v. Rich Garces

15: Barry Bonds (SF-N)
August 31-September 4, 1998

1	8/31:	IBB; 8th inning
2-6	9/01:	2-for-2, 3 BB
7-10	9/02:	3-for-3, 1 BB
11-15	9/04:	4-for-4, 1 BB
End	9/05:	K; 1st inning
		v. Chan Ho Park

15: John Olerud (NY-N)
September 16-22, 1998

1	9/16	1B; 9th inning
2-6	9/18	3-for-3, 2 BB
7-10	9/19	3-for-3, 1 BB
11-14	9/20	2-for-2, 2 BB
15	9/22	BB; 1st inning
End		GO 4-3; 3rd inning
		v.Mike Thurman

Table 2. Other Long Streaks of Reaching Base Safely

TOB	PLAYER	TEAM-LG	START	END	1B	2B	3B	HR	BB	HBP
17	Frank Ward	BAL/CIN-N	06/16/1893	06/19/1893	7	0	1	0	8	1
16	Ted Williams	BOS-A	09/17/1957	09/23/1957	2	0	0	4	9	1
15	Frank Thomas	CHI-A	05/16/1997	05/20/1997	6	3	0	1	5	0
15	Barry Bonds	SF-N	08/31/1998	09/04/1998	5	2	0	2	6	0
15	John Olerud	NY-N	09/16/1998	09/22/1998	6	1	0	2	6	0
14	Billy Hamilton	PHI-N	07/20/1893	07/24/1893	7	0	1	0	6	0
14	Pinky Higgins	BOS-A	06/19/1938[1]	06/21/1938[2]	10	2	0	0	2	0
14	Pedro Guerrero	LA-N	07/23/1985	07/26/1985	2	3	0	2	6	1
14	Manny Ramirez	BOS-A	08/21/2002	08/24/2002	6	1	0	2	5	0
13	Roger Connor	STL-N	05/30/1895[1]	06/01/1895	5	3	1	0	4	0
13	Joe Kelley*	BAL-N	09/17/1898	09/21/1898	8	2	0	0	2	1
13	Jim Dwyer	BAL-A	09/29/1982	10/02/1982	6	2	0	0	5	0
13	Harold Baines	BAL-A	04/30/1993	05/04/1993	5	3	0	0	5	0
13	Barry Larkin	CIN-N	05/25/1997	05/27/1997	6	1	1	0	4	1
13	Bill Spiers	HOU-N	06/03/1997	06/11/1997	3	0	0	0	9	1
13	Bernie Williams	NY-A	08/14/2002	08/17/2002	9	2	0	0	2	0
13	Barry Bonds	SF-N	09/11/2002	09/14/2002	4	2	0	0	7	0
13	Brian Giles	SD-N	06/19/2005	06/22/2005	4	3	1	0	5	0
12	Jake Stenzel	PIT-N	07/15/1893	07/18/1893	7	2	1	0	2	0
12	Tris Speaker	CLE-A	07/08/1920[1]	07/10/1920[1]	10	1	0	0	1	0
12	Max Carey	PIT-N	07/06/1922	07/07/1922	5	2	1	1	3	0
12	Ted Williams	BOS-A	08/12/1939	08/15/1939	5	2	1	1	3	0
12	Vada Pinson	CIN-N	05/02/1959	05/03/1959[2]	3	3	0	2	3	1
12	Reggie Jackson	NY-A	06/14/1978	06/16/1978	5	0	2	0	5	0
12	Ben Oglivie	MIL-A	06/26/1978	06/28/1978[1]	3	1	1	2	5	0
12	Bobby Grich	CAL-A	09/14/1984	09/17/1984	4	2	0	2	4	0
12	Dave Collins	CIN-N	10/01/1987	10/03/1987	5	2	0	0	3	2
12	Eric Young	COL-N	09/19/1993	09/24/1993	7	0	1	0	4	0
12	Rick Wilkins	HOU-N	04/12/1996	04/16/1996	5	1	0	1	5	0
12	Jim Edmonds	STL-N	04/10/2000	04/12/2000	4	3	0	2	3	0
12	Frank Catalanotto	TEX-A	04/21/2000	05/18/2000	9	1	0	0	2	0

Superscript numbers on game dates refer to first or second games of doubleheaders.
*Kelley reached base safely on 12 consecutive occasions, then hit a sacrifice fly, then singled.

exhibition game in Ohio in 1894, the fans nicknamed Ward "Baby Ruth," after the three-year old daughter of President Cleveland.[2] So, while Ted Williams can't claim the record anymore for consecutive times reaching base, we can say that only "Baby Ruth" himself is known to have surpassed The Kid.

#

TRENT MCCOTTER *lives in Chapel Hill, NC, where he is currently a student at the University of North Carolina.*

NOTES

1. The *Chicago Tribune* article I quoted was featured in the May 22, 1997, edition on page 11.
2. The quote about Ward being called Baby Ruth was in the September 23, 1894, *Washington Post* on page 15.

SOURCES

I utilized the following newspapers when gathering details of Ward's streak: *Baltimore Sun, Baltimore American, Louisville Courier–Journal, Cincinnati Enquirer, Cincinnati Post,* and the *Cincinnati Commercial–Gazette.*

(If you know of a long streak of reaching base that does not appear on the list in Table 2, please send it to me at my address in the SABR member directory.)

ACKNOWLEDGMENTS

It took a team to put together and verify all the information in this article, and many acknowledgments are due. Pete Palmer wrote the program that found the long streaks in the chart above, so I owe him a huge thanks. He used Retrosheet data in his program, so everyone who's done work for the most important baseball research project ever also deserves a big thank-you from me for all their work. For having the opportunity to find Ward's streak, I thank Tim Wiles and Jim Gates at the National Baseball Hall of Fame, who allowed me access to the daily sheets without having to travel to Cooperstown. Greg Rhodes and Chris Eckes with the Cincinnati Reds also helped finding details on Ward's streak. Brian Rash, Gabriel Schechter, Steve Gietschier, and Bill Deane all sent copies of daily sheets that I used in finding other long streaks of reaching base. Baltimore's Enoch Pratt Library and The Public Library of Cincinnati provided extremely helpful newspaper copies. Finally, I'd like to thank Jim Charlton, the editor of this journal, for his continued guidance and help with my work on this article, as well as the other piece I wrote for this publication.

Baseball Geography and Transportation

In 1876, at the time of the National League's inception, the only reasonable way for a baseball team to travel from New York (home of the Mutuals) to St. Louis (home of the Brown Stockings) on a regular basis was by train. Stagecoach was too slow. Buses, and roads good enough to support them, were over half a century away, and jet airplanes over three-quarters. Major league baseball teams therefore relied almost exclusively on the railroad for nearly 80 years.

The "travel day" between series, which today often amounts to a day off, was quite necessary in the era of rail transportation. At the turn of the century it took over 20 hours to go between New York and Chicago, and well over 24 between New York and St. Louis. These trips would usually be avoided by strategic scheduling, but even a short run like New York City to Buffalo took longer than seven hours.

But the change from rail to air and the proliferation of the automobile have affected far more than how the players get around. New modes of transportation have influenced the shape of the field of play itself and made possible one of the most heartwrenching moves in baseball franchise history.

Jet Airplanes, Player Culture, and a Transplanted Rivalry

On June 8, 1934, Cincinnati GM Larry MacPhail flew 19 of his players to Chicago for a series with the Cubs,[1] making the Reds the first team to travel by airplane. A dozen years later the Yankees became the first team to do it on a regular basis, chartering a Douglas DC-4 dubbed the "Yankee Mainliner" in the 1946 season.[2]

Still, airplane travel was far from a regular occurrence until the 1950s when jet engine technology made traveling longer distances faster, cheaper, and more comfortable. The 1950s also saw the birth of the Interstate Highway System (though a rudimentary system of transcontinental roads had been in place since the 1920s). The increased mobility of the general population gave real estate businessman and Brooklyn Dodger owner Walter O'Malley the opportunity to move both his team and their crosstown rivals, the New York Giants, to California after the 1957 season. Prior to this move no team had been west of Kansas City, and baseball's geographical center was near the Pennsylvania-Ohio border, relatively unchanged since 1876. All teams were within a day's train ride of each other. O'Malley's move shifted the center nearly as far west as Chicago and almost doubled the distance of the average commute between parks.

Table 1. Distance Between Major League Ballparks

Year	Maximum	Average	Change
1882	1036 mi	430 mi	--
1901	1036 mi	417 mi	-3%
1955	1248 mi	469 mi	+12%
1958	2693 mi	872 mi	+86%
1962	2693 mi	898 mi	+3%
1969	2693 mi	1158 mi	+29%
1977	2693 mi	1119 mi	-3%
1993	2731 mi	1143 mi	+2%
1998	2731 mi	1170 mi	+2%
2005	2731 mi	1155 mi	-1%

What else changed in the shift from rail to air? Don Zimmer, who played for the Brooklyn Dodgers in the 1950s, relates: "On trains, we were together. You get on a plane, and you're only talking to one person—the guy next to you. There isn't the

The Evolving Map of Baseball Cities

● NATIONAL LEAGUE
○ AMERICAN LEAGUE OR AMERICAN ASSOCIATION

1882

1901

1955

closeness now that there was then. We'd eat in the same dining car, we were always together. I'm not saying it was better, that was just the biggest difference."[3]

Relations with the media were different, too. "The lives of the baseball players and the writers who covered them were interwoven, since travel by train, not plane, created situations in which avoidance was difficult, if not impossible."[4]

Finally, relationships with fans became more distant. "Train travel had facilitated a traditional practice of whistle-stop barnstorming at the end of spring training, as teams would often make several stops along the way home from Florida or Arizona, playing additional exhibition games and/or making publicity appearances. Plane travel helped phase out this custom in the 1950s."[5]

The Automobile, Suburbs, and Ballpark Symmetry

Professional baseball teams must play in places where fans can go to see them. Before the 1950s this meant that they played in cities, where the population was dense and public transportation available. In the 1950s, however, as cars became affordable and good roads the rule rather than the exception, the growing class of car owners began to move to the suburbs. It was no longer necessary to locate a ballpark in the city, and it became common practice to build on the outskirts, where land was cheaper, parking safer, zoning rules more lax, and events generally less disruptive.

The move to open sites has had profound effects on ballpark design. Most parks built in the 1960s and 1970s (Candlestick Park, Dodger Stadium, Shea Stadium, Olympic Stadium, San Diego Stadium, Astrodome, Kauffman Stadium, etc.) are round structures with symmetrical field layouts. Since they are located on the outskirts of their respective towns, the architects weren't concerned with keeping the buildings within the bounds of city streets (for example, Lansdowne in Boston or Sullivan and McKeever in Brooklyn). Rather, without restrictions on shape or size they

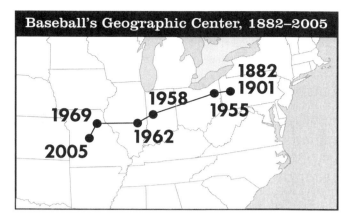

Baseball's Geographic Center, 1882–2005

constructed symmetrical fields circumscribed by high, raked seating that placed fans farther from the action.

What does the future hold? While baseball used to go where the life was, some recent ballparks have been situated such that they bring life where it is needed or desired in sleepy downtown areas. Can we expect to see this trend continue? Baseball in Canada has not been a great success, but what about Mexico? Latin America? Japan? With frequent and inexpensive flights, the increasing number of MLB players coming from other countries and the advent of the World Baseball Classic, such ideas begin to sound distinctly plausible.

# # #

NOTES

1. "Cincinnati Reds Will Fly Here For Cub Series." *Chicago Daily Tribune*, June 7, 1934: 23.
2. "Yankees' Plane Is in St. Louis." *New York Times*, May 14, 1946: 33.
3. Newman, Mark. "Finding ways to get to 100 Series." MLB.com. September 21, 2003. Viewed January 24, 2006. http://mlb.mlb.com/NASApp/mlb/mlb/news/mlb_news.jsp?ymd=20030921&content_id=537248&vkey=news_mlb&fext=.jsp
4. Friend, Harold. "Joe DiMaggio: It's None of Your Business." BaseballLibrary.com. March 6, 2002. Viewed January 24, 2006. http://www.baseballlibrary.com/baseballlibrary/submit/Friend_Harold7.stm
5. Treder, Steve. "Dig the 1950s." The Hardball Times. March 23, 2004. Viewed January 24, 2006. http://www.hardballtimes.com/main/printarticle/dig_the_1950s/

ALEX REISNER *is a freelance computer programmer who enjoys music, photography, design, bicycling, the Marx brothers, playing, watching, and thinking about baseball.*

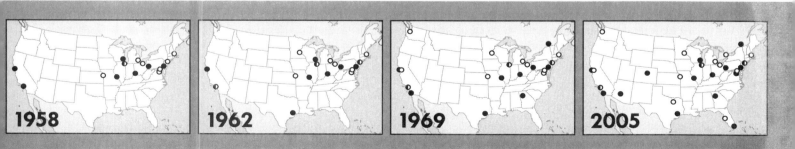

MONTE CELY

The Cy Young Award

Individual or Team Recognition?

The Cy Young Award is Major League Baseball's premier annual recognition of pitching achievement. While only one outstanding pitcher in each league is presented the award, is that honor fundamentally an individual, or a team, recognition?

The Cy Young Memorial Award was established in 1956 by baseball commissioner Ford Frick to honor the best pitcher in major league baseball. The award is named for pitching great and all-time wins leader Denton True "Cy" Young, who had passed away in 1955. The Cy Young Award winners are selected by the Baseball Writers Association of America. During the first 11 years of the award, from 1956 to 1966, only a single winner was selected for all of Major League Baseball. Don Newcombe of the Brooklyn Dodgers was the first recipient. Immediately after Commissioner Frick retired, the rules were amended to provide for a winner from each league.[1]

After a voting tie in 1969 resulted in the American League award being given to both Denny McLain and Mike Cuellar, the voting rules were adjusted to allow the BBWAA voters to cast "weighted" votes for first, second, and third places.[2] Criteria for the voting is minimal, with the ballot instructing the sportswriters to "vote for the best pitcher."

Data Collection

To test the existence of a fundamental influence in Cy Young Award selection, a set of statistics needed to be collected and categorized.

In his book *The Neyer/James Guide to Pitchers* (co-authored with Rob Neyer), Bill James presents a method, based upon past statistics, to predict the winner of the Cy Young Award. His method determines a number of Cy Young "points" (or CYP) awarded to a pitcher, based upon a linear equation using various weightings of the following statistics: Innings Pitched, Earned Runs, Strikeouts, Saves, Shutouts, Wins, Losses, and a Victory Bonus. The Victory Bonus is awarded if the pitcher's team wins their respective division championship. James' CYP formula did indeed predict two of the four CYA winners in 2004 and 2005: Johan Santana (AL 2004) and Chris Carpenter (NL 2005).[3]

As in the earlier NL edition of this paper, my purpose is not to propose a new or enhanced method to predict Cy Young Award winners, but rather to look retrospectively at the relative influence of team versus individual accomplishments on that selection. I found James' CYP formula useful as a guide toward the key statistics. Consequently, I continue to use the following performance statistics for this study:

Individual Performance
ERA, Strikeouts, WHIP, Innings Pitched

Team Performance
Wins, Win %, Saves, Team Wins & Team Finish

Analyses and Discussion

Appendix 1 recaps the 46 National League Cy Young Award winners, their pertinent statistics, and league rankings for those statistics.[4] Correlations, in descending frequency, in terms of the number of times that the NL Cy Young Award winner led in the performance categories, are as follows:

Table 1. Key Statistical Correlations,
National League, 1956–2005

	Won CYA	%(n=46)
Wins	29	63%
Team Finish	27	59%
Innings Pitched	19	41%
Strikeouts	18	39%
Earned Run Average	15	33%
Winning %	13	28%
WHIP x 9	12	26%
Saves	5	11%

This high-level analysis shows that two team-oriented accomplishments, Wins and Team Finish, are most highly correlated with winning the NL Cy Young Award, and in fact are the only statistics in this study that reflect frequencies of higher than 50% in the National League. Among the individual-oriented statistics, Innings Pitched had the highest frequency, at 41%—ahead of the stats that seem to get the most attention, ERA

(33%) and Strikeouts (39%).

Let's look at the American League Cy Young Award winners. Appendix 2 lists the 44 AL award winners, their key statistics, and season rankings for those statistics. (Remember that during the first 11 years of the Cy Young Award, only one award was given for the entire major leagues. There was also a tie resulting in two AL awards being given in 1969. Consequently, the number of awards for the NL and AL are not equal.) Key correlations are as follows:

Table 2. Key Statistical Correlations,
American League, 1956–2005

	Won CYA	%(n=44)
Wins	28	64%
Team Finish	27	61%
Earned Run Average	15	34%
Winning %	15	34%
WHIP x 9	12	27%
Innings Pitched	11	25%
Strikeouts	8	18%
Saves	2	5%

As is the case in the National League, Wins and Team Finish are most highly correlated with winning the AL Cy Young Award. In fact, the correlation is slightly (though not significantly) stronger than in the NL. ERA leadership is most highly correlated among the individual statistics in the AL, at 34%. Strikeouts and innings-pitched leadership show a much lower correlation in the AL than in the NL.

Evaluating the impact of league statistical leadership is problematic when it comes to those relief pitchers that have won the Cy Young Award. In general, relievers either don't rank or don't qualify (due to their lower number of innings pitched) for leadership in many of the key statistical pitching categories. It is noteworthy that, of the four AL relief pitchers that have won the Cy Young, two of them (Sparky Lyle in 1977 and Willie Hernandez in 1984) did not lead in saves during their award-winning seasons. Over in the NL, all five of the Cy Young Award–winning relievers ranked number one in saves during their honored season.

With team finish having one of the stronger correlations to the Cy Young Award, would we expect to find the award-winning pitchers concentrated on "big market" teams? Or would the alleged East Coast–West Coast biases of baseball pundits have an effect on Cy Young Award selection? These could be classified as team-oriented effects, if they exist. Here's the data on Cy Young Award winners by team:

Table 3. Team Affiliation of Cy Young Award
Winners, National League, 1956–2005

Team	Awards	Multiple Winners
Dodgers	9	Koufax-3
Braves	7	Maddux-3, Glavine-2
Phillies	6	Carlton -3
Cubs	4	
Diamondbacks	4	Johnson-4
Mets	4	Seaver-3
Cardinals	3	Gibson-2
Padres	3	
Astros	2	
Pirates	2	
Expos/Nats	1	
Giants	1	

Table 4. Team Affiliation of Cy Young Award
Winners, American League, 1956–2005

Team	Awards	Multiple Winners
Orioles	6	Palmer-3
Red Sox	6	Clemens-3, Martinez-2
Phillies	6	Carlton-4
Yankees	5	
Athletics	5	
Blue Jays	4	Clemens-2
White Sox	3	
Tigers	3	McLain-2
Twins	3	
Royals	3	Saberhagen-2
Brewers	2	
Angels	2	
Mariners	1	
Indians	1	

The key drivers here appear to be the numbers of league and division championships won by the team combined with the presence of dominant Hall of Fame (or future HoF)–caliber pitchers. The "big-market" and "East Coast–West Coast" effects are probably secondary in nature.

An additional analysis is to study the trend, over time, of how leadership in these performance accomplishments has correlated to winning the Cy Young Award. There have been 46 Cy Young winners from the National League and 44 AL winners across the 50 seasons that the award has been bestowed. Has there been any "shift" in emphasis on the various statistics over time? (See Table 5 and Table 6.)

A better trend line might be evident by the end of this decade. However, it does not appear at present that there is any fundamental shift in the correlations, with the possible exception of fewer

Table 5. Key Statistical Categories Led by National League Cy Young Award Winners, 1958–2005

Decade(#CyAs)	ERA	K	WHIP	IP	Wins	Win%	Finish	Saves
1956-1969(10)	4	5	4	3	8	3	8	0
1970-1979(10)	2	3	2	3	7	2	3	2
1980-1989(10)	2	5	1	6	6	2	6	2
1990-1999(10)	5	2	4	6	7	3	7	0
2000-2005 (6)	2	3	1	1	1	3	3	1
Totals (46)	15	18	12	19	29	13	27	5

Table 6. Key Statistical Categories Led by American League Cy Young Award Winners, 1958–2005

Decade(#CyAs)	ERA	K	WHIP	IP	Wins	Win%	Finish	Saves
1958-1969 (8)	1	1	0	5	7	3	6	0
1970-1979(10)	5	0	3	1	7	1	7	0
1980-1989(10)	2	0	4	1	6	6	6	1
1990-1999(10)	5	5	3	3	5	3	4	1
2000-2005 (6)	2	2	2	1	3	2	4	0
Totals (44)	15	8	12	11	28	15	27	2

Win leaders receiving the award in the NL in the 2000s.

Summary and Conclusions

In reviewing the eight statistical categories used for this paper (Wins, Winning Percentage, Saves, Team Finish, ERA, Strikeouts, WHIP, and Innings Pitched), the winning pitcher or his team (in every case except one—David Cone of the 1994 Royals)—finished first in at least one of the key statistics. In one case, Sandy Koufax in 1965, a starting pitcher finished first in *all seven* of the pertinent statistical categories (excluding saves).

Of course, the statistics representing these accomplishments are highly interrelated. It is of particular interest that leadership in Strikeouts and Innings Pitched were more often correlated with the award in the NL than was leadership in ERA. ERA was indeed the most correlated individual statistic studied in the AL. A potentially confounding factor here is that the relief pitchers that have won the award are generally not eligible for the ERA leadership due to their lower number of innings pitched. I do not believe that this would affect the statistical comparisons of this paper, as it could also be argued from the team accomplishments perspective that winning a wild card could be counted as a team finish of comparable weight with winning a division championship.

The fundamental conclusion of this paper is that leadership in team-oriented accomplishments (defined as Wins, Winning Percentage, Saves, and Team Finish) has more often, over the last 50 years in both the National League and the American League, influenced the selection of the Cy Young Award winner than does leadership in individual accomplishments (defined as ERA, Strikeouts, WHIP, and Innings Pitched). There may be some evidence that this trend is changing in the 21st century, although Bartolo Colon would argue against that premise.

#

NOTES

An earlier version of this paper examined key individual and team statistics for Cy Young Award winners in the National League and attempted to draw conclusions as to which factors most directly, or most often, influenced selection to this prestigious award.

1. Baseball Almanac website, www.baseball-almanac.com
2. Online Baseball Library, www.BaseballLibrary.com
3. Bill James & Rob Neyer. *The Neyer/James Guide to Pitchers* (New York: Fireside, 2004).
4. Sources and clarifications for the statistical table presented in Appendices 1 and 2: (1) Statistics are from the Baseball Almanac website, unless noted below. (2) WHIP calculations were derived from individual pitching statistics listed on the SABR Online Encyclopedia. (3) WHIP and innings-pitched league rankings are from Baseball Reference (www.baseball-reference.com). (4) All NL relievers that have won the Cy Young Award also finished first in the league that year in saves (1974, 1979, 1987, 1989, 2003). Of the AL relievers that have won the Cy Young Award, the 1981 and 1992 winners also led in saves. Sparky Lyle in 1977 finished second in saves; in 1984, Willie Hernandez finished third in saves. (5) Various statistics for the 1981 and 1994 seasons may seem "low" due to work stoppages. (6) Rick Sutcliffe was credited with wins leadership in 1984 due to his four wins credited in the AL prior to his trade to the Cubs.

Thanks go to SABR members Bill Gilbert, Jan Larson, Jim Charlton, and Bernie Miklasz for their advice and insights in the formulation of this topic and development of the paper.

Thanks to my friend and baseball memorabilia collector Jerry Adamic for his encouragement, and to my son and fellow baseball fan Matt Cely for his support and proofreading of the paper.

Finally, thanks to my wife Linda for helping me track down statistical sources for use in this paper, and for her patience as I labored at my computer.

MONTE CELY *is a second-year SABR member. He is retired from the telecommunications business and lives in Round Rock, Texas, home of the popular minor league affiliate of the Houston Astros. Monte is a longtime St. Louis Cardinals fan, having seen his first major league baseball game with his dad at Sportsman's Park (Busch Stadium) in 1959.*

Appendix 1

Statistics and Rankings for NL Cy Young Award Winners, 1956–2005

Rankings appear in superscript. x = pitcher did not finish in Top 25 of this statistical category. y = relief pitcher did not qualify for league ERA leadership consideration. z = pitcher did not finish in Top 5 of this statistical category.

| | | INDIVIDUAL STATISTICS | | | | TEAM STATISTICS | | | | | |
		ERA	K	H+W/9IP	IP	W	L	Win%	Saves	TmW	Finish
1956	D. Newcombe	3.06^5	139^7	8.90^1	268^4	27^1	7	0.794^1	—	93	1
1957	W. Spahn	2.69^3	111^{13}	10.59^5	271^2	21^1	11	0.656^3	3	95	1
1960	V. Law	3.08^6	120^{18}	10.16^2	271^4	20^3	9	0.690^2	—	95	1
1962	D. Drysdale	2.83^4	232^1	10.03^3	314^1	25^1	9	0.735^3	1	102	2
1963	S. Koufax	1.88^1	306^1	7.87^1	311^3	25^1	5	0.833^2	—	99	1
1965	S. Koufax	2.04^1	382^1	7.71^1	335^1	26^1	8	0.765^1	2	97	1
1966	S. Koufax	1.73^1	317^1	8.86^2	323^1	27^1	9	0.750^2	—	95	1
1967	M. McCormick	2.85^{16}	150^{19}	10.34^z	262^z	22^1	10	0.688^2	—	91	2
1968	B. Gibson	1.12^1	268^1	7.70^1	304^3	22^2	9	0.710^3	—	97	1
1969	T. Seaver	2.21^4	208^{10}	9.36^5	273^z	25^1	7	0.781^1	—	100	1
1970	B. Gibson	3.12^4	274^2	10.71^z	294^3	23^1	7	0.767^1	—	76	4
1971	F. Jenkins	2.77^9	263^2	9.44^3	325^1	24^1	13	0.649^7	—	83	4
1972	S. Carlton	1.97^1	310^1	8.95^2	346^1	27^1	10	0.730^2	—	59	6
1973	T. Seaver	2.08^1	251^1	8.78^1	290^3	19^2	10	0.655^4	—	82	1
1974	M. Marshall	2.42^4	143^{16}	10.69^z	208^z	15^{12}	12	0.556^{21}	21	102	1
1975	T. Seaver	2.38^3	243^1	9.80^4	280^3	22^1	9	0.710^3	—	82	3
1976	R. Jones	2.74^6	93^x	9.26^1	315^1	22^1	14	0.611^{13}	—	73	5
1977	S. Carlton	2.64^4	198^4	10.11^4	283^3	23^1	10	0.697^6	—	101	1
1978	G. Perry	2.73^6	154^9	10.63^z	260^4	21^1	6	0.778^1	—	84	4
1979	B. Sutter	2.22^y	110^{23}	8.82^z	101^z	6^x	6	0.500^x	37	80	5
1980	S. Carlton	2.34^2	286^1	9.86^3	304^1	24^1	9	0.727^3	—	91	1
1981	F. Valenzuela	2.48^8	180^1	9.42^2	192^1	13^2	7	0.650^7	—	63	1
1982	S. Carlton	3.10^8	286^1	10.34^z	295^1	23^1	11	0.676^4	—	89	2
1983	J. Denny	2.37^2	139^{14}	10.49^5	242^z	19^1	6	0.760^1	—	90	1
1984	R. Sutcliffe	2.69^4	155^6	9.72^z	150^z	16^1	1	0.941^1	—	96	1
1985	D. Gooden	1.53^1	268^1	8.71^2	276^1	24^1	4	0.857^2	—	98	2
1986	M. Scott	2.22^1	306^1	8.31^1	275^1	18^3	10	0.643^8	—	96	1
1987	S. Bedrosian	2.83^y	74^x	10.82^z	89^z	5^x	3	0.625^x	40	80	5
1988	O. Hershiser	2.26^3	178^7	9.47^4	267^1	23^1	8	0.742^3	1	94	1
1989	M. Davis	1.85^y	92^x	9.49^z	92^z	4^x	3	0.571^x	44	89	2
1990	D. Drabek	2.76^6	131^{16}	9.58^3	231^5	22^1	6	0.786^1	—	95	1
1991	T. Glavine	2.55^3	192^3	9.88^3	246^2	20^1	11	0.645^7	—	94	1
1992	G. Maddux	2.18^3	199^3	9.10^2	268^1	20^1	11	0.645^7	—	78	4
1993	G. Maddux	2.36^1	197^3	9.44^1	267^1	20^4	10	0.667^8	—	104	1
1994	G. Maddux	1.56^1	156^3	8.06^1	202^1	16^1	6	0.727^3	—	68	2
1995	G. Maddux	1.63^1	181^3	7.32^1	209^1	19^1	2	0.905^1	—	90	1
1996	J. Smoltz	2.94^4	176^1	9.04^2	253^1	24^1	8	0.750^1	—	96	1
1997	P. Martinez	1.90^1	305^2	8.40^1	241^4	17^5	8	0.680^6	—	78	4
1998	T. Glavine	2.47^4	157^{22}	10.85^z	229^z	20^1	6	0.769^2	—	106	1
1999	R. Johnson	2.48^1	364^1	9.20^2	271^1	17^8	9	0.654^9	—	100	1
2000	R. Johnson	2.64^2	347^1	10.09^3	248^3	19^3	7	0.731^1	—	85	3
2001	R. Johnson	2.49^1	372^1	9.11^1	249^2	21^3	6	0.778^3	—	92	1
2002	R. Johnson	2.32^1	334^1	9.28^3	260^1	24^1	5	0.828^1	—	98	1
2003	E. Gagne	1.20^y	137^x	6.26^z	82^z	2^x	3	0.400^x	55	85	2
2004	R. Clemens	2.98^5	218^5	10.43^z	214^z	18^2	4	0.818^1	—	92	2
2005	C. Carpenter	2.83^5	213^2	9.52^5	241^2	21^2	5	0.808^2	—	100	1
#1 Rankings		15	18	12	19	29		13	5		27

Statistics and Rankings for AL Cy Young Award Winners, 1956–2005

Rankings appear in superscript. x = pitcher did not finish in Top 25 of this statistical category. y = relief pitcher did not qualify for league ERA leadership consideration. z = pitcher did not finish in Top 5 of this statistical category.

		INDIVIDUAL STATISTICS				TEAM STATISTICS					
		ERA	K	H+W/9IP	IP	W	L	Win%	Saves	TmW	Finish
1958	B. Turley	2.97^6	168^3	11.24^z	245^4	21^1	7	0.750^1	1	92	1
1959	E. Wynn	3.17^{10}	179^3	11.33^z	255^1	22^1	10	0.688^3	—	94	1
1961	W. Ford	3.21^{10}	209^2	10.62^z	283^1	25^1	4	0.862^1	—	109	1
1964	D. Chance	1.65^1	207^3	9.05^2	278^1	20^1	9	0.690^{15}	4	82	5
1967	J. Lonborg	3.16^{18}	246^1	10.25^z	273^2	22^1	9	0.710^2	—	92	1
1968	D. McLain	1.96^4	280^2	8.15^3	336^1	31^1	6	0.838^1	—	103	1
1969	M. Cuellar	2.38^3	182^5	9.05^2	290^3	23^2	11	0.676^9	—	109	1
1969	D. McLain	2.80^7	181^7	9.83^z	325^1	24^1	9	0.727^6	—	90	2
1970	J. Perry	3.03^8	168^{10}	10.17^2	279^5	24^1	12	0.667^3	—	98	1
1971	V. Blue	1.82^1	301^2	8.57^1	312^3	24^2	8	0.750^2	—	101	1
1972	G. Perry	1.92^2	234^3	8.80^3	343^2	24^1	16	0.600^{10}	1	72	5
1973	J. Palmer	2.40^1	158^{10}	10.27^4	296^z	22^3	9	0.710^2	—	97	1
1974	C. Hunter	2.49^1	143^{17}	8.87^1	318^5	25^1	12	0.676^4	—	90	1
1975	J. Palmer	2.09^1	193^4	9.28^2	323^2	23^1	11	0.676^3	—	90	2
1976	J. Palmer	2.51^5	159^7	9.68^2	315^1	22^1	13	0.629^{11}	—	88	2
1977	S. Lyle	2.17^y	68^x	10.77^z	137^z	13^{25}	5	0.722^2	26	100	1
1978	R. Guidry	1.74^1	248^2	8.51^1	273^z	25^1	3	0.893^1	—	100	1
1979	M. Flanagan	3.08^4	190^3	10.67^3	266^3	23^1	9	0.719^2	—	102	1
1980	S. Stone	3.23^7	149^7	11.65^z	251^z	25^1	7	0.781^1	—	100	2
1981	R. Fingers	1.04^y	61^x	7.85^z	78^z	6^x	3	0.667^x	28	62	1
1982	P. Vuckovich	3.34^6	105^x	13.56^z	223^z	18^2	6	0.750^1	—	95	1
1983	L. Hoyt	3.66^{17}	148^8	9.22^1	260^4	24^1	10	0.706^4	—	99	1
1984	W. Hernandez	1.92^y	112^x	8.49^z	140^z	9^x	3	0.750^x	32	104	1
1985	B. Saberhagen	2.87^3	158^9	9.52^1	235^z	20^2	6	0.769^2	—	91	1
1986	R. Clemens	2.48^1	238^2	8.72^1	254^5	24^1	4	0.857^1	—	95	1
1987	R. Clemens	2.97^3	256^2	10.58^5	281^2	20^1	9	0.690^1	—	78	5
1988	F. Viola	2.64^3	193^3	10.22^5	255^z	24^1	7	0.774^1	—	91	2
1989	B. Saberhagen	2.16^1	193^3	8.65^1	262^1	23^1	6	0.793^1	—	92	2
1990	B. Welch	2.95^6	127^{21}	11.00^z	238^3	27^1	6	0.818^1	—	103	1
1991	R. Clemens	2.62^1	241^1	9.42^2	271^1	18^4	10	0.643^{10}	—	84	3
1992	D. Eckersley	1.91^y	93^x	8.21^z	80^z	7^x	1	0.875^z	51	96	1
1993	J. McDowell	3.37^{11}	158^{13}	11.60^z	256^2	22^1	10	0.688^7	—	94	1
1994	D. Cone	2.94^2	132^6	9.65^2	171^z	16^2	5	0.762^4	—	64	3
1995	R. Johnson	2.48^1	294^1	9.41^1	214^4	18^2	2	0.900^1	—	79	1
1996	P. Hentgen	3.22^2	177^7	11.25^4	265^1	20^2	10	0.667^5	—	74	4
1997	R. Clemens	2.05^1	292^1	9.27^1	264^1	21^1	7	0.750^3	—	76	5
1998	R. Clemens	2.65^1	271^1	9.86^3	234^3	20^1	6	0.769^2	—	88	3
1999	P. Martinez	2.07^1	313^1	8.31^1	213^z	23^1	4	0.852^1	—	94	2
2000	P. Martinez	1.74^1	284^1	6.63^1	217^z	18^4	6	0.750^2	—	85	2
2001	R. Clemens	3.51^9	213^3	11.33^z	220^z	20^2	3	0.870^1	—	95	1
2002	B. Zito	2.75^3	182^3	10.21^5	229^5	23^1	5	0.821^2	—	103	1
2003	R. Halladay	3.25^5	204^3	9.64^2	266^1	22^1	7	0.759^1	—	86	3
2004	J. Santana	2.61^1	265^1	8.29^1	228^2	20^2	6	0.769^2	—	92	1
2005	B. Colon	3.48^8	157^8	10.43^3	222^7	21^1	8	0.724^4	—	95	1
#1 Rankings		15	8	12	11	28		15	2		27

CYRIL MORONG

Are Balanced Teams More Successful?

If a team scores 10% more runs than average and allows 10% fewer than average, they could be said to be perfectly balanced. Do such teams win more games than those that are less balanced? For example, if a second team scores 15% more runs than average and allows 5% fewer than average, they would be less balanced than the first team—but does the first team win more games due to greater balance, even though they seem to have about the same level of performance as the second?

To measure a team's offensive performance, I divided their runs scored per game by the league average. Then that was park adjusted using the park factors from the Sean Lahman database. The 1980 Orioles, for example, scored 4.97 runs per game. That divided by the league average of 4.51 leaves 1.10. But their park factor was 99, meaning that 1% fewer runs were scored in their park than average. So the 1.10 was divided by .99 to get 1.114, which is then multiplied by 100 to get 111.4, meaning the Orioles were 11.4% better than average in scoring. I performed similar calculations for runs allowed. In that case, the Orioles got 111.77, meaning they gave up 11.77% fewer runs than average (I'm following the convention that Pete Palmer uses, so above 100 means the team was better than average at preventing runs).

To measure balance, I found the difference between their runs-scored measure for offense (OFF) and their runs-allowed measure for defense (DEF) and then found the absolute value of balance (BAL). So the nearer the value of OFF and DEF, the more balanced the team. The Orioles had a BAL of .374 (slightly different than what the numbers imply due to rounding).

Is this balance factor important or relevant? To test this, I first ran a regression in which team winning percentage was the dependent variable and OFF and DEF were the dependent variables. The equation was:

$$(1) \quad -.476 + (.49 \times OFF) + (.482 \times DEF)$$

(I divided both OFF and DEF by 100 for the regression so, for example, instead of using 110 for BAL, I used 1.10). The coefficient on DEF is not negative for reasons explained above. The standard error for 162 games was about four wins. I looked at all teams from 1980 to 2004, then ran the regression with the balance variable added in. The results:

$$(2) \quad -.476 + (.486 \times OFF) + (.488 \times DEF) - (.032 \times BAL)$$

The standard error was still about four wins for 162 games. It did fall by about .02 wins. So adding in a balance factor does not explain winning much better. The BAL variable was statistically significant with a T-value of -2.6. It has the right sign needed if balance is to help winning. As BAL gets larger (meaning the teams get less balanced), they win less. But notice that its impact is only about 1/16 of OFF and DEF. Adding BAL also had very little impact on the equation itself, which you can see by comparing equation (2) to equation (1).

It is also helpful to look at how much a one standard deviation increase in any of the variables would change a team's winning percentage. Standard deviation (SD) is a measure of dispersion or the spread of the numbers. The SD of OFF was 9.51. If we multiply that by .486, we get 4.62. Since I divided both OFF and DEF by 100 for the regression, we have to divide 4.62 by 100, which leaves .0462. Over 162 games, that is about 7.5 more wins. The SD of DEF was 9.07. That multiplied by .488 leaves 4.43. Over a full season, that is 7.17 more wins. For BAL, the SD was 8.11. Using the -.032 coefficient, over 162 games we get about .42 more wins. Therefore, making a significant improvement in a team's balance adds less than one win per season.

I also looked to see if teams that exceeded their "Pythagorean" winning percentage were more balanced than other teams. The Pythagorean winning percentage was invented by Bill James, and it says that a team should have a winning percentage equal to runs scored squared divided by (runs scored squared plus runs squared allowed). The correlation between the BAL variable and how much teams exceeded their Pythagorean winning percentage was .0025, meaning that there is no connection. Being more balanced did not increase a team's number of expected wins.

How did the most balanced teams do? The teams with the lowest 25 BAL scores are listed in Table 1.

Table 1. The Most Balanced Teams

Rank	Team	Year	OFF	DEF	BAL	PCT
1	NYN	1999	110.08	110.13	0.047	0.595
2	KCA	1983	95.23	95.28	0.049	0.488
3	NYA	1997	112.67	112.62	0.050	0.593
4	SDN	1980	95.60	95.53	0.068	0.451
5	PHI	1997	89.58	89.66	0.085	0.420
6	BOS	1995	106.40	106.51	0.103	0.597
7	CHN	1987	95.21	95.32	0.113	0.472
8	TBA	2004	92.17	92.00	0.173	0.435
9	ATL	1985	90.49	90.27	0.224	0.407
10	TBA	1999	92.07	91.84	0.226	0.426
11	MON	1983	102.25	102.50	0.251	0.506
12	CLE	2003	95.46	95.13	0.329	0.420
13	CHN	1990	94.68	95.03	0.353	0.475
14	BAL	1980	111.40	111.77	0.374	0.617
15	NYN	1982	92.89	92.51	0.375	0.401
16	COL	1997	100.63	101.02	0.387	0.512
17	NYN	1994	97.87	98.29	0.415	0.487
18	MON	2002	100.96	101.40	0.438	0.512
19	PIT	1981	98.09	97.63	0.464	0.451
20	CAL	1996	89.65	90.14	0.486	0.435
21	PHI	1990	94.85	94.36	0.488	0.475
22	MIL	1998	94.02	93.53	0.490	0.457
23	BOS	1986	107.05	106.56	0.491	0.590
24	NYA	1982	99.76	99.26	0.502	0.488
25	CAL	1986	106.39	106.92	0.539	0.568

Table 2. The Least Balanced Teams

Rank	Team	Year	OFF	DEF	BAL	PCT
1	KCA	1987	88.32	117.16	28.845	0.512
2	DET	1993	119.10	90.18	28.924	0.525
3	TEX	1991	116.43	87.47	28.952	0.525
4	SEA	1983	73.87	103.06	29.194	0.370
5	HOU	1995	120.43	91.04	29.387	0.528
6	TEX	1983	89.22	118.80	29.585	0.475
7	TOR	1991	90.52	120.32	29.797	0.562
8	ATL	1995	94.81	124.75	29.940	0.625
9	KCA	1993	85.13	115.35	30.225	0.519
10	SLN	2003	122.14	91.04	31.096	0.525
11	CIN	2004	108.46	77.07	31.390	0.469
12	TOR	1982	82.36	113.80	31.441	0.481
13	TOR	1996	82.80	114.35	31.543	0.457
14	TEX	2001	113.04	81.34	31.702	0.451
15	BOS	1992	79.96	111.98	32.024	0.451
16	ANA	2001	82.02	114.33	32.304	0.463
17	ARI	2003	86.46	118.88	32.422	0.519
18	SFN	1999	120.86	87.80	33.068	0.531
19	BOS	1993	83.31	117.97	34.658	0.494
20	TOR	1997	81.06	116.25	35.188	0.469
21	ML4	1982	129.90	94.64	35.259	0.586
22	SDN	1997	114.63	77.00	37.635	0.469
23	TBA	1998	73.44	113.49	40.053	0.389
24	MON	2003	80.65	121.04	40.389	0.512
25	LAN	2003	82.61	126.31	43.696	0.525

The average winning percentage is .491, so these teams did not win any more games than normal. Table 2 lists the 25 least balanced teams. Their average winning percentage was .497.

Table 3 lists the top 25 teams in winning percentage from 1980 to 2004. Their average BAL score was 11.737, while the average for all teams was 10.138. So, the best teams are just a little less balanced than normal (remember that zero is perfect balance).

A couple of teams in Table 3 are interesting. One is the 2002–2003 Braves. In 2002 they rank 17th, having an OFF of just 98.83 and a DEF of 126.79. So they had great pitching and about average hitting. But the following year the team ranks 25th; they were very unbalanced, but in the opposite direction. They had great hitting (an OFF of 125.16) and so-so pitching (a DEF of 97.93). The other is the 2001–2002 A's. In 2001, they were very balanced, with a BAL of 1.452. Their winning percentage was .630. The next year, they became very imbalanced when BAL rose to 25.215. But they actually saw a slight rise in their winning percentage, to .636. So for the A's, going from being very balanced to being very imbalanced did not hurt their record.

Table 4 lists the lowest 25 teams in winning percentage. Their average BAL was 10.165. So the worst teams are just about as balanced as anyone else. Lack of balance is not why they lost so much.

Table 3. The Best Teams

Rank	Team	Year	OFF	DEF	BAL	PCT
1	SEA	2001	126.60	118.04	8.561	0.716
2	NYA	1998	121.31	118.79	2.513	0.704
3	CLE	1995	115.25	117.67	2.416	0.694
4	NYN	1986	119.28	111.23	8.059	0.667
5	ATL	1998	108.76	128.15	19.385	0.654
6	MON	1994	109.94	116.04	6.104	0.649
7	SLN	2004	117.27	110.64	6.635	0.648
8	DET	1984	116.93	109.15	7.785	0.642
9	OAK	1988	116.84	108.16	8.674	0.642
10	ATL	1993	103.40	130.09	26.689	0.642
11	NYA	2002	118.18	108.89	9.289	0.640
12	NYA	1980	114.63	106.95	7.677	0.636
13	OAK	1990	109.59	116.13	6.540	0.636
14	SFN	1993	115.74	109.77	5.971	0.636
15	ATL	1999	110.23	116.51	6.273	0.636
16	OAK	2002	98.71	123.92	25.215	0.636
17	ATL	2002	98.83	126.79	27.959	0.631
18	HOU	1998	119.78	115.28	4.498	0.630
19	OAK	2001	116.95	118.41	1.452	0.630
20	NYN	1988	119.16	108.57	10.590	0.625
21	ATL	1995	94.81	124.75	29.940	0.625
22	SLN	1985	114.52	112.88	1.637	0.623
23	ATL	1997	103.99	128.35	24.357	0.623
24	NYA	2003	115.31	107.33	7.988	0.623
25	ATL	2003	125.16	97.93	27.225	0.623

Table 4. The Worst Teams

Rank	Team	Year	OFF	DEF	BAL	PCT
1	CIN	1982	80.68	103.19	22.513	0.377
2	CLE	1987	92.56	84.60	7.962	0.377
3	SDN	1993	90.65	97.02	6.374	0.377
4	MIN	1981	78.82	99.60	20.776	0.376
5	SDN	1981	95.48	87.93	7.544	0.373
6	MIN	1982	87.96	92.09	4.132	0.370
7	SEA	1983	73.87	103.06	29.194	0.370
8	CLE	1985	99.75	85.74	14.006	0.370
9	CHN	1981	85.82	90.98	5.164	0.369
10	SEA	1980	82.23	94.47	12.234	0.364
11	DET	1989	90.49	83.56	6.930	0.364
12	NYN	1993	96.26	94.81	1.447	0.364
13	KCA	2004	93.35	86.13	7.219	0.358
14	PIT	1985	87.62	92.49	4.867	0.354
15	CLE	1991	78.49	96.68	18.193	0.352
16	TOR	1981	71.86	100.10	28.231	0.349
17	MIL	2002	90.61	85.16	5.445	0.346
18	DET	2002	79.83	84.26	4.429	0.342
19	TBA	2002	86.90	84.37	2.531	0.342
20	ATL	1988	85.11	89.68	4.567	0.338
21	BAL	1988	80.82	87.14	6.313	0.335
22	FLO	1998	93.32	78.25	15.071	0.333
23	DET	1996	90.63	79.91	10.714	0.327
24	ARI	2004	79.44	86.12	6.678	0.315
25	DET	2003	79.01	80.60	1.591	0.265

The interesting team in Table 4 is the 1981–1982 Twins. In 1981, their BAL was 20.776. So they were unbalanced, and they had a winning percentage of just .376. The next year, their BAL fell to 4.132, meaning they became more balanced. Yet their winning percentage also fell to .370.

The most balanced team was the 1999 Mets. They boasted very good hitting and pitching, with their OFF and DEF both being just about 110. This led to an excellent .595 winning percentage, a wild card birth in the playoffs, and a tough loss to the Braves in the NLCS (equation (1) predicts that they would have a .594 winning percentage). They boasted a star-studded lineup. Table 5 shows how the Met regulars hit: fifth in runs scored, averaging 5.23 runs per game.

Table 6 shows the statistics of the key Met pitchers. The team was fifth in ERA in the NL at 4.28. The pitching staff was helped by the fact that the Mets also only made 68 errors that year, by far the lowest in the league, and also a record at that time. Every other team made at least 100.

The least balanced team was the 1987 Royals. They had a fairly weak hitting attack, with an OFF of just 88.32. Table 7 shows the Royals' key hitters. Seitzer, Tartabull, and Brett all had good years, but the rest of the hitters did not. The Royals were last in runs scored, averaging 4.41 runs per game (and tied for next-to-last in OPS). Their park factor was 106 that year, meaning it was a slightly better than average run environment.

Table 8 displays the Royals' pitchers. Saberhagen, the leader of the staff, was a two-time Cy Young Award winner. The Royals were second in the league in ERA at 3.87, only .13 behind the league-leading Toronto Blue Jays (a little impressive since their park was favorable to hitters). Frank White (2B) won the last of his eight Gold

Table 5. 1999 Mets Hitting

	AB	HR	RBI	AVG	SLG	OBP	OPS	SB
Edgardo Alfonzo	628	27	108	.304	.502	.385	.886	9
John Olerud	581	19	96	.298	.463	.427	.890	3
Robin Ventura	588	32	120	.301	.529	.379	.908	1
Mike Piazza	534	40	124	.303	.575	.361	.936	2
Rey Ordonez	520	1	60	.258	.317	.319	.636	8
R. Henderson	438	12	42	.315	.466	.423	.889	37
Roger Cedeno	453	4	36	.313	.408	.396	.804	66
Brian McRae	298	8	36	.221	.349	.320	.669	2
Benny Agbayani	276	14	42	.286	.525	.363	.888	6

Table 6. 1999 Mets Pitching

Pitcher	W	L	SV	IP	BB	SO	ERA
Al Leiter	13	12	0	213	93	162	4.23
Orel Hershiser	13	12	0	179	77	89	4.58
Masato Yoshii	12	8	0	174	58	105	4.40
Rick Reed	11	5	0	149.1	47	104	4.58
Octavio Dotel	8	3	0	85.1	49	85	5.38
Turk Wendell	5	4	3	85.2	37	77	3.07
Armando Benitez	4	3	22	78	41	128	1.85
Kenny Rogers	5	1	0	76	28	58	4.03
Pat Mahomes	8	0	0	63.2	37	51	3.68
Dennis Cook	10	5	3	63	27	68	3.86
Bobby Jones	3	3	0	59.1	11	31	5.61
John Franco	0	2	19	40.2	19	41	2.88

The 1987 Kansas City Royals

Gloves. Willie Wilson had one career Gold Glove, but not in 1987.

Balance seems to matter very little. More balance, holding everything else constant, only slightly increases winning percentage. The most balanced teams don't win more than the least balanced teams. The teams with the best and worst winning percentages are no more or less balanced than other teams. Even in specific cases where teams saw a big change in balance, like the 1981–82 Twins, the 2001–02 A's, and the 2002–03 Braves, winning percentage hardly changed. General managers should concentrate on improving teams in any way that they can and should not worry if their team is balanced or not.

# # #

CYRIL MORONG, *a member of SABR since 1995, teaches economics at San Antonio College and is a lifelong White Sox fan. This article benefited from comments made by David Gassko. An earlier version of this article originally appeared at the Beyond the Boxscore website.*

Table 7. 1987 Royals Hitting

	AB	HR	RBI	AVG	SLG	OBP	OPS	SB
Kevin Seitzer	641	15	83	.323	.470	.399	.869	12
Danny Tartabull	582	34	101	.309	.541	.390	.931	9
Willie Wilson	610	4	30	.279	.377	.320	.698	59
Frank White	563	17	78	.245	.400	.308	.708	1
George Brett	427	22	78	.290	.496	.388	.884	6
Bo Jackson	396	22	53	.235	.455	.296	.750	10
Steve Balboni	386	24	60	.207	.427	.273	.700	0
Jamie Quirk	296	5	33	.236	.345	.307	.652	1
Angel Salazar	317	2	21	.205	.246	.219	.465	4

Table 8. 1987 Royals Pitching

Pitcher	W	L	SV	IP	BB	SO	ERA
Bret Saberhagen	18	10	0	257	53	163	3.36
Mark Gubicza	13	18	0	241.2	120	166	3.98
Charlie Leibrandt	16	11	0	240.1	74	151	3.41
Danny Jackson	9	18	0	224	109	152	4.02
Bud Black	8	6	1	122.1	35	61	3.60
Steve Farr	4	3	1	91	44	88	4.15
Jerry Don Gleaton	4	4	5	50.2	28	44	4.26
Dan Quisenberry	4	1	8	49	10	17	2.76
John Davis	5	2	2	43.2	26	24	2.27
Bob Stoddard	1	3	1	40	22	23	4.28
Dave Gumpert	0	0	0	19.1	6	13	6.05
Gene Garber	0	0	8	14.1	1	3	2.51

One-Team Players

Most articles written about Craig Biggio or Jeff Bagwell will contain a statement similar to the following: "Biggio and Bagwell are the last of a dying breed. In these days of free agency, it is rare for players to remain with the same team for their entire career. It isn't like the old days." Is that statement true? I compiled a list of all players who played at least 15 years in the major leagues and spent their entire career with one team.

The results are shown in the accompanying table. There have been 63 players who qualify, and they are sorted in the table by their debut dates.

The first one to do it played his entire career in the 19th century. Considering the instability of the franchises in that era, it is surprising that anyone could play his entire career with one team, but Bid McPhee broke in with Cincinnati in the American Association in 1882. When the franchise was absorbed into the National League in 1890, McPhee went along and stayed with them until his career ended in 1899.

Two players debuted in the decade of the 1900s, two debuted in the 1910s, ten debuted in the 1920s, six in the 1930s, four in the 1940s, nine in the 1950s, eleven in the 1960s, ten in the 1970s, six in the 1980s, and two in the 1990s. There are three players still active entering the 2007 season who have played their entire career with one team: Craig Biggio with the Astros, John Smoltz with the Braves, and Bernie Williams with the Yankees. The most long-term, one-team players active at any one time was in 1946, when eight of them were active. Ted Lyons and Mel Ott were in their 21st season, Mel Harder was in his 19th, Bill Dickey was in his 17th, Tommy Bridges was in his 16th, and Luke Appling, Frank Crosetti, and Stan Hack were in their 15th. As recently as 1988, there were six active: Dave Concepcion, George Brett, Robin Yount, Jim Rice, Mike Schmidt, and Frank White. Of course, in 1988 you heard the same talk about those guys being the "last of a dying breed" as well.

A few facts emerge from looking at the table. Of the 63 players in the table, 57 are eligible to be elected to the Hall of Fame. Thirty-four have been elected, or 59.6% of them. Ripken and Gwynn were the most recent to join this elite group in 2007. At least they don't have to spend time wondering what cap will be shown on their plaque. There are 22 different teams represented. With nine players the Tigers have the most: Hooks Dauss, Charlie Gehringer, Tommy Bridges, Al Kaline, Bill Freehan, Mickey Stanley, John Hiller, Alan Trammell, and Lou Whitaker. No team ever had more than two players active at the same time. The teammates who played together the longest were Alan Trammell and Lou Whitaker, who played together for 19 years. Interestingly enough, in over 100 years of baseball, the Philadelphia/Kansas City/Oakland Athletics have never had anyone play their entire career with them who played longer than 13 years (Pete Suder and Ed Rommel). It looks like Connie Mack and Charlie Finley had at least one similarity as owners.

Four of these players were originally signed by other organizations. Pee Wee Reese was originally signed by the Pittsburgh Pirates in 1938. After the Pirates sent him to Louisville, he became a part of the Boston Red Sox organization. The Dodgers purchased him from the Red Sox for $35,000. Roberto Clemente was originally signed by the Brooklyn Dodgers and was drafted by the Pirates out of their organization in 1954. John Smoltz was drafted by the Detroit Tigers in the 1985 June draft. He was traded to the Braves for Doyle Alexander in 1987. Jeff Bagwell was drafted by the Boston Red Sox in the 1989 June draft. He was traded to the Astros in 1990 for pitcher Larry Andersen. Needless to say, the teams that let these players get away were wailing and gnashing their teeth for the next 15 to 20 years.

The conclusion that can be drawn from all of this is that a player playing his entire career with one club has always been a rarity, and while players like Jeff Bagwell, Craig Biggio, John Smoltz, and Bernie Williams may not be a dying breed, they are certainly unique and should be appreciated for their loyalty to their clubs.

# # #

BILL CARLE *is chairman of SABR's Biographical Research Committee and a diehard fan of the Kansas City Royals.*

Player	Debut	Last Game	Years	Team	Player	Debut	Last Game	Years	Team
Bid McPhee	05-02-82	10-15-99	18	CIN	Bill Mazeroski	07-07-56	10-04-72	17	PIT
Walter Johnson	08-02-07	09-30-27	21	WAS	Bob Gibson	04-15-59	09-03-75	17	SLN
Clyde Milan	08-19-07	09-22-22	16	WAS	Carl Yastrzemski	04-11-61	10-02-83	23	BOS
Hooks Dauss	09-28-12	09-19-26	15	DET	Bill Freehan	09-26-61	10-03-76	15	DET
Red Faber	04-17-14	09-20-33	20	CHA	Tony Oliva	09-09-62	09-29-76	15	MIN
Pie Traynor	09-15-20	08-14-37	17	PIT	Willie Stargell	09-16-62	10-03-82	21	PIT
Ossie Bluege	04-24-22	07-13-39	18	WAS	Ed Kranepool	09-22-62	09-30-79	18	NYM
Travis Jackson	09-27-22	09-24-36	15	NYG	Mickey Stanley	09-13-64	09-28-78	15	DET
Lou Gehrig	06-15-23	04-30-39	17	NYY	Jim Palmer	04-17-65	05-12-84	19	BAL
Ted Lyons	07-02-23	05-19-46	21	CHA	John Hiller	09-06-65	05-27-80	15	DET
Charlie Gehringer	09-22-24	09-27-42	19	DET	Roy White	09-07-65	09-27-79	15	NYY
Mel Ott	04-27-26	07-11-47	22	NYG	Johnny Bench	08-28-67	09-29-83	17	CIN
Mel Harder	04-24-28	09-07-47	20	CLE	Bill Russell	04-07-69	10-01-86	18	LAD
Carl Hubbell	07-26-28	08-24-43	16	NYG	Dave Concepcion	04-06-70	09-15-88	19	CIN
Bill Dickey	08-15-28	09-08-46	17	NYY	Paul Splittorff	09-23-70	06-26-84	15	KCR
Tommy Bridges	08-13-30	07-20-46	16	DET	Mike Schmidt	09-12-72	05-28-89	18	PHN
Luke Appling	09-10-30	10-01-50	20	CHA	Frank White	06-12-73	09-30-90	18	KCR
Frank Crosetti	04-12-32	10-03-48	17	NYY	George Brett	08-02-73	10-03-93	21	KCR
Stan Hack	04-12-32	09-24-47	16	CHN	Robin Yount	04-05-74	10-03-93	20	MIL
Bob Feller	07-19-36	09-30-56	18	CLE	Jim Rice	08-19-74	08-03-89	16	BOS
Ted Williams	04-20-39	09-28-60	19	BOS	Jim Gantner	09-03-76	10-03-92	17	MIL
Pee Wee Reese	04-23-40	09-26-58	15	BK-LA	Lou Whitaker	09-09-77	10-01-95	19	DET
Bob Lemon	09-09-41	07-01-58	15	CLE	Alan Trammell	09-09-77	09-29-96	20	DET
Stan Musial	09-17-41	09-29-63	22	SLN	Cal Ripken	08-10-81	10-06-01	21	BAL
Carl Furillo	04-16-46	05-07-60	15	BK-LA	Tony Gwynn	07-19-82	10-07-01	20	SD
Vernon Law	06-11-50	08-20-67	16	PIT	Barry Larkin	08-13-86	10-03-04	19	CIN
Whitey Ford	07-01-50	05-21-67	16	NYY	Edgar Martinez	09-12-87	10-03-04	18	SEA
Mickey Mantle	04-17-51	09-28-68	18	NYY	Craig Biggio	06-26-88	Active	19	HOU
Al Kaline	06-25-53	10-02-74	22	DET	John Smoltz	07-23-88	Active	18	ATL
Ernie Banks	09-17-53	09-26-71	19	CHN	Jeff Bagwell	04-08-91	10-02-05	15	HOU
Roberto Clemente	04-17-55	10-03-72	18	PIT	Bernie Williams	07-07-91	Active	16	NYY
Brooks Robinson	09-17-55	08-13-77	23	BAL					

Pee Wee Reese—a Dodger his entire career.

BILL GILBERT

Salary Arbitration: Burden or Benefit?

The salary arbitration process is not well understood and it is frequently described in a negative way by media, as well as the clubs and players. I hope to improve the understanding of the process and how it works in this article.

Salary arbitration was instituted as part of the collective bargaining agreement between the Major League Baseball Players Association (MLBPA) and Major League Baseball (MLB) in the early 1970s. The purpose was to provide a system for players not yet eligible for free agency to be compensated based on a comparison with their peers.

The first hearings were held in 1974. The highest number of cases filed in any year was 162 in 1990. In 2007, 106 cases were filed with 99 being settled before a hearing was held. The number of cases that actually went to an arbitration hearing peaked in 1986 (35). Over the years, 476 cases have been heard by arbitrators with the clubs winning 273 (57%) and the players winning 203 (43%).

Eligibility for Salary Arbitration

Two classes of players are eligible for salary arbitration. The first class is players with 3-5 years of major league service (MLS) and the top 17% in seniority of MLS-2 players. This class accounts for over 90% of the cases filed with most of them involving players with 3 or 4 years of major league service.

The second class of eligible players includes free agents with 6+ years of ML service. Clubs have the option to offer arbitration to free agents who were with the club the previous season and these players then have the option of accepting or declining. If the player accepts arbitration, he is bound to the club and is no longer a free agent. Cases involving this class of players rarely go to a hearing. When Todd Walker won his arbitration case in 2007, he was the first MLS-6+ free agent to go to a hearing since 1991 when Dickie Thon, Jim Gantner and Dan Petry, all with 11+ years of MLS, went to hearings and lost.

The Arbitration Process

The arbitration process enables clubs to retain control of players with less than six years ML service, while the advantage to the players is that they receive salaries that are influenced by the market and their performance. The benefit to both sides is that the process is designed to promote a settlement without a hearing. If a case goes to a hearing, the arbitrators must award either the player's

filing or the club's filing—there's nothing in between. Thus both sides are taking a substantial risk if they allow a case to go a hearing. In the last 10 years, over 90% of the cases filed have settled prior to a hearing.

Of the 106 players who filed for salary arbitration in 2007, 50 reached contract agreements with their clubs before players and clubs exchanged salary figures on January 16. Of the remaining 56 cases, only 7 went to hearings with the clubs winning 4 and the players winning 3. The other 49 cases were settled prior to the hearings, as follows:

10 players signed multi-year contracts.

4 players signed one-year contracts for a figure above the mid-point of the two figures.

12 players signed one-year contracts at the mid-point.

23 players signed one-year contracts below the mid-point.

This is the way the arbitration process is supposed to work, with very few cases going to hearings. Players eligible for arbitration for the first time typically are in a position to negotiate a large increase in salary since the possibility of arbitration gives them leverage that they didn't have in their pre-arbitration years when their salaries are under control of the clubs. Players who have been through the process before also generally receive salary increases depending on their performance in the preceding year.

Conduct of a Hearing

A hearing panel consists of three arbitrators with one designated as the chairperson. Others present include the player (and sometimes his wife), his representatives and representatives from the MLBPA. Respected baseball analysts like Bill James and Gary Skoog have been used in hearings and several former players; Phil Bradley, Bobby Bonilla, Mark Belanger, Mike Fischlin and Tony

Bernazard among others, have been employed by the MLBPA and have been present at hearings. The club is represented by an official, usually the general manager, and also typically by an experienced arbitration practitioner to present the case. Others present are representatives from the Labor Relations Department of MLB, usually including General Counsel–Labor, Frank Coonelly.

The player is given one hour to present his case followed by an hour for the club to present its side. After a break to prepare rebuttals, each side is allowed 30 minutes for rebuttal. The arbitrators then have 24 hours to render their decision. There has been at least one occasion where a case was settled after a hearing. In a 1994 case involving the Houston Astros and relief pitcher, Tom Edens, the hearing was held with both sides anticipating a decision the following day. However, in the evening after the hearing, the agent for Edens called Bob Watson, then the Houston General Manager, and suggested that they settle at the mid-point of the filings. Watson agreed and the arbitrator (there was only one back then) was relieved of the responsibility of reaching a decision.

Arbitration Criteria

The collective bargaining agreement is specific regarding what is admissible and non-admissible in a hearing. Admissible items include the quality of the player's performance, the length and consistency of his performance, his record of past compensation, any physical or mental defects and comparative baseball salaries. The arbitrators are directed to give particular attention to contracts of players not exceeding one service group above that of the player.

Non-admissible items include the financial position of the player or the club, press comments on the player's performance and prior offers by either side.

Arbitration Hearing Strategies

In the player's case, emphasis is given to the strength of his performance and his awards or achievements. He is compared with players in the same service class with high salaries. The objective is to build evidence that supports a salary higher than the mid-point in the case. Sometimes another player will be brought in to testify in support of the player. A classic example was the 1998 Charles Johnson case when Scott Boras brought in

Kevin Brown to testify that he had pitched to both Johnson and Ivan Rodriguez and that Johnson was better at working with pitchers. In his 1994 case vs. Kansas City, Brian McRae also benefited from first-hand testimony about his defense by David Cone and Willie Wilson.

The challenge of the club is to point out deficiencies in the performance of the player *without personally demeaning the player*. This is tricky but it is essential since the player is part of the club. The club can point out the lack of awards and achievements and will strive to compare the player with players in the same service class with relatively low salaries. The objective is to build evidence that supports a salary lower than the mid-point in the case.

In a typical case, each side will use a different group of players they deem comparable to support their cases. An exception was the 1994 Brian McRae case. It was the last hearing on the 1994 docket so essentially all other relevant salaries had been established. Both sides used exactly the same group of National League outfielders as comparables, all with three years of MLS and one-year contracts for 1994 at salaries close to the mid-point of $1.6 million in the McRae case. The players were Ray Lankford, Moises Alou, Luis Gonzalez, Orlando Merced and Bernard Gilkey. McRae's agent argued that his player's performance placed him among the leaders in this group and the Club argued that his performance did not measure up to these players. McRae won the case (but subsequent years have shown that he probably ranked last in this group on a career basis).

Arbitration Hearing Results

The trend in recent years is for more cases to be settled prior to hearings. This is due to several reasons, one of which is that both sides now have a better grasp of a player's value in the arbitration process and file accordingly, anticipating a settlement around the mid-point:

	Average # Hearings/Yr.	% Won by Players
1980-1992	21	45%
1993-2001	11	37%
2002-2007	6	34%

Clubs have won a majority of decisions in each of the last 11 years.

Salary Case Studies

These three examples illustrate how a player's salary may change as he moves from club control in his first three years, through arbitration, to his eligibility for free agency after six years.

B. J. Ryan

Ryan's case is typical of a player whose role and performance increases as he moves through his arbitration years. In his first two arbitration years, he settled with Baltimore near the mid-point before a hearing, and in the third year a salary was agreed upon before figures were exchanged. Ryan became a very effective closer in 2005 and signed a five-year contract with Toronto when he became a free agent after six years.

Year	MLS	Salary Status	Salary, $K	Arbitration Filings Player	Club
2000	0	Club Control	204	--	--
2001	1	Club Control	240	--	--
2002	2	Club Control	300	--	--
2003	3	Eligible	762.5	700	825
2004	4	Eligible	1,275	1,000	1,500
2005	5	Eligible	2,600*	(settled early)	
2006	6	Free Agent	4,000**	--	--

*Earned an additional $225K in performance and awards bonuses.
**First year of five-year, $47M contract.

Jarrod Washburn

Washburn had a big year (18-6, 3.15 ERA) prior to his first year of arbitration eligibility. This gave him the leverage to command a big contract as an MLS-3. His salary continued to increase the next two years when he was essentially an average major league starting pitcher. In all three of his arbitration years, he settled on a contract with the Angels before figures were exchanged. He signed a four-year contract with Seattle when he became a free agent after six years.

Year	MLS	Salary Status	Salary, $K	Arbitration Filings Player	Club
2000	0	Club Control	222.5	--	--
2001	1	Club Control	270	--	--
2002	2	Club Control	350	--	--
2003	3	Arb. Eligible	3,875	(settled early)	
2004	4	Arb. Eligible	5,450	(settled early)	
2005	5	Arb. Eligible	6,500	(settled early)	
2006	6	Free Agent	7,450*	--	--

*First year of four-year, $37.0 M contract.

Michael Barrett

Barrett was one of the fortunate players who became eligible for free agency as an MLS-2. In his first two arbitration years, he agreed on a contract with Montreal before figures were exchanged. However, his career hit a bump in 2003 when he batted .208 and lost his job as the starting catcher. He was traded to the A's and then to the Cubs who did not tender him a contract. This took away the leverage he would have had as an arbitration eligible player and the Cubs signed him to a contract with a salary far below what he was paid the previous year. He responded with a breakout season and signed a three-year contract with the Cubs in his final year of arbitration eligibility after figures were exchanged.

Year	MLS	Salary Status	Salary, $K	Arbitration Filings Player	Club
2000	0	Club Control	265	--	--
2001	1	Club Control	285	--	--
2002	2+	Arb. Eligible	1,150	(settled early)	
2003	3	Arb. Eligible	2,600	(settled early)	
2004	4	Arb. Eligible	1,550	(non-tendered)	
2005	5	Arb. Eligible	3,133*	3,400	3,900
2006	6	Multi-Year	4,333	--	--

*First year of three-year., $12M contract. Earned an additional $50K award bonus.

Conclusions

- The arbitration process provides benefits to both clubs and players.

- Clubs retain player control for 6 years.

- Players receive market-influenced salaries 3 years before free agent eligibility.

- The process has been in place since 1974 and has survived numerous labor negotiations.

- The vast majority of salaries are determined by the process, not by an arbitration award.

#

A SABR member since 1984, BILL GILBERT has given 11 presentations at SABR Conventions and has also written articles for The National Pastime, The Baseball Research Journal, and other publications.

The Curse of the...Hurlers?

Consequential Yankees–Red Sox Trades of Note

The Curse of the Bambino hovered over the Boston Red Sox for more than 80 years, from the time they sold Babe Ruth to the New York Yankees after the 1919 season until early in the 21st century. The team that won four world championships in the 1910s didn't win another until 2004. A close look at the Red Sox–Yankee trades of that era reveals that—as great as the Babe was for the Yankees—it really was the trade of Boston pitching talent to New York that solidified the Yankees' march to greatness in the 1920s. The Curse of the Hurlers would really have been a more appropriate moniker.

Carl Mays, Waite Hoyt, Sam Jones, Joe Bush, George Pipgras, and Herb Pennock—five of these six pitchers were members of the Boston Red Sox pitching staff before 1923. (George Pipgras was the property of the Red Sox, though he never played for them, at least not until 1933.) They were traded to the Yankees in a four-year span, from December 1918 to January 1923. They went on to win more than 600 games for the Yankees, more than 500 of them in the 1920s.

What was a greater loss to the Boston Red Sox, the mighty Ruth or this impressive collection of pitching talent? They got fewer headlines than the Babe got, and they were certainly less colorful. Yet without these men, how many pennants would the Yankees have won? The Yankees simply would not have dominated the 1920s without them, even though they had Ruth. This is especially true because in this first decade of the Lively Ball era, good pitching was at a premium.

In the 1920s, with Colonel Ruppert's money, Ed Barrow's trading acumen, and Paul Krichell's scouting ability, whose numbers could the Yankees have replaced more easily, the run production of Ruth or the run prevention of these pitchers?

The following table presents the annual contributions of these pitchers and what they meant to both the Red Sox and the Yankees (OBA = opponents' batting average; OOBA = opponents' on-base average).

Two of the former Red Sox pitchers, Hoyt and Pennock, were with the Yankees for about a decade and consistently ranked at or near the top of the American League in many pitching categories.

Waite Hoyt

Year	Category	Stat	Rank
1923	Win Percentage	.654	3
	ERA	3.02	2
	OBA	.253	2
	OOBA	.307	2
1924	Games (tie)	46	3
1926	OOBA	.316	3
1927	Wins (tie)	22	1
	Win Percentage	.759	1
	ERA	2.63	2
	Complete Games	23	3
	Shutouts (tie)	3	2
1928:	Wins	23	3
	Win Percentage	.767	2

Herb Pennock

Year	Category	Stat	Rank
1923	Win Percentage	.760	1
1924	Wins	21	2
	Win Percentage	.700	2
	Complete Games	25	3
	Shutouts (tie)	4	3
	Innings Pitched	286.1	3
	ERA	2.83	3
1925	ERA	2.96	2
	Complete Games	21	3
	Innings Pitched	277	1
	OBA	.254	3
	OOBA	.303	1
1926	Wins	23	2
	Win Percentage	.676	2
	Innings Pitched	266.1	3
	OOBA	.313	1
1928	Shutouts	5	1
	ERA	2.56	2

The others—Mays, Bush, Jones, and Pipgras—were with the Yankees an average of only four seasons each. They took turns having outstanding seasons, helping propel the Yankees to the top of the AL.

Carl Mays

Year	Category	Stat	Rank
1920	Shutouts	6	1
	Wins	26	2
	Win Percentage	.703	2
	Games (tie)	45	3
1921	Wins (tie)	27	1
	Win Percentage	.750	1
	Innings	336.2	1
	Games	49	1
	Complete Games (tie)	30	2
	ERA	3.05	3
	OBA	257	2
	OOBA	.303	2

Joe Bush

Year	Category	Stat	Rank
1922	Wins	26	2
	Win Percentage	.788	1
	OBA	.252	2
	Strikeouts (tie)	125	2

Sam Jones

Year	Category	Stat	Rank
1923	Wins (tie)	21	2
	Win Percentage	.724	2
1923	OBA	.257	3

George Pipgras

Year	Category	Stat	Rank
1928	Wins (tie)	24	1
	Shutouts (tie)	4	2
	Games	46	3
	Innings	300.2	1
	Strikeouts	139	2
1929	Strikeouts	125	3

The Trades

The New York Yankees acquired this pitching talent in a series of six trades with the Boston Red Sox. Baseball historian Fred Lieb and Boston reporter Burt Whitman referred to them as part of "The Rape of the Red Sox." Red Sox owner Harry Frazee has been vilified for giving up the heart of his team in terrible one-sided deals. But how did these trades look at the time they were made, without the benefit of hindsight?

A close review of the deals reveals a very different picture. They were quite balanced and not one-sided. The recent performances of the players involved, as well as their potential and prospects in the future, suggested equitable trades. The comments in the press of both cities reflected the perceived evenness of the transactions. However, over time these deals did prove to be very one-sided in favor of the Yankees.

> His [Frazee's] friends who are many admire his courage and energy; his enemies who are not few, must at least respect his aggressive fearlessness.
> —F.C. Lane, *Baseball Magazine*, March 1919

Thus was Harry Frazee described before the controversial Carl Mays deal. He made two big trades with the Philadelphia Athletics before the start of the 1918 season. His acquisition of Stuffy McInnis, Amos Strunk, Wally Schang, and Joe Bush was a key driver of the last Red Sox world championship of the 20th century, in 1918. Frazee also spent $60,000 in one of those deals. He was aggressive in building a winner and spent money willingly. Moreover, he made deals that helped his ball club, as reflected in that 1918 title.

> Curious how this club is always able to supply a horde of fine players for the other teams, and yet put up a formidable front each season. . . . Is Frazee a foxy baseball general or is the chubby magnate blessed with uncanny luck?"
> —W. A. Phelon, *Baseball Magazine*, February 1922

Thus was Harry Frazee described after the Ruth deal and two blockbuster December trades with New York, in 1920 and 1921. The 1918 world champion Red Sox finished in sixth place in 1919 with Ruth. They finished in fifth place in both 1920 and 1921 without him. They also improved their record from 1919 to 1921. Fred Lieb noted in the December 23, 1921, *New York Evening Telegram* that Harry Frazee couldn't be accused of weakening his club the way Connie Mack did because Frazee always insisted on getting players in return in his deals.

Here is a close look at his six trades of pitchers to the Yankees, other than the Babe Ruth deal, starting with one he made less than three months after the Red Sox won that 1918 World Series.

Harry Frazee

Trade No. 1
December 18, 1918

TO NEW YORK	TO BOSTON
Ernie Shore, P	Ray Caldwell, P
Dutch Leonard, P	Slim Love, P
Duffy Lewis, OF	Frank Gilhooley, OF
	Roxy Walters, C
	$25,000 cash[1]

This trade seemed very favorable to the Yankees when it was made. They acquired three veterans with proven track records, stars of Boston's 1915 and 1916 championship clubs. Shore was 3–1 in those two series; Leonard was 2–0; Lewis had hit .400.

The trio were still in the prime of their careers: Leonard was 26, Shore was 27, and Lewis was 30. From 1915 to 1917, Shore and Leonard won 97 games between them. Lewis had hit close to .300 in his Red Sox career and was part of baseball's finest outfield along with Tris Speaker and Harry Hooper.

The Yankees gave up players who had not yet achieved their full potential. Caldwell, at 30, was the oldest. He was a very talented pitcher and a good hitter. He won 37 games for weak New York teams in 1914 and 1915. The Washington Senators had offered Walter Johnson for him straight up early in 1915 (when both were flirting with the Federal League), and the new Yankee owners turned the deal down.[2] But Ray also had a strong affinity for alcohol and "not obeying training rules."

Slim Love had an incredible fastball; the *New York Evening Journal* reported that only Walter Johnson threw faster than he did in the American League. But Love also had control problems; he led the league with 116 walks in 1918. Walters was a classic good-field, weak-hit catcher with a great arm. Gilhooley had otherwise promising seasons ended by injuries in 1916 and 1917, and had rebounded with a solid 1918 season, hitting .276.

Burt Whitman of the *Boston Herald* noted that the Red Sox had a surplus of talent that could be traded without hurting the team, as they did a year earlier. With Ruth, Mays, Bush, and Jones, he wrote that Boston still had the best pitching staff in the league. He continued, "Walters . . . may add strength and snap to the world champions where they need it considerably. Love may develop into a second Rube Waddell."[3]

The New York press was enthusiastic; the *New York Times* called it "the most important baseball trade locally for years. . . . In Shore, Huggins has one of the best pitchers of the game, and Lewis is the first real outfielder that the Yanks have been able to land in many seasons." The *New York Herald* called it "a master stroke."[4]

There seems to be an overall consensus that the Yankees had come out on top on this deal. *The Sporting News* wrote of Miller Huggins "electrifying the baseball world . . . in snaring three of the Red Sox most brilliant stars." The paper continued, "Shore and Leonard are two great pitchers . . . while Lewis was a tower of strength in the offense and defense of the champions."[5]

The paper noted the loss of the talented Caldwell, but seasoned their praise with a reference to his "frequent and prolonged" escapades. In the same issue Joe Vila wrote, "It's a cinch that Shore and Leonard will prove their real worth in the box."

The trade ended up a wash, helping neither team very much. The "sure deal" for New York was anything but, and Shore and Lewis, who missed the 1918 season in the Navy, never regained their old form. Shore won only seven games for New York, and Lewis played in only 275 more games. Leonard got into a contract dispute with the Yankees, who sent him to Detroit before he played a single game for New York. One report said that Leonard insisted his salary be placed in escrow to ensure that he would receive it. Yankees owner Colonel Jacob Ruppert apparently did not appreciate the implications of this proposal.

Caldwell lasted less than a season with Boston, but had a stunning comeback with the Cleveland Indians. Late in the 1919 season, he no-hit the Yankees, and he then won 20 games for the 1920 world champions. Love won only six more games in the bigs. Walters hung around for seven more years, yet he hit above .201 twice and played in more than 54 games only once. Frank Gilhooley's last major league season was 1919, but he went on to a sensational career in the International League. Four times in the 1920s, he garnered 200 hits, and he hit above .340 three times in that decade.

Trade No. 2
July 29, 1919

TO NEW YORK	TO BOSTON
Carl Mays, P	Allan Russell, P
	Bob McGraw, P
	$40,000 cash

This trade is most remembered for the battle it triggered between American League president Ban Johnson and the Yankees' owners, who were supported by Harry Frazee and the White Sox's Charles

Comiskey. Mays walked out on the Red Sox, and Frazee sent him to New York in July 1919. Johnson wanted the deal rescinded to punish Mays and the Red Sox and to keep players in line, but the Yankees prevailed in court. It was a setback that marked the beginning of the end of Ban Johnson's iron rule over the league.

There is no doubt that Mays was a talented pitcher. He had won 61 games for the Red Sox the previous three years. He is also the answer to the trivia question, "Who was the last pitcher to clinch a world championship for the Red Sox in the 20th century?" His 2–1 three-hitter on September 11, 1918, was his second win in the series by that score.

Mays was no stranger to controversy. In his few years in the majors, he had been involved with a number of beanball incidents. He was also not an easy person to get along with. Red Sox manager Ed Barrow didn't want Mays back, calling the pitcher "a chronic malcontent."[6] In time, Yankees manager Miller Huggins would come to share this sentiment about Mays. The trade received a great deal of attention in the papers; most of it focused on Ban Johnson's efforts to overturn the deal and the legal battles with the Yankees. There is little discussion about the merits of the trade itself.

Any evaluation of the trade must take into account the fact that Mays had put the Red Sox in a difficult position. It was likely that he would not pitch for the team again, so Frazee had cut the best deal he could. He insisted on getting pitching in return, not simply money. The White Sox, for example, wanted Mays and offered only cash. In his discussions with the Yankees, Ed Barrow expressed interest in "Rubberarm" Russell. The Yankees also included McGraw, whom the *New York Evening Journal* had once called a "real comer."[7]

The trade seemed to favor the Yankees, and Frazee seemed to make the best of a bad situation. Even Ernest Lanigan, no fan of the Boston owner, noted Frazee would likely benefit from the deal: "Mays always was a trouble-maker in Boston . . . who came very near being expelled from the American League once." In return, Frazee "gets a couple of pitchers who look like fair prospects and a wad of dough."[8] The "wad" was nearly as much as the Red Sox had received for selling Tris Speaker to Cleveland.[9]

That season Frazee's side of the trade looked good. Mays went 9–3 for New York, but Russell had a record of 10–4 for Boston. Later Mays was instrumental in the Yankees' pennant drives of 1920 and 1921. Allan Russell and Bob McGraw never rose above journeyman status; Russell ended his career as a key member of the 1924 and 1925 pennant winners, the Washington Senators, making 67 relief

appearances those two seasons, and McGraw finished his career with an ERA of exactly 5.00.

The Yankee owners were eager to acquire Mays as a step in their building a winner, but manager Huggins was strangely silent about the deal. During the lengthy court battles between Ban Johnson and the Yankees, he showed little enthusiasm for his new pitcher. By 1922 the Yankees had soured on Mays and sold him to Cincinnati after the 1923 season for far less than Frazee got for him. Yet Mays still had some good years left. He won 20 games in 1924 and 19 games for the 1926 Reds, who fell just two games short of the pennant and a World Series matchup with his former team, the Yankees.

Trade No. 3
December 15, 1920

TO NEW YORK	TO BOSTON
Waite Hoyt, P	Hank Thormahlen, P
Harry Harper, P	Muddy Ruel, C
Mike McNally, IF	Del Pratt, IF
Wally Schang, C	Sammy Vick, OF
	$50,000 cash

This was the first of two blockbuster deals transacted almost exactly one year apart. In this trade both teams gave up talent and promise to get the same in return. It seemed like a balanced deal at the time.

The teams traded promising pitchers, Hoyt and Thormahlen; they swapped catchers, a proven veteran (Schang) for a prospect (Ruel); they exchanged utility players McNally and Vick. (Sammy Vick had been the Yankees' starting right fielder in 1919 before the arrival of Babe Ruth.) The Red Sox also got Del Pratt, one of the best second basemen in the game, and gave up marginal pitcher Harry Harper. Pratt had come to Yankees three years earlier and dramatically improved the team's middle infield. He averaged close to .300 those seasons, including .314 in 1920.

At the time of the trade Hoyt seemed unpredictable at best, and unmanageable at worst. The New York Giants originally signed Hoyt, and when manager John McGraw assigned him to Newark late in 1918, he refused to report. He instead joined the Baltimore Dry Docks (a shipyard team). The following year McGraw assigned him to Rochester; again Hoyt ran off to join the Dry Docks. After refusing another assignment in New Orleans, the headstrong Hoyt ended up on the Boston Red Sox.

Hoyt's 1920 season was shortened by a serious injury. A double hernia and a stomach abcess kept him out of the game for about three months. There was no question he had promise. Whether he would take direction from management and whether he would fully recover from his operation were open to speculation.

Hank Thormahlen seemed at least as promising as Hoyt. After winning 25 games for Baltimore of the International League in 1917, the Yankees bought him for about $7,500. He was a sensational prospect. Two of baseball's most respected sportswriters wrote glowingly about him. Veteran scribe Sam Crane said, "He will show later and show big, mark me."[10] Joe Vila called Thormahlen "one of the best southpaw prospects I have ever seen."[11] While the pitcher's 1920 season (9–6, 4.14 ERA) was less impressive than 1919 (12–10, 2.62 ERA), he still had stuff. A week after the trade The Sporting News wrote, "[Thormahlen] appears to have the makings of a fine pitcher, a much better prospect than Harper."[12]

Fred Lieb was critical of this deal in his 1947 Red Sox team history, calling it "another of [Frazee's] infamous deals with the Yankees." Yet he wrote something quite different in his "Cutting the Plate" column that appeared in the New York Evening Journal in 1931: "That was one of the most even deals [the Yankees] made with Frazee."[13] Boston writers were positive about the trade, seeing it as a clear win for the Red Sox. Burt Whitman of the Boston Herald was ecstatic; he called Pratt and Ruel the keys to the deal, though he liked Thormahlen too. "The Red Sox got by far the best of the deal. All Boston fans must applaud the move."[14] He further gushed that the deal must have been "conscience money" from the Yankees for the Babe Ruth deal, "for surely the Sox get the cream of the talent."

Whitman also noted (somewhat prophetically) that Hoyt "may make the trade look good for the Yankees." The Boston Globe weighed in: "Schang and Pratt are the two big players in the deal, with Hoyt something of a speculation, and unless the latter should develop into a great pitcher, it looks as if the Yankees were stung."[15]

The opinions of the New York press were balanced. The New York Times saw the deal as "even Steven," and the New York Herald said that the deal would help both teams. Sam Crane recognized Pratt's enormous value in the New York Evening Journal, calling the second baseman "a tower of strength for the Yankee team." Yet there were problems. Dan Daniel noted that Pratt "is not a great organization man."[16] Miller Huggins faced criticism both inside and outside the clubhouse, and Pratt was stirring things up—even jockeying for Huggins' job. "A lack of amenability to reason,

or at least to the constitutional authority," was how the Times phrased it.[17]

Joe Vila was more outspoken in The Sporting News: "Miller Huggins got out the old chloroform bottle. . . . Huggins actually gave up nothing for something."[18] Vila's comments were based on the report that Pratt had left Organized Baseball for a coaching job at the University of Michigan—his relationship with Miller Huggins had deteriorated so badly that had he not been traded, Pratt would have stayed at the college job. The terms of the trade were that it would go through even if Pratt didn't report.

Shortly after the trade, Baseball Magazine wrote, "Ruel is a classy little catcher who should improve greatly with age and experience."[19]

The December 16, 1920, New York Tribune predicted Ruel would prove to be a better player than Schang in five years, but "New York is too valuable a territory to waste on architectural plans." Win, and win now—Huggins was being pressured to deliver a pennant quickly. In Schang he was getting a proven star who had caught for two world champion teams, the 1913 Athletics and the 1918 Red Sox. If Pratt was the key to the deal for Boston, Schang was the man for New York.

Shrewd observer Sam Crane of the New York Evening Journal was noncommittal. "Let's stand pat on the trade" before declaring who got the better of the deal, he wrote on December 16.

Hoyt was the wild card, a gamble. If he didn't prove out, then "New York certainly got the worst of the deal."[20] The New York World summed it up: "Opinions have been freely expressed on the big baseball trade last week . . . the value of the trade from a New York point of view hinges entirely on Waite Hoyt. The possibilities of this youthful pitcher cannot be overestimated."[21]

Schang delivered for the Yankees, hitting .316 and .319 his first two seasons with the team, and New York won three straight pennants. Ruel did eventually become a star—for Washington. The Red Sox sent Allan Russell and Ruel to the Senators in 1923, where they became key parts of the 1924 and 1925 pennant winners.

Later, Miller Huggins said that giving up Muddy Ruel was his biggest trading mistake. The diminuitive backstop (5'9", 150 pounds) was durable—enough to play an average of more than 124 games a year, most as a catcher, hitting above .275 in six of eight seasons. Yet just what Huggins thought about Ruel as a ballplayer is unclear. Many years later, Frank Graham quoted Huggins in the New York Journal-American: "Muddy was one of the finest young men I'd ever known. If I ever had a son, I'd like him to be like Muddy. But I simply couldn't see him as a catcher."[22]

After the trade, Boston sent Pratt a blank contract and let him fill in the salary (he inserted $11,500 a year for two years). He resigned from his Michigan position[23] and went on to hit .324 for the 1921 Red Sox. Pratt continued to excel with the bat and hit above .300 in each of his next three seasons, though he did slow down in the field by 1924, his final season.

Harper and Thormahlen never came close to stardom. Harper won only four more games, three more victories than Thormahlen tallied after the deal. McNally and Vick never became regulars; McNally was a key sub in 1921 when Frank Baker was injured, but Vick tore ligaments in his knee in the off-season following the trade and was out of the bigs after 1921.

Ultimately, Waite Hoyt "made" this deal for New York. He delivered 38 wins in his first two seasons in New York, and gave up no earned runs in 27 innings in the 1921 Series.

Trade No. 4
December 20, 1921

TO NEW YORK	TO BOSTON
Joe Bush, P	Jack Quinn, P
Sam Jones, P	Bill Piercy, P
Everett Scott, IF	Rip Collins, P
	Roger Peckinpaugh, IF
	$150,000 cash[24]

One year later the teams completed another blockbuster deal. The key for the Yankees was receiving two veteran pitchers (Bush and Jones, both 29 years old) in exchange for, in essence, two young arms (Piercy and Collins, both 25) and veteran spitballer Jack Quinn. Again the Yankees were looking to "win now," giving up prospects for proven veterans. *The Sporting News* noted something that has been true of the Yankees since the early 1920s: "The insistence of the [Yankees] club owners and their patrons on an immediate winner has worked against the retention and development of these prospects."[25]

Quinn was 38 years old at the time of the deal and was an anchor on the 1920 Yankees staff with 18 wins—but he had slipped badly in 1921 (8–7). This was the second time New York had given up on him; they thought he was getting old when they sent him to Rochester in 1912. Jones had a fine season in 1921, winning 23 games for the Sox, and Bush continued a remarkable comeback from a "dead arm," with a 16–9 record in 1921.

Rip Collins (not to be confused with Ripper Collins of the Cardinals in the 1930s) was a talented pitcher with a lot of promise. "He has blinding speed, more sheer stuff, perhaps, than any pitcher has shown since Walter Johnson," wrote F.C. Lane in *Baseball Magazine* in August 1927. And Collins delivered, winning 25 games for the Yankees in 1920–1921 with only 13 losses.

Bill Piercy was another arm with potential. He was a Coast League star in 1919–1920, when he pitched more than 600 innings and won 39 games with an impressive 2.34 ERA. Piercy is perhaps best known as the answer to the trivia question, "Who was the pitcher that Judge Landis suspended along with Babe Ruth and Bob Meusel, for barnstorming after the 1921 World Series?" By the time Piercy served that suspension, he was a member of the Red Sox.

The swap of shortstops, two of the league's best, seemed to be fair. Everett Scott, the younger of the pair, was not as accomplished a hitter as Roger Peckinpaugh, but had the edge with his glove. Peck had been an anchor on the Yankees since 1913—the heart of the team—and even managed New York briefly at the end of the 1914 season, when he was only 23 years old.

Peck had recently made a critical miscue in the eighth game of the just-concluded 1921 Series. A ground ball went through his legs and brought in the game's only run, giving the New York Giants the clincher, a 1–0 win over Waite Hoyt. Yankees co-owner Til Huston was furious over the error, though just what role he played in trading Peckinpaugh remains unclear. (For what it's worth, Peck would later commit a record eight errors in the 1925 Series.)

As with Del Pratt a year earlier, Miller Huggins was again dealing with unrest in the clubhouse. His detractors—Ruth reportedly being among them—pushed the Yankee shortstop as a replacement for Huggins. Peck was not party to this, but his transfer helped secure Huggins' position.

Opinion was split as to who got the better end of the deal. The *Boston Herald* and the *Boston Post* were critical of Frazee. In the *Herald*, Burt Whitman called the trade "an insult to Boston fandom" and wailed that "the great Red Sox armada . . . has been scrapped. . . . Frazee has junked his ball club." The *Post*'s Paul Shannon declared Boston was no longer a major league city.[26] The *Globe* rationalized that Jones and Bush "were as good as they were ever going to be."

Joe Vila was of the opinion in *The Sporting News* that "Frazee was either chloroformed or hypnotized."[27] Focusing mainly on the pitching talent the Yankees received, the *New York Times* called the deal "a sensational surprise."[28]

The December 21 *New York World* did not agree. "Both Bush and Quinn are about through as far as the major leagues are concerned," and "Piercy and Collins are young pitchers of high promise." Fred Lieb noted in the *New York Evening Telegram* that Collins had as much "latent talent" as any pitcher of his years. In the *New York Evening Mail* of December 17, 1921, Hugh Fullerton noted the Yankees were taking a chance of raising "two Shockers" against them, promising young arms that would come back to haunt—and beat—them.

The *New York Tribune* saw great promise in the young arms New York had surrendered:

Piercy in every action and movement is the nearest approach of baseball history to the great and only Christy Mathewson. Collins has the speed of Walter Johnson. He was what Johnson never had in his prime—a good curve ball. They will come back next year, as Urban Shocker did after he was traded to the Browns, to make Huggins rue his bargain.[29]

While Piercy and Collins never lived up to these lofty expectations, the passage illustrates the luxury of hindsight. No less of an astute observer than John McGraw felt Frazee's critics were being unduly harsh. "They are hopping a little hard on Frazee. If a couple of young pitchers show anything or get fixed up with ambition, that club may kick up trouble."[30]

The Yankees had now given up on Quinn for the second time—and a second time he surprised them. He would go on to win another 122 games in 12 more years in the bigs, belying Joe Vila's assertion that Quinn was "through."[31] The heralded Bush would win only 87 more games over seven years. The Yankees also gave up on Jones prematurely in 1926. He went on to win 94 more games in his career.

The Yankees got only two or three strong years from Jones and Bush. Unlike the Hoyt deal, the payoff was short-term. From 1922 to 1924, Jones and Bush helped New York to two pennants (and barely missing a third). Their timing was excellent; after terrific 1920 and 1921 seasons, Carl Mays fell off badly. Bush took over with a 26–7 record in 1922, and Jones followed with a 21–8 mark the following year.

Collins won 14 games for the last-place Red Sox in 1922. Near the end of that season, Collins and Quinn beat the Yankees, 3–1 and 1–0 in back-to-back games, nearly denying them the pennant. In a 1927 *Baseball Magazine* article, F.C. Lane said of Collins, "He might have been a marvelous hurler. He has been merely good." His obituary noted that Collins "loved a good time and liquid refreshment." When he was once asked why he looked older than his 32 years, Collins replied, "You can't buck liquor and Broadway lights without getting marked up."

Scott would go on to play five more years and 558 games, and Peckinpaugh appeared in 707 games over the next six years. Yet Peck never took the field for the Red Sox. They traded him to Washington in a three-way deal three weeks later, bringing third baseman Joe Dugan to Boston.[32] Peckinpaugh anchored the infield of the pennant-winning Senators of 1924 and 1925 and won the American League Award (forerunner of the MVP).

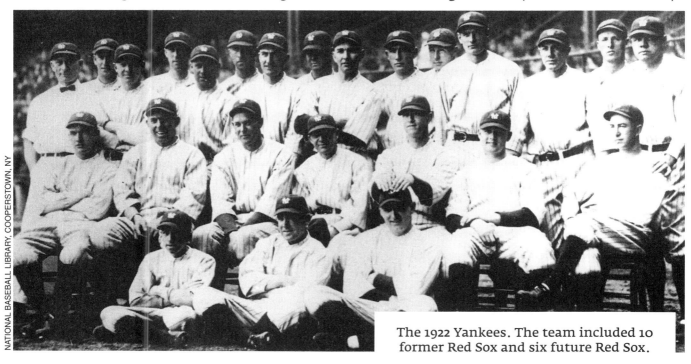

The 1922 Yankees. The team included 10 former Red Sox and six future Red Sox.

Trade No. 5
January 3, 1923

TO NEW YORK	TO BOSTON
George Pipgras, P	Al DeVormer, C
Harvey Hendrick, OF	cash?[33]

At the time this deal was considered a minor transaction and got little press. Pipgras and Hendrick were relatively obscure minor leaguers—the biggest name was DeVormer, a starting catcher in Vernon's Coast League champions of 1918–1920. The Yankees had given the Vernon club three prospects for him late in 1920; when New York released Ping Bodie to Vernon a year later, the *New York Times* reported that he was sent as part of the DeVormer deal. Yet the catcher was no more than a reserve player for the Yankees, appearing in 46 games in 1921–1922.

What little coverage this transaction exists favors the Red Sox. The *New York Times* wondered what the Yankees would do with another right-handed pitcher (Pipgras). What they really lacked was a lefty in the rotation. In Boston, Burt Whitman of the *Boston Herald* was excited: "Keep your seats, fans and fannies, and get a double nelson on your hats. The Red Sox are on the big end of a deal."[34]

This trade was significant for the Yankees, though it took five years for this to become apparent. Pipgras, 23 years old at the time of this trade, did not develop into a big winner for the Yankees until the late 1920s. At first he had control problems, then spent two years on the bench and two more in the minors. He didn't begin to contribute for New York until late in the 1927 season.

The Yankees' timing was either very good or very lucky. After the rest of the righties in their rotations of the early 1920s (other than Hoyt) were gone or at the end of the line, Pipgras took over. At the end of the decade, from late 1927 through 1929, he won 52 games for New York. Without his arm the Yankees would not have come close to winning the 1928 pennant.

"The first time I saw him I knew he was a good pitcher," said Huggins of Pipgras in 1927. After Huggins' death, Ford Frick noted in the September 26, 1929, *New York Evening Journal*, "Once Hug was convinced that a man would make a real ball player he would stay with him for years."

DeVormer played in fewer than 200 games in the majors. Hendrick became a decent player, hitting .308 over an 11-year career, mainly with Brooklyn.

Trade No. 6
January 30, 1923

TO NEW YORK	TO BOSTON
Herb Pennock, P	George Murray, P
	Norm McMillan, OF–3B
	Camp Skinner, OF
	$50,000[35]

Less than a month later the Yankees acquired a lefty for the rotation: Herb Pennock. Pennock did not carry impressive credentials from Boston. In the preceding two years he had compiled a 23–31 record with an ERA of more than 4.00. The three players the Red Sox acquired were fairly young (mid-20s) and unproven, with Murray showing the most promise. Now that the Yankees had Joe Dugan at third base, McMillan had become expendable.

Once again the Yankees were thinking of their immediate needs, and had a couple of things on their minds when they made the deal. First, they had just come away from another World Series loss to the Giants. Unlike 1921, they didn't even win one game in the 1922 series. They had to get a proven southpaw into their starting rotation—they really hadn't had one since George Mogridge in 1915–1920.[36] Second, they were working on a big trade for Eddie Collins, and the White Sox were insisting that Waite Hoyt be included in the deal—all the more reason for New York to add a veteran to the staff, to bolster their ranks for 1923. When Huggins decided not to offer Hoyt, the White Sox deal collapsed.

Yankees owner Jacob Ruppert found himself on the defensive after announcing the Pennock deal. The immediate sentiment was very negative. Ruppert emphasized that Huggins felt strongly about the lefty Pennock, and that he (Ruppert) felt strongly about Huggins. He then outlined the Yankees' philosophy, one not unlike that of the present-day club:

> John McGraw once was accused of being an "opportunist." We are opportunists in this case. We are taking Pennock to make reasonably sure of the present. We are willing to take a chance on the future. Other Murrays and McMillans will come along.[37]

In Boston there was a broad spectrum of opinion. Burt Whitman of the *Boston Herald* canvassed many baseball observers, who told him they weren't concerned about the trade from Boston's perspective. He went on to suggest that the Red Sox had acquired "all promising if not brilliant material for [manager] Frank Chance."[38] The *Boston Globe* was mildly positive, yet the *Boston Post* was very critical:"Frazee took the leap yesterday, making the wreck of a once great aggregation complete."[39]

In New York the writers were very clear: the Yankees had given up too much on a gamble for an average veteran. The *New York World* wrote that the Yankees had been "gypped" and that Miller Huggins was as much of a "sap" as when he traded Urban Shocker away in 1918.[40]

The *New York Times* wrote, "Murray, one of the best young pitchers in the big leagues, has been hailed by all good judges as a sure comer. . . . [E]ither Murray or McMillan is as valuable as the aging Pennock" and called it "one of the most one-sided trades in the history of the American League."[41] In a rare glimpse of organizational schism, the paper quoted an unnamed Yankees official who considered the deal to be "the worst trade the Yanks ever made." The *New York Herald*'s Dan Daniel was equally concerned: "The Yankees have indulged in a flight of extravagance to land Pennock . . . In another year Murray may be one of the outstanding stars of the game."[42]

In *The Sporting News*, Joe Vila noted the difference of opinion on the deal, yet came down on the side of the Red Sox. "The Boston manager has received three very promising colts in exchange for a passing veteran."[43]

That "passing veteran" went on to a long Yankee career, one that garnered him entry into the Baseball Hall of Fame. Considered one of the greatest clutch pitchers in World Series history, Herb Pennock won 162 games for the Yankees. Skinner played in a total of seven games for Boston, the balance of his major league career. "Can't miss" Murray—whom Fred Lieb said had "the makings of a Johnson or Alexander"—won just 16 more games in the majors. He broke his arm in 1925 while throwing a curveball. McMillan had modest success as the starting third baseman on the 1929 pennant-winning Chicago Cubs. That was one of two years that he played in more than 76 games.

Summing Up

Six trades with the Red Sox for pitching talent helped build the Yankees dynasty of the 1920s. Six trades built the foundation of baseball's most winning franchise. While so much attention has been focused on the acquisition of a former pitcher—the incomparable slugger Babe Ruth—six other trades brought the club a precious and rare 1920s commodity: pitching talent. The sale of Ruth symbolized the power shift to New York. The trades of these pitchers cemented that transfer of power.

History has been unkind to Harry Frazee, yet these transactions seemed quite equitable when they were made, in the eyes of the press as well as the past performances of the men involved. This analysis does not even include the cash Frazee received ($315,000) that could have been used to acquire other playing talent.

After the December 1921 blockbuster deal (Trade No. 4), F.C. Lane wrote, "Such are the uncertainties of baseball that no opinion beyond a guess can be hazarded as to the probable outcome of this deal."[44] Yet the fact remains that these trades turned out to be famously one-sided for New York. The Yankees ended up with a wealth of pitching talent without which their dynasty could not have risen. The Red Sox ended up with little to show for their side of the ledger. Why did so many trades turn out so favorably for the Yankees? Were they guessing? Were they simply lucky? Or were they good? Consider these factors.

1. ED BARROW

The Red Sox manager of 1918–1920 became the Yankees' business manager in October 1920, just before the first of the two blockbuster deals (Trade No. 3). When that deal was announced, Fred Lieb wrote in the *New York Evening Journal*, "The fine hand of Ed Barrow is seen in this latest deal." Lieb noted that Barrow was the man "who made a real pitcher out of Sam Jones."

Barrow knew these pitchers better than anyone else knew them. Jones and Bush played key roles for Boston's 1918 pennant winners. Bush, Jones, and Pennock won well over 50% of the Red Sox 1920 victories, and Hoyt had glimpses of brilliance in Boston.

While Barrow was not a modest man and took credit for things that weren't totally his doing (such as converting Ruth from a pitcher to an everyday hitter), did he have some special insight into the potential of these former Red Sox pitchers? Did he see the likelihood of success in a youngster like Hoyt and a veteran like Pennock that others could not see so clearly? Did he grasp that youngsters like Thormahlen and Collins and Murray would not become stars?

Barrow also had an acute understanding of the importance of the manager's authority in the clubhouse. He therefore didn't hesitate to deal away an active challenger to Huggins' leadership—such as Del Pratt—or a passive lightning rod for an anti-Huggins clique—such as Roger Peckinpaugh. Finally, was it just a coincidence that Trade No. 1, which appeared to be so favorable to the Yankees but didn't turn out that way, was made before Ed Barrow joined the Yankees?

The Yankees' brain trust, summer of 1922. Left to right: manager Miller Huggins,
owner Jacob Ruppert, and business manager Ed Barrow.

2. MILLER HUGGINS

Huggins had an uncanny knack for evaluating talent. He honed that skill as the manager of the St. Louis Cardinals, where he gained the reputation as a shrewd trader. A close look at the December 1920 trade gives some insight to his capacity to assess personnel.

After working with Thormahlen for three years, Huggins saw his inconsistency and inability to deliver in the heat of the 1920 pennant race. *The Sporting News* reported on December 23, 1921, that the deal that brought Hoyt to New York was held up for two months by Huggins' reluctance to part with Muddy Ruel. The Yankees skipper finally did go ahead with the deal, and a few months later he revealed a key reason for doing so. Huggins told the *New York Evening Mail* before the start of the 1921 season that Waite Hoyt was "a pitcher of infinite promise."[45]

A year later, Huggins surprised many observers when he gave up on Collins and Piercy. Joe Vila of the *New York Sun* was the sportswriter with whom Huggins was closest and sometimes confided in. Vila was also the New York correspondent of *The Sporting News*, where he was probably reflecting the skipper's assessment when he wrote on December 29, 1921, "Collins and Piercy never will make good in fast company." He—Vila or Huggins, or both—was right.

Another year later, the *New York World* was shocked by the prospects the Yankees gave up in the Pennock deal. "The Yankees paid a big toll. They gave a stunning price." Miller Huggins reacted with aplomb. He knew what he did, and why he did it. "We must have a lefthander of experience . . . For my purposes, I had to have Pennock."

Taken together, Barrow and Huggins had a powerful sense of evaluating personnel that left other teams behind. By the mid-1920s, other teams refused to make major deals with the Yankees, so fearful were they that they'd be taken advantage of. This forced the Yankees to turn to the minor leagues for personnel. Once again, Barrow and Huggins worked their magic. With the help of their scouts, first Bob Connery and then Paul Krichell, they also developed a system for identifying future Yankees. While Earle Combs, Lou Gehrig and Tony Lazzeri didn't come cheaply, they came to the Yankees having never played a major league game . . . and succeeded brilliantly at baseball's highest level.

Good Teams Make Good Players Better

Throughout Yankees history there have been players who excelled with the Yankees to a far greater degree than they did on other teams they played for, before and/or after their Yankee stints. Perhaps one of the best examples of this synergy was another Yankee acquisition from the Red Sox, one that is outside the time frame of this paper.

Red Ruffing, traded from Boston to New York in 1930, went from mediocrity to greatness as a pitcher once he joined the Yankees. Is there something to this phenomenon, something that can be measured?

It is ironic that until the Yankees built a winning tradition in the 1920s, they were known for a very different effect on ballplayers who joined them. Good players elsewhere seemed to play "down" when they joined the Yankees. The press often talked about a "fatality," a bad karma that followed the team. Sportswriters referred to Frank "Home Run" Baker as an example of this in the early Ruppert years. His Yankee seasons were not nearly as good as his Philadelphia years, though he should have been entering the peak of his career. When Duffy Lewis and Ernie Shore were also unable to bring their great performances to New York, the "jinx" of the Yankees seemed to be continuing.

# # #

NOTES

1. The amount of cash included in this and all the other deals has been gleaned from the New York Yankees' general ledger and player salary notebooks, courtesy of SABR member Dan Levitt. There were differing amounts mentioned in different newspaper accounts; the numbers were not made public. Ed Barrow says in his autobiography that this deal involved $50,000.
2. Joe Vila, *New York Sun*, March 16, 1919, and Fred Lieb, *New York Evening Telegram*, January 15, 1922.
3. *Boston Herald*, December 19, 1918.
4. *New York Herald*, December 19, 1918.
5. *The Sporting News*, December 26, 1918.
6. Meany, Tom. *The Yankee Story*.
7. *New York Evening Journal*, March 27, 1918.
8. *The Sporting News*, August 14, 1919.
9. During the Mays negotiations, the Red Sox made another transaction that was barely noticed. They purchased a young pitcher named Waite Hoyt. A few weeks later, on September 24, Hoyt caught the Yankees' attention with a remarkable pitching performance, throwing nine perfect innings of relief against New York (though he lost in the 13th inning, 2–1).
10. *New York Evening Journal*, April 27, 1918.
11. *The Sporting News*, December 26, 1918.
12. *The Sporting News*, December 23, 1920.
13. *New York Evening Journal*, September 29, 1931.
14. *Boston Herald*, December 16, 1920.
15. *Boston Globe*, December 16, 1920.
16. *New York Herald*, December 17, 1920.
17. *New York Times*, December 16, 1920.
18. *The Sporting News*, December 23, 1920.
19. *Baseball Magazine*, February 1921.
20. *The Sporting News*, December 23, 1920.
21. *New York World*, December 20, 1920.
22. *New York Journal–American*, November 7, 1945.
23. Pratt's former Yankees teammate Ray Fisher took the post. He would coach Michigan to 637 wins over the next 38 years, including 15 conference championships.
24. Writing about this trade in his autobiography, Ed Barrow comments, "Of course, the hard-pressed Frazee also got a check."
25. *The Sporting News*, January 12, 1922.
26. *The Boston Post*, December 21, 1921.
27. *The Sporting News*, December 29, 1921.
28. *The New York Times*, December 21, 1921.
29. Quoted in *The Sporting News*, January 5, 1922.
30. *New York Evening Telegram*, December 23, 1921.
31. *The Sporting News*, December 29, 1921.
32. The Red Sox dealt Dugan to the Yankees a few months later, in July 1922. The only pitcher involved in that deal went *to* the Red Sox. While he won only one big league game, this pitcher became one of the game's greatest hitters, with a .349 career batting average. His name? Lefty O'Doul.
33. Cash for Boston was rumored to have been part of this deal but remains unconfirmed.
34. *Boston Herald*, January 4, 1923.
35. Sportswriter William McGeehan wrote of this deal: "Mr. Frazee now has the largest collection of Colonel Ruppert's checks in existence." *New York Herald*, January 31, 1923.
36. The Yankees also gave up Mogridge too soon; he would win 65 games for Washington from 1921 to 1924.
37. *New York World*, January 31, 1923.
38. *Boston Herald*, January 31, 1923.
39. *Boston Post*, January 31, 1923.
40. *New York World*, February 1, 1923.
41. *New York Times*, January 31, 1923.
42. *New York Herald*, January 31, 1923.
43. *The Sporting News*, February 8, 1923.
44. *Baseball Magazine*, February 1921.
45. *New York Evening Mail*, April 9, 1921.

ACKNOWLEDGMENTS

This article is based on many sources, including numerous primary source newspaper accounts. I want to acknowledge in particular the following sources: Ed Linn, *The Great Rivalry*; Lyle Spatz, *Yankees Coming, Yankees Going*; and Glenn Stout, *Red Sox Century* and *Yankees Century*, as well as Lenny Jacobson's NWSABR presentation and Dan Levitt's analysis of New York Yankees' financial data.

STEVE STEINBERG *focuses on early 20th century baseball in New York and St. Louis. He is working with Lyle Spatz on a book on the 1921 season, tentatively entitled* 1921, The Battle for Baseball Supremacy in New York.

New Light on an Old Scandal

My interest in the "Black Sox scandal" began at summer's end in 2002, and by the following June, I was sufficiently addicted to the subject that I simply had to visit Milwaukee. Why Milwaukee? Because I had learned that in 1924 that city was the site of a trial that pitted Shoeless Joe Jackson against his old employer, the Chicago White Sox, who were incorporated in Wisconsin. For B-Sox addicts, it was the Trial of the Century.

Jackson had signed a three-year contract in 1920, and when he was suspended in September that year, he had two years left—that is, unless his contract contained the standard "ten days clause" (if it did, the Sox could release him on short notice without cause). Jackson contended that the clause had been negotiated out of his contract; his team said otherwise. Acquitted with seven other players of conspiracy charges in 1921, Jackson sued for back pay, forcing the Sox to prove that he had done *something*, on the field or off, to deserve termination.

It seemed only Donald Gropman, a sympathetic biographer of Jackson, and Jerome Holtzman, a most unsympathetic historian, used the material from the 1924 trial in their writings. While Gropman thought this information exonerated Jackson, Holtzman believed it condemned him. I had to see for myself.

Jackson was not, however, my main interest. I was focused on the cover-up of the Fix, and how it finally came undone, almost a year later. My Milwaukee research in June 2003 into "the trial nobody noticed" became the first chapter of *Burying the Black Sox: How Baseball's Cover-Up of the 1919 World Series Fix Almost Succeeded*, released in March 2006 by Potomac.

But the B-Sox story is a cold case, not a closed case. Since June 2003 I have learned a lot more, and am still learning. I have often wondered what I missed in Milwaukee on that first visit. How many more pieces to this giant puzzle remained in that treasure trove? So when SABR offered me the chance to return and do more digging (via a Yoseloff grant), I could not resist. Here is what I found, the second time around.

Surveying the Terrain

On my first visit I had set the goal of trying to read through the nearly 1,700 pages of trial transcripts. Skimming here and there, I did that, and I also mapped the three volumes that contain the proceedings.

This time I wanted to go through all of the other material, mostly depositions but also the exhibits: reports from Comiskey's detectives, some newspaper clippings, and handwriting samples used by the experts who testified. This trial hinged on the circumstances under which Jackson had signed his 1920 contract—did the illiterate plaintiff sign in his house, with his wife handy to read it and check for the ten-days clause that Jackson believed was *not* in the contract? Or did he sign in his car, with only team secretary Harry Grabiner present?

Incidentally, among the treasures in Milwaukee is a kind of "Rosetta Stone." Attached to the pretrial depositions of Sox owner Charles Comiskey and Grabiner are "photostatic copies" of Jackson's 1919 and 1920 contracts. In 1919 (and previous years), Kate Jackson signed for her husband; in 1920, Joe signed himself. This document enables us to distinguish between the signatures when Jackson's autograph appears.

Lawyer Ray Cannon had filed three different lawsuits, on behalf of Oscar "Happy" Felsch, Joe Jackson, and Charles "Swede" Risberg. Their cases were numbered 64442, 64771, and 64772 respectively, indicating that his first client was Felsch. Cannon then contacted Jackson and Risberg, who both agreed to file similar suits. Jackson's went to trial first, in January 1924. The material that was collected in preparation for all three suits was used. A former ballplayer, Cannon was hoping that these cases would attract more players to another cause, a players union that would enable them to battle the reserve clause, which bound players to their teams.

The Risberg and Felsch Cases

All three cases were prepared along the same lines. Each player asked for $1,500 they felt was owed them from 1917; they said that Comiskey had promised each player would receive $5,000 for winning the pennant, no matter what the Series gate receipts turned out to be. When the players' shares turned out to be around $3,500, they all expected another $1,500. In the Jackson trial, the jury said they believed that the promise was made, but they awarded no money, because there was nothing in writing—no contract. This prompted Commy's lawyers to get Schalk, Collins, and Faber on record, stating that their manager in 1917, Pants Rowland, had made no such promise to the team.

The players also asked for the balance due from the contracts they claimed were breached when they were suspended in 1920 and later released. (Monies due from the Sox's second-place finish in 1920 was mentioned, but that was a bone to pick with the league or Commissioner Landis, so it was not featured in these suits.)

Initially, the players also asked for $100,000 in damages to their reputations and careers. In Felsch's suit, filed first, another $100,000 was asked for, because Happy had been blacklisted and unable to play ball in any professional league. These items were eventually removed from each suit when the plaintiffs were unable to substantiate the charges with facts.

Risberg's case is the easiest to summarize. He asked for $750 still due from his 1920 salary; for a $1,500 bonus that he said he was promised in 1920 for "good and efficient baseball"; for the $1,500 from 1917; and (initially) $100,000 because his reputation and career had been "annihilated." Risberg settled out of court in February 1925 for $288.88 plus interest ($75.23) and court costs ($37.20), or a total of $401.31.

Felsch had asked for $1,120 from 1920 (he claimed a paycheck had been missed), the 1917 bonus, and initially those large damages, which were later dropped. In his initial suit, we get a hint of where Ray Cannon was heading. Comiskey's lawyers succeeded in having the following removed, because it was "a sham, frivolous, irrelevant and scandalous": The Sox had been guilty of a cover-up

> in order to prevent the American public from discovering and learning the true facts about the deception, trickery and fraud that had been practised by the defendant [the Sox]... in fooling and deceiving the public as to the baseball games and in deliberately causing games to be lost and won by certain clubs or teams as the defendant... desired.

Cannon had intended to complicate things for Comiskey and his lawyers by bringing up three different "scandals" from 1917 involving the White Sox and the Detroit team. Detroit lost back-to-back doubleheaders to the Sox around Labor Day; they also beat the Sox's rival, Boston, later in the pennant race; then, after the pennant was clinched, the Sox lost three games to Detroit. The Sox had taken up a collection and paid off the Detroit pitchers that month. Was it a bribe, for tossing games to the Sox? Or a reward, for knocking off Boston? Did the Sox then pay back the favor by helping Detroit get closer to third-place money? These were old questions—Ban Johnson, American League czar, knew all about them, and Landis had looked into them soon after taking office in 1921. But they were ammunition for Cannon. The loose ends would not be tied up in these cases, however, and became front-page news in 1927, after Swede Risberg went public with the charges when the Cobb–Speaker allegations were in the news.

Felsch's case was settled in February 1925, too, for the two 1920 paychecks ($583.33 each, plus 6% interest, or $1,470.15), and court costs of $105.20.

Among the fascinating items in the Felsch material is a note from Ray Cannon to Comiskey's lawyers when he was preparing the complaint. This laundry list of questions that he wanted to ask appeared in the papers—Cannon was knowledgeable about using the press. It appears that Cannon had picked up from some player(s) a story that he asked the Sox about:

> 14. What steps were taken and what threatened through Louis Comiskey [Commy's son and team officer], with the aid of a battery of detectives in the spring of 1920, to scare and intimidate the players... to admit connection with the framing of the 1919 World Series, and against what players were the threats made, and by what persons were they made, and what statements were made by Louis Comiskey and others, to the effect that all members of the Chicago White Sox baseball team who were connected to the 1919 World Series scandal, were to be *handcuffed together on the opening day of the 1920 pennant race in Chicago, and displayed before the large audience in the grandstand and bleachers, and then led away to jail?* [Emphasis added]

This could be sheer and unfounded bluff on the part of Cannon, but it's nevertheless a striking image. He was sending the Sox a message that he knew what they knew on Opening Day, that they had signed seven of eight players who had been publicly accused (in the press, not by baseball) of suspicious play the previous October, and of at least plotting with known gamblers.

How the Plot Thickened . . . Then Fizzled

The gambling–fixing side of the B-Sox story is by far the murkiest, where little is certain—something I tried to convey in my book by a *Who's on First?* sketch which would be comic relief if only the subject were not so sad. The 1920 grand jury seemed ready to indict gamblers from several syndicates and a roster of cities that stretched from Pittsburgh to New Orleans. But most of those fellows vanished along with Hal Chase (after California refused to extradite him). So the main impression we have today of what happened is from *Eight Men Out*, a version heavily colored by interviews with Abe Attell and by newspaper accounts of the 1921 trial, focused on just one syndicate.

In the Milwaukee depositions of Bill Burns and Billy Maharg, we get—in the words of those two go-betweens—an account of events in unprecedented detail. This may or may not be the way things unfolded, but it's a fascinating tale.

The testimonies of Burns and Maharg agree substantially with those they gave at the 1921 trial, but there are some differences, and a comparison of the two versions is another project.

When he was deposed on October 5, 1922, Bill Burns was a confectioner, running a chocolate shop in Texas. But in 1919 he sold oil leases, and his sales route took him to Cincinnati, Chicago, New York, Montreal, and Philadelphia. Here is Burns' story, along with that of Maharg (whose role in this seems to be that of Burns' bodyguard):

With three weeks to go in the season, before the Sox had clinched the pennant, Eddie Cicotte told Burns in the Ansonia Hotel in New York that "something good was coming up," and if it went through—if the Sox got into the Series—Burns would be informed. A few days later at the same spot, Burns saw Cicotte again, this time with Chick Gandil. Billy Maharg, visiting Burns from Philadelphia, was also present.

Burns had known Maharg for years; they often hunted and fished together near Burns' Texas home. Burns had wired Maharg an invitation to come to New York for a social visit. Maharg stayed at the Ansonia several days, seeing most of the Sox. But what he overheard at the Ansonia that day would change his life.

Burns was told that six were willing to deal: Cicotte, Gandil ("the chief spokesman"), Risberg, McMullin, Williams, and Felsch. When Burns testified at the 1921 trial that the players initiated the Fix, some who had been sympathetic (thinking that vulnerable, gullible, underpaid athletes had been victimized) were shocked. The asking price was $100,000. Maharg recalled just five names (not McMullin), but also recalled that the players "would throw the first two, or all five in a row—whichever way the financiers wanted it."

Burns left New York City for a ten-day stop in Montreal, and Maharg returned to Philadelphia. There, a gambler friend called "Chrissy" or "Rossy" said "only one man" had the funding for such a project. Rossy gave Maharg a letter of introduction to Arnold Rothstein, then called The Big Bankroll on the phone and told him Maharg was coming over to Considine's, a 42nd Street saloon. But Rothstein was a no-show, and Maharg left.

Burns sent Maharg a telegram from Canada. He'd be back in New York in a few days and would call. Burns met with Maharg in Philadelphia, and this time they made an appointment to see Rothstein, traveling together to the Aqueduct race track on Long Island. But "A.R." was busy "making book," so they agreed to meet at the Astor at 9:00 P.M. Rothstein listened to the scheme, then "said he would not handle it."

Four or five days later, Burns ran into Hal Chase. What seemed a poor risk to Rothstein looked like "a sure shot" to Chase. Burns had received a letter from a Sox player, from St Louis, saying that now *eight* Sox were in the deal, and that is what Burns told Chase.

Within three or four days Burns and Chase met again, at the Ansonia. Enter Abe Attell and a fellow who went by "Bennett"—as it turned out, this was David Zelcer. Attell claimed to be representing Rothstein, and said A.R. was backing The Big Fix.

Burns remained in New York until two days before the Series, then bought a train ticket to Cincinnati. Before he left, he telegrammed Maharg again, telling him to meet him on the 4:30 train, that the fix was in, and Rothstein was backing it.

With "financiers" lined up, Burns still had to make the connection between the fixers and the players. The day before the Series started, in Cincinnati, Burns met with Attell and Zelcer at the Gibson Hotel, then walked them over to the Sinton, where the White Sox were staying. Seven players were waiting in 708 [Gandil and Risberg's room]; Joe Jackson was not present. Burns announced that Arnold Rothstein was behind the plan.

Burns then introduced the players all around to Attell, "the Little Champ," and "Bennett." Burns recalled that the door to 708 was partly open, and Weaver checked constantly so that manager Kid Gleason would not join the meeting. The negotiation went on until 1:00 or 2:00 A.M. Gandil insisted on $20,000 before Game One ... then the players insisted that their $100,000 be held by someone. Finally, the deal was made: $20,000 paid after each loss. The money would be divided nine ways, eight players—and Bill Burns. Burns had the impression that Lefty Williams was "kind of representing Jackson," and that anything Williams OK'd would be OK with the star outfielder.

Maharg was not in Cincinnati yet. He arrived the morning of Game One. Burns said he saw the players that morning again, in the Sinton lobby. He saw Attell again, too, in the Haviland Hotel.

Neither Burns nor Maharg attended Game One.

After the game, which the Reds won 9–1, Maharg caught up with Burns, and they went to a hotel (it's not clear which, the Haviland or the Gibson or the Sinton) looking for Attell and the payoff. When they caught up with him, Attell said the money was "out on bets."

Burns delivered the bad news to the players at the Sinton. He met with Risberg, McMullin, Cicotte, Gandil, and Williams, telling them that Attell was collecting money and they'd have to wait till the morning. Gandil was angry and said Attell was "not living up to his agreement." Burns saw Williams and Gandil again after dinner, and there was a meeting with Attell and Zelcer on a side street. Abe was upbeat, and the conversation was all about tossing game two.

On the next morning Burns and Maharg saw Attell again, at the Haviland, but instead of showing him the money, Attell showed him a telegram, saying that Rothstein had wired him cash. Maharg recalled the message: "Have wired you 20 grands. Waived identification. A.R." Burns was skeptical and took the telegram, with Attell in tow, to the nearest telegraph office. There was no sign of it in the log. Attell said the office "must've lost or misplaced the record." Then Attell said that he would go and get the money due, and Maharg could come with him. Maharg could then give the cash to Burns, who would signal the players that all was going smoothly.

But, as Maharg put it, it "never came off that way." "I told him that I thought he [Attell] was a liar, myself," Maharg said. Burns took the telegram—it was all he had—to the Sinton, and went to Room 708. It was about 10:00 A.M. The two pitchers were present, along with the three pals, Gandil, Risberg, and McMullin. Gandil was now sure Attell was double-crossing them. Chick and Swede did all the talking. Burns held out hope that the $20,000 would still appear before game time. Attell would get it to Burns, and Burns would signal the players "in the lines"—that is, from the front row of the stands.

Burns received no cash, gave no signal. He did not go to the park.

After game two, Attell and his men were jubilant and flush with winnings. Burns and Maharg "had a date" to meet Attell at the Haviland. They waited, and Attell no-showed. But they caught up

with him at the Sinton; he was in his room [660] with the Levi Brothers, Ben and Lou, and Zelcer (whom Maharg described as "Rothstein's First Lieutenant"). Burns told Attell that the players were "sore" and asked for the $40,000 they were due. Attell reached under a mattress and extracted a roll of money—$10,000—and lobbed it to Burns. Attell and Zelcer then complained that "everybody in the East and West" knew about the fix, and it was really hard to make anything in the betting.

Burns took the ten grand to the players by himself, while Maharg waited with Attell. It was about 9:00 P.M. Risberg, McMullin, and Cicotte were there, and Burns also thought Weaver was present. Then Gandil and Felsch came in and the counting commenced. It was done on a bed, with all of the players standing around, watching: 10G—not 40. Burns reported, "One of the boys put it under his pillow"—if they were in 710, that would have been Cicotte's pillow, but Burns didn't say. Gandil and Risberg again were noisy about the double-crossing going on. Burns said maybe Attell was swindling them. "I was not." Burns said the meeting then amounted to a lot of swearing.

Burns was upset and returned to Attell, telling him that he was "jamming the whole thing up." Maharg recalled that while Burns was gone (about thirty minutes), someone said Rothstein had bet "about 300 G" ($300,000) on the Series. Attell was sorry about the shortfall, but it couldn't be helped. "Another ring is in on it." The players would have to wait until the Series was over to get the rest. "They asked Burns to ask the players if they would try to win the next game, so they could get better odds for their money. Burns said he would ask them."

Burns left again, then came back. The players had said no, they would not win for "a Busher" (Dickie Kerr, a rookie in 1919; it "was generally known," according to Maharg, that Kerr was getting the start in Game Three). "The same way tomorrow." Maharg: "Burns said the players were not satisfied, and they hollered like hell." Burns set a date to meet with them again the next day, in Chicago. The trains left Cincinnati about midnight.

The morning of Game Three, Maharg and Burns saw Attell at the Sherman Hotel. Attell asked Burns to phone Gandil. Chick told him it was "going the same way." Burns relayed the message to Attell.

But Game Three did not "go the same way"— Kerr pitched brilliantly, and the Sox won, 3–0. Gandil knocked in two runs.

Burns and Maharg went to Zelcer's room at the Astor (next to the Sherman Hotel) after the game. Attell was there, too. Zelcer wanted Burns to go to the players and talk to them about Game Four, but Burns protested that they would not trust him. Zelcer understood, and said he'd put up $20,000 of his own money, give it to Burns to hold as a bet—if the Sox lost, Burns would turn the money over to the players. Burns could bet the money on the Reds. Burns agreed to take the offer to the players, and hailed a cab.

Burns found Gandil at his apartment. Chick said they won Game Three because they had been double-crossed. The fix was off, the players were through. Burns ran into Risberg and McMullin on the street later, and Swede confirmed that the players had met by themselves before Game Three and decided to win it. But Swede added that *he* "was going through with it." [There is some evidence that Swede Risberg was the most sensitive about the dangerous position the players put themselves in; crossing Arnold Rothstein could indeed be hazardous to one's health. If Burns' recollection is accurate, Swede may have been sending A.R. the message that he, at least, was keeping his part of the bargain.] McMullin said nothing; he was riding the bench in this Series.

Burns returned to the Sherman Hotel and told Attell and Zelcer—no deal. Maharg's glum comment: "The next day, Cincinnati won anyway."

Attell was disappointed. It was just hard luck that the money was out on bets; it would be there after the Series was lost. Too bad the players couldn't wait.

This is where Maharg's story ends. He left Chicago for Cincinnati, but had no further doings with the plot. He said he never saw Attell again; and he next saw Zelcer at the 1921 trial. When he read about the 1920 grand jury looking into the Fix, he went to "Jimmie Isaminger," a personal friend and reporter on a Philadelphia newspaper. Why? I "wanted his opinion of it more than anything else, of what they would do with me when this thing came up."

Ain't Over Till It's Over

But for Bill Burns there was one more meeting. It was arranged by Abe Attell, and there Burns was introduced to a group of gamblers from St Louis, including a "short, red-complected man"—Carl Zork. They wanted to offer more money to the players, put the fix back in.

Burns went to the players one more time and made the offer. They rejected it. Burns gave Attell the information. To the best of Bill Burns' knowledge, no more money was exchanged between the

Eddie Cicotte and Dutch Reuther, starting pitchers in Game One of the 1919 World Series.

gamblers and the players. He did not speak with the players again.

In the Wake of the Fix

Bill Burns lived in Texas. He did not travel to Chicago to give this deposition because he was anxious to tell his story. No, he was asked to make the trip by Ban Johnson, at the suggestion of Alfred Austrian, Comiskey's lawyer—for Buck Weaver's suit against the Sox. As in 1921, when Burns came north for the trial, the American League paid his expenses.

Burns was questioned about why he had not come forth sooner with the tale. He said that right after the Series, he went to New York, then right back to Texas. He spoke with "several private men down there" about the fix but no reporters. When his name popped up in one of Hugh Fullerton's articles about the rumors (in December 1919), he did nothing.

During the 1920 season, Burns said that he did speak with several ballplayers and a manager about the fix. But he refused to name anyone else. After Landis' edict banning anyone connected in any way to fixing games, implicating more men could ruin their careers.

Burns did not mention that he had received a telegram from Judge McDonald, inviting him to come and talk to the grand jury in September 1920. McDonald said that he invited Maharg, Attell, and Rothstein, too, but couldn't force anyone from another state to testify. (Rothstein did come, voluntarily.)

Asked why he did not go for the $10,000 reward that Comiskey had offered, Burns replied, "Well, I didn't want that kind of money ... I didn't want to bring the ballplayers out." Asked if his motive now was "solely revenge," Burns repeated that he did not want to harm any players. Why then, did he tell all (in the trial) in 1921? "They had it planned to lay everything on me." Maharg, when he tracked Burns down in Texas, had told him that unless he came north to defend himself, he'd be "the fall guy" in the trial. "So you didn't do it for revenge?" Burns: "Well, I did to a certain extent, yes sir."

Burns seemed upset that Cicotte, Jackson, and Williams "started the whole thing"—the unraveling of the cover-up—by going to the 1920 grand jury. He recalled that when he came to Chicago and told his story to Hartley Replogle (the assistant state's attorney), Replogle told him that his account of things "dovetailed" with the versions the players gave the grand jury.

Judge McDonald's Recollection

The Cook County grand jury had been called together in September 1920 by Judge Charles A. McDonald. Ban Johnson said that he had given McDonald the green light to hand the grand jury the duty to investigate the ties between gambling and baseball. When the focus fell on the 1919 World Series, McDonald had a problem. He was a baseball fan, and his team, the White Sox, were in another dandy pennant race. He discussed this with Alfred Austrian, and they agreed that no Sox would be subpoenaed until the race had been decided. So the appearance of Cicotte and Jackson on September 28 must have been upsetting.

McDonald had known Comiskey "very well and very favorably" for about 25 years. In the 1924 trial he appeared for the defense (Comiskey). He was quizzed about his meeting with Joe Jackson on September 28, 1920.

Earlier, McDonald had spoken with Eddie Cicotte, then accompanied him for moral support to the grand jury chamber. Cicotte had mentioned Jackson as one of the players involved in the plot. So when Jackson phoned McDonald, from Austrian's office, to say that he wanted to clear his name, McDonald told him it was too late, that Cicotte had given him up, along with six others.

McDonald had no notes from the meeting that followed. Austrian brought Jackson to the courthouse, introduced him to McDonald, and left. The judge said that he did not go with Jackson to the grand jury after their talk.

And that is significant, because McDonald and Jackson sparred in the press after some reporters characterized his grand jury statement as a confession—to throwing games. Jackson disputed that he said that, and the statement we have from the grand jury seems to bear that out. McDonald, recalling only what Jackson had told him earlier (that he might have played harder) and what Cicotte had told him, concluded that Jackson had helped throw the Series. McDonald never heard Jackson tell the grand jury that he played every game to win.

What Did Eddie Say?

The statements made by the three players were among the documents that vanished the winter after the grand jury. But they were reconstructed from stenographer's notes for the 1921 trial. Ray Cannon, deposing Charles Comiskey in March 1923, had pressed Commy's lawyers for a copy of Jackson's grand jury statement. George Hudnall, the Sox's lead lawyer in the 1924 trial, objected when Cannon asked Comiskey if the team had a copy. He instructed Commy not to answer, because "the grand jury proceeding is supposed to be secret. If he got it, he has no business to it."

When Cicotte and Williams were first deposed in 1923, neither were cooperative. But apparently sometime later that year the grand jury statements were deemed admissible evidence, and in January 1924, just weeks before the Jackson case went to trial, Cicotte and Williams were deposed again (separately). This time their grand jury statements were read into the record.

Joe Jackson's testimony from 1920 did not appear until the trial in Milwaukee was under way. George Hudnall produced it from his briefcase. Jackson had given a different version of events in 1924 (for example, he said he received the $5,000 from Williams after the Series, instead of after Game Four), so his 1920 grand jury statement meant that he was guilty of perjury, either in 1920 or 1924; that fact ruined his case and caused the judge to set aside the jury's verdict, which had gone for Jackson on every count by 11–1.

It is not clear that the Milwaukee trial depositions contain every word from the 1920 statements, but they contain a substantial amount of fascinating material, in Q and A format, embedded in the "live" questioning. This is especially important for Cicotte, because we have little from his 1920 statement today (unlike Jackson and Williams), and it is not clear that what we have is reliable, or whether it was embellished by the press.

And the Cicotte grand jury testimony for the 1924 trial has more information than that which was read into the 1921 trial, because many names of players and gamblers were omitted in 1921 at the direction of the judge.

Before Cicotte was deposed, his lawyer advised him not to say anything that might incriminate himself. Cicotte wound up saying very little. When his grand jury testimony was read, he did not disagree with anything he had said in 1920. "What I told the grand jury was the truth." Some highlights of what he said:

¤ Cicotte indeed named all of the players later banished to the grand jury. He said the idea of the fix had originated in a conversation with Gandil and McMullin, and maybe one other teammate. Gandil: "We ain't getting a devil of a lot of money, and it looks like we could make a big thing." Asked how much it would take for Cicotte to join in, he replied, $10,000.

¤ He recalled a pre-Series meeting in his room at the Warner Hotel that followed soon after, with Gandil, Felsch, Weaver, and perhaps McMullin and Williams. "I was the first one that spoke about the money end of it. I says, there is so much double-crossing stuff, if I went in the Series ["to throw ball games"] I wanted the money put in my hand." Gandil assured him that he'd get his money in advance. Cicotte left his room to visit with teammates Red Faber and Shano Collins, while the other players left, one by one, to avoid the appearance of having been in a meeting. When he later returned to his room, about 11:30 P.M., there was $10,000 under his pillow. He pocketed the cash and took it to Cincinnati.

¤ After the Series, he said he took the money home to Detroit and hid it. Four thousand dollars paid off the mortgage on his farm; the rest went to put in new floors in the barn and house and to buy livestock and feed. Cicotte didn't know where the money had come from: "I never asked them" [his teammates]. Some gamblers, he supposed.

¤ Cicotte admitted that he put on base the first batter he faced in Game One, Morrie Rath. He tried to walk him, but instead hit him. He made no mention that this was a signal that the fix was in. "You wanted Rath to get on base?" "Yes. But after he passed, after he was on there, I don't know, I guess I believe I tried too hard. I didn't care, they could have had my heart and soul out there. That is the way I felt. I felt—I didn't want to be that way after I had taken the money."

¤ Cicotte spoke at some length about a play in the fourth inning that started his undoing. "That's the play they incriminate me on, but I was absolutely honest on that play." With a runner on first, Cicotte stopped Kopf's smash up the middle and threw to Risberg for the force-out at second. Swede stumbled or threw slowly to first, and the runner beat it out, keeping the inning alive. "Everybody saw me make that play," Cicotte insisted. All of the hits that inning "was clean base hits." Cicotte did not think Swede intended to miss the runner on that play.

¤ After the 9–1 loss, "I went up in the room. I was too ill, I had the headache after the game. I stayed in my room and was sick all night long. I couldn't hit in St Louis." [The lawyers were puzzled by this phrase, and Cicotte did not offer to explain it.] His roommate, Felsch, offered him some aspirin tablets. "Happy, this will never be done again."

¤ According to Cicotte, the players did not discuss the fix after Game One, "because we didn't trust nobody."

¤ Cicotte said he saw nothing fishy in game two, except that Williams was wild. Asked if he thought the walks were intentional, he said, "Sure, that is the way I thought."

¤ Back in Chicago for Game Three, Cicotte did not tell his brother about the fix or the money. His wife was in Detroit, and he didn't tell her, either. "She don't know I paid off the mortgage," he told the grand jury. In Game Three, "Kerr pitched great."

¤ The next game Cicotte pitched, Game Four, "I tried to make good but I made two errors. I was very anxious to get the ball and I didn't make any runs. [The Sox lost, 2–0.] If we could make four or five runs—I would have won that game." Asked if he had tried to make a bad throw in that game, Cicotte said, "No sir, I didn't, I tried to get my man." "I tried to win [Game Four]."

Cicotte said in effect that he had played the Series to win. "I was going to take a chance. I wanted to win. I could have given [the money] back with interest, if they only let me win the game that day." Tris Speaker consoled Cicotte after the Game Four loss (Spoke was covering the Series for a Cleveland paper).

Asked by someone in the grand jury how he could win with seven players on his own team against him, Cicotte said, "They never talked to me at all. If they talked to me, I was deaf ears. I was a man of another country."

Cicotte said that he never saw any other players receive any money. Asked by Replogle if he would come back to the grand jury if they wanted to hear more from him, he replied, "Yes, sir." He was not asked back.

The newspapers had their story: Cicotte confirmed that the fix had been in: the Sox sold out the Series for $100,000. Never mind that Cicotte and Jackson both said they played the Series to win. Their admission that some players had plotted with gamblers was immediately translated into eight Sox playing crooked for the entire eight-game series. Down in history.

Historian Harold Seymour thinks that the spin given to the players' stories may have been for their protection—that is, for the consumption of the gamblers. See, they tried to lose. Victor Luhrs in his 1966 *The Great Baseball Mystery* argued that Cicotte played to win. But *Eight Men Out* had appeared in 1963, and the film version would color perceptions even more.

The material from the 1924 Milwaukee trial suggests that the fix was in—but not for very long. And that even players assumed to be committed to the fix—like Cicotte—may have played to win.

# # #

A SABR member since 1991, GENE CARNEY *is the author of* Burying the Black Sox: How Baseball's Cover-Up of the 1919 World Series Fix Almost Succeeded *(Potomac, 2006). He has addressed the topic at the last three SABR national conventions. Gene has edited* Notes from the Shadows of Cooperstown *since 1993; since 1999* Notes *is at www.baseball1.com/notes.*

DiMaggio's Challengers

Joe DiMaggio's record hitting streak of 56 games is probably the most famous, as well as the most studied, of all sports records. Since 1991 there have been five articles in SABR publications on his 56-game hitting streak, and one on his 61-game streak in the Pacific Coast League.

One question that is frequently asked is: "Has anyone else ever come close to matching DiMaggio's feat?" Traditional record books show that the closest anyone else has gotten to 56 games was the 45 in a row that Wee Willie Keeler had over the 1896 (one game) and 1897 (44 games) seasons. That means that even the second-longest hitting streak in history was still 11 games short of the mark set by DiMaggio in 1941.

However, that way of looking at long hitting streaks can be misleading. What if, after Keeler's 45-game hitting streak had ended, he immediately started another 10-game hitting streak? If he'd just had a hit in that one game between the streaks, his overall stretch would've been 56 games in a row, matching DiMaggio. Has there ever been a player who came just one hitless game away from matching—or beating—DiMaggio's high-water mark? To see if anyone had ever actually come that close to putting together 56 games in a row with a hit, I looked through dozens of the top hitting seasons of all time; and, thanks to Retrosheet, I also checked every season since 1957.

There has in fact been a player who came within one game of beating Joe DiMaggio's hitting streak. In 1894, Chicago Colt Bill Dahlen hit in 42 straight games from June 20 through August 6, then snapped his streak the next day going 0-for-6. In his next game he began a 28-game hitting streak, lasting from August 8 through September 9. Over the stretch of 71 games from June 20 through September 9, Dahlen had a hit in 70 of them. That one 0-for-6 on August 7, while his teammates collected 20 hits, kept Dahlen from making Joe DiMaggio take a back seat.

Four other players have come within two games of having a hitting streak of 56 or more games. Willie Keeler had two such streaks, while Sam Thompson, Gene DeMontreville, and Ed Delahanty had the other two. Thompson had his streak over the last part of 1895 and the beginning of 1896; over a 56-game span, only an 0-for-3 on September 17, 1895, and an 0-for-2 on May 5, 1896, kept him from a hitting streak of exactly 56 games. The end of 1896 and the beginning of 1897 saw the next two close calls. Gene DeMontreville of the Washington Senators had a hit in 62-out-of-64 games from August 7, 1896, through May 17, 1897. The only things standing in the way of a new record hitting streak were hitless games on August 19(G2) and September 7(G2). Over the stretch containing the last game of 1896 and the first 60 games of 1897, Willie Keeler had a hit in 59 of them. Just hitless games on June 19 and July 1, 1897, kept him from a 61-gamer. Keeler's other streak was in 1898. From July 2 through September 6, first game, Keeler played in 56 games and hit safely in 54 of them; the two hitless games were July 30, second game, and August 6. The last player known to have come within just two games of a 56-game streak was Ed Delahanty, who almost hit in 63 consecutive games in 1899. From June 5 through August 18(G2), Delahanty had a hit in 61 of his 63 games. Had he managed to get a hit on June 29 and July 14, Delahanty's hitting streak would have been seven games longer than DiMaggio's.

Eleven more players had just three hitless games over a stretch of 56 games (see table 3). Johnny Damon, in 2005, was only the third player in the past 50 years to come within three games of hitting in 56-or-more consecutive games. If Damon had not been held hitless on July 18, July 24, and August 15, then he would have had a 57-game hitting streak from June 10 through August 20, and there'd be a new hitting streak for everyone else to chase after.

Although most of the men listed in the chart of oh-so-close hitting streaks are Hall of Famers, there were some unlikely seasons that almost saw a record hitting streak. For instance, if Pete Browning, a neglected 19th century player, had had a hit in three games in which he actually went hitless in 1890, then he would be listed in the record books with an unsurpassed mark of 61 games in a row. During his close-call, Gene DeMontreville had a 36-game hitting streak that was discovered for the first time as I researched this article. While DeMontreville had several good seasons, few people would have thought the mostly unknown 19th century player would have put together the 10th longest hitting streak ever. Amazingly, two players came so close to having a long hitting streak without even putting together a 20-gamer at any point during the stretch.

Amazingly, two players came so close to having a long hitting streak without even putting together a 20-gamer at any point during the stretch. Even though most people will continue to consider Willie Keeler's 45-game stretch to be the closest any player has come to matching DiMaggio, that feat really belongs to Bill Dahlen. Just one bad day cost Dahlen a 71-game hitting streak, which would have been 26 games longer than the next-longest National League streak in history. If Willie Keeler could have had a few of his hitless games turned around, then he could be the proud holder of separate hitting streaks of 61, 57, and 56 games.

Pete Browning

There have been many essays done on how mathematically unlikely a 56-game hitting streak is, but we can see how close players like Bill Dahlen, Ed Delahanty, Sam Thompson, and Willie Keeler came to matching or topping it. It may be just a matter of time before someone finally manages to avoid going hitless in a few critical games and equals or beats DiMaggio's great feat.

# # #

TRENT McCOTTER *is currently working on his SABR-Yoseloff Research Grant identifying errors in 1920s American League statistics.*

Table 1. Players with One Hitless Game Precluding a 56-Game Streak

Player	Team	Year	Dates	Total	Streaks	Hitless Dates
Bill Dahlen	CHI-N	1894	06/20-09/09	71g	42g-28g	08/07

Table 2. Players with Two Hitless Games Precluding a 56-Game Streak

Player	Team	Year	Dates	Total	Streaks	Hitless Dates
Sam Thompson	PHI-N	1895-96	08/22-05/19	56g	22g-21g-11g	09/17, 05/05
Gene DeMontreville	WAS-N	1896-97	09/07[2]-05/17	64g	11g-15g-36g	08/19[2], 09/07[1]
Willie Keeler	BAL-N	1896-97	09/26-07/13	61g	45g-5g-9g	06/19, 07/01
Willie Keeler	BAL-N	1898	07/02-09/06[1]	56g	25g-4g-25g	07/30[2], 08/06
Ed Delahanty	PHI-N	1899	06/05-08/18[2]	63g	18g-12g-31g	06/29, 07/14

Table 3. Players with Three Hitless Games Precluding a 56-Game Streak

Player	Team	Year	Dates	Total	Streaks	Hitless Dates
Pete Browning	CLE-P	1890	06/25-09/05	61g	15g-15g-18g-10g	07/12, 07/31, 08/26
Willie Keeler	BKN/BAL-N	1893-94	08/24-07/04[1]	57g	25g-6g-18g-5g	05/23, 06/05, 06/27
Jesse Burkett	CLE-N	1896	04/25-07/10[2]	60g	18g-1g-19g-19g	05/22, 05/26, 06/19
Ty Cobb	DET-A	1911	04/23-07/02	61g	11g-4g-3g-40g	05/04, 05/10, 05/14
Tris Speaker	BOS-A	1912	05/22-07/19[1]	58g	3g-20g-30g-2g	5/25, 6/16, 07/17[1]
George Sisler	STL-A	1917	06/30[2]-09/04	67g	21g-13g-4g-26g	7/18, 8/6,& 08/11[1]
Rogers Hornsby	STL-N	1922	07/17-09/19	56g	6g-12g-2g-33g	7/23, 8/9[1], 08/12
George Sisler	STL-A	1922	07/04[2]-09/17	60g	7g-5g-4g-41g	07/11, 07/20, 07/26
Joe DiMaggio	NY-A	1937	06/19-8/20	60g	7g-22g-20g-8g	06/26, 07/22, 08/13
George Brett	KC-A	1980	05/22-08/18	56g	4g--10g-9g-30g	05/26, 06/07, 07/17
Benito Santiago	SD-N	1987-98	08/18-04/26	57g	5g-34g-7g-8g	08/23, 10/03, 04/13
Johnny Damon	BOS-A	2005	06/10-8/20	57g	29g-5g-15g-5g	07/18, 07/24, 08/15

Superscript numbers on game dates refer to first or second games of doubleheaders.

DAVID W. SMITH

Effect of Batting Order (Not Lineup) on Scoring

This present study is an outgrowth of my presentation in 2004 at SABR34 in which I addressed the pattern of scoring in a game, such as the possible importance of one-run wins, come-from-behind wins, etc. The first point to establish is the rate of scoring by home and road teams in each inning. The results for 1957–2005 are in Figure 1.

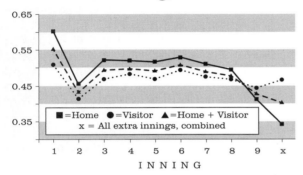

Figure 1. Average Runs in Each Inning, 1957–2005

■=Home ●=Visitor ▲=Home + Visitor
x = All extra innings, combined

INNING

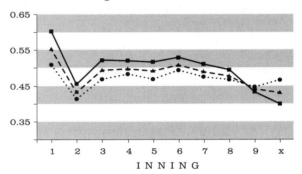

Figure 2. Average Runs in Each Inning, Normalized per Three Outs, 1957–2005

INNING

Two points of special note are:
1. More runs are scored in the first inning than any other, and this difference is by a wide margin, especially for the home team.
2. The home team averages more runs than the visitors in each of the first eight innings, although that pattern reverses in the ninth inning and later.

This second point deserves an additional comment. At first glance, it might seem surprising that the home team scoring drops so dramatically in the ninth and extra innings. However, most of this apparent decline is accounted for by the fact of "walk-off" wins. That is, when the home team gets enough runs to win in the ninth inning or later, they stop batting, with the result that fewer total runs are scored. For the period studied here, 1957–2005, there were 9,053 walk-off wins, which works out to one in every 10.5 games. This sizable number would seem to be enough to account for a substantial portion of the observed drop. Included in this total are 4,646 extra-inning wins by the home team, all of which are, of course, walk-offs.

My friend Clem Comly suggested a different way to look at scoring rate for these innings, which is to normalize scoring per three outs made in each inning. In this way the partial innings of the walk-offs will be mitigated to some extent. The result of that recalculation is seen in Figure 2.

The values for the first eight innings are, of course, unchanged, as are those for the visitors in the ninth and extra innings. The rates for the home team in these last two categories are increased, as expected, but they don't quite catch up to the visitors because there are still many potential runs that are not scored due to the walkoffs.

It occurred to me and to several who saw these results at SABR34 that a good place to start in trying to figure out the underlying factors causing this pattern was to consider which batters were likely to bat in each inning. Therefore, I began my journey into the land of lineup studies, territory already well staked out by Mark Pankin (see, for example: http://www.pankin.com/markov/btn1191.pdf). However, Mark's pioneering work has concentrated on the starting lineup and how variations there can affect scoring. He also made great use of sophisticated modeling to explore these questions in very interesting ways. Tom Ruane has also done some Markov modeling work on the effect of lineups (www.retrosheet.org/Research/RuaneT/lineup_art.htm).

My approach here is a bit different in two ways. First, I looked at actual performance data, not model results, and second, I focused on the consequences of different lineup positions batting first in a given inning, not on the starting lineup. It is essential to distinguish clearly between the starting lineup and the batting order in a given inning. When I refer to the starting lineup, I will use the term "lineup slots," whereas when I refer to the batting order in an inning, I will speak of the first batter, second batter, etc.

This analysis requires play-by-play data and I used the Retrosheet files from 1957 through 2005, as summarized in Table 1.

Table 1. Data for Present Study, 1957–2005

Seasons	Games	Half-Innings
49	95,755	1,719,857

Note: There were actually 95,979 games played from 1957 to 2005, but Retrosheet has not yet acquired play-by-play data for 224 games from 1957 to 1973. Therefore, 99.8% of games played from the last 49 seasons were available.

The basic pattern of which batter leads off an inning is shown in the following two tables, with raw totals in Table 2 and the same information in percentage form in Table 3, which allows much easier comparisons.

There are several interesting features here. First of all is the surprise that there was actually a first inning in which the batter in the 8th slot batted first! This occurred on June 9, 1961 (game

2) in Boston when the Angels had a batting out of order situation which resulted in the first- and eighth-place batters swapping places the first time through the order. The lineup slot which bats first most often in an inning moves around the lineup fairly smoothly as the game progresses. The highlighted boxes in Table 3 indicate the three lineup slots which lead off each inning most frequently. Those marked in boldface are those in which the three most frequent slots to bat first are at least 40% of the total. Those underlined are less than 40%. In the second inning, the leading three slots (number 4 through 6) comprise over 81% of the total and by the ninth inning, the three most frequent are just under 36%, reflecting the expected randomization in the first slot as the game proceeds.

It is not surprising that the first three men in the lineup are quite unlikely to lead off the second inning, but the low totals for the number 4, 5, and 6 men to lead off the third are perhaps a bit unexpected. Finally, note that the clear leader in times leading off the second inning is the fourth batter in the lineup. This takes us to a related concept, which is somewhat of a mirror image of which batter leads off an inning, namely which position makes the last out (that statement does not do

Table 2. Number of Times Each Lineup Slot Batted First in an Inning

Slot	1	2	3	4	5	6	7	8	9	Extra	Total
1	191509	1992	36609	16260	25562	26305	20948	24872	15844	5063	364964
2	0	616	20841	26610	16393	26203	17268	23309	15157	4661	151058
3	0	273	12578	33101	11886	25889	17936	22164	16361	4660	144848
4	0	68494	6678	31786	11935	23353	19707	19798	16758	4167	202676
5	0	52683	3957	27726	17365	20528	22067	18761	17514	4288	184889
6	0	34656	2205	22373	24039	17558	24138	18885	18032	4523	166409
7	0	19377	26877	16194	28312	15324	24361	19459	17348	4258	171510
8	1	9268	41042	10857	29527	16627	23642	20885	16138	4478	172465
9	0	4151	40723	6603	26484	19526	20999	22723	15239	4590	161038

Note: "Extra" refers to all extra half innings. The 40,688 extra half innings reported here occurred in 8971 games, an average of 4.5 per game.

Table 3. Percentage of Times Each Lineup Slot Batted First in an Inning, 1957–2005

Slot	1	2	3	4	5	6	7	8	9	Extra	Total
1	100	1.0	19.1	8.5	13.3	13.7	11.0	13.0	10.7	12.4	21.2
2	0	0.3	10.9	13.9	8.6	13.7	9.0	12.2	10.2	11.5	8.8
3	0	0.1	6.6	17.3	6.2	13.5	9.4	11.6	11.0	11.5	8.4
4	0	35.8	3.5	16.6	6.2	12.2	10.3	10.4	11.3	10.2	11.8
5	0	27.5	2.1	14.5	9.1	10.7	11.5	9.8	11.8	10.5	10.8
6	0	18.1	1.2	11.7	12.6	9.2	12.6	9.9	12.2	11.1	9.7
7	0	10.1	14.0	8.5	14.8	8.0	12.8	10.2	11.7	10.5	10.0
8	0	4.8	21.4	5.7	15.4	8.7	12.4	10.9	10.9	11.0	10.0
9	0	2.2	21.3	3.4	13.8	10.2	11.0	11.9	10.3	11.3	9.4

justice to innings which end on caught-stealing or pickoff plays). This means that the most common single result of the first inning (35.8% of the time) is that the side is retired in order or one runner reached base and was retired on a double play, caught stealing or via pickoff. This is true even though the scoring rate is highest in this inning.

The last column in Table 3 shows that the batter in the leadoff slot is the first batter in 21.2% of all innings with the other eight positions fairly evenly distributed in comparison. Of course, this predominance of the leadoff batter is greatly influenced by the first inning reality. If the first inning totals are removed and the numbers renormalized, then there is much evenness across the slots. In fact, after the first inning the fourth and fifth slots in the starting lineup are the most likely to bat first. These percentages are presented in Figure 3.

Figure 3. Percentage of Time Each Lineup Slot Batted First in All Innings and in All Innings after the First

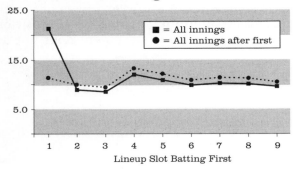

The possibility of differences between the visiting and home teams must also be considered. I did that comparison, and only one of the 90 entries in Table 3 showed even a one percent difference between visitors and home. That is, the fourth-place slot batted first in the second inning for the visiting team 37.5% of the time and 34.0% of the time for the home team. This means that the visitors went out in order in the first inning more often than the home team did. This is reflected in the higher average number of first inning plate appearances for the home team: 4.42 as compared to 4.28 for the visitors. This percentage difference appears small, but does represent over 13,000 more home team batters in the first inning over the 49 years studied.

Of course, the most important measurement is scoring. Figure 4 presents the average number of run scored in each inning when the first batter in the inning was in the indicated lineup slot. The numbers here are the averages across all innings.

As expected, I found some variation between individual innings, but I am not reporting those details here for two reasons. First, as we have seen, each inning/batter combination occurs with greatly varied frequency, so comparisons become less valuable. For example, the batter in the third slot bats first in the second inning only 0.1% of the time, so the runs scored in those innings don't have much meaning in a comparative sense. Second, tables with 90 data points in them are cumbersome and not easy to read. This figure will be the standard format for the bulk of the presentation.

Figure 4. Average Runs Scored per Inning When First Batter Occupied Indicated Lineup Slot

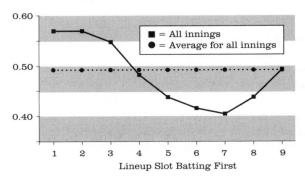

There is a remarkable relationship between the first batter in an inning and the chance of scoring. The first two slots in the lineup are equally valuable as first batters in terms of scoring, followed by a steady but non-linear decline to the seventh place batter, ending with a definite upturn for the last two spots. This pattern may be unexpected at first, especially the observation that when the men in the fourth- and fifth-place slots bat first, the result is virtually the same as when the inning begins with the ninth- and eighth-place batters, respectively. However, we must remember that the scoring is the result of everyone who bats in that inning, not just the first batter. On average across all innings there are about 4.3 batters per inning (data not shown). Therefore, when the fourth slot leads off, then the eighth and ninth slots bat as the fourth and fifth men that inning. On the other hand, when the eighth-slot batter leads off, then the inning gets back to the top of the order in three batters which leads to more scoring, even if the man starting the inning made an out. I wanted to be sure that the high results when the leadoff man bats first were not overwhelmed by the first inning effect. When those totals are removed, then the average number of runs scored when the leadoff man bats first in an inning other than the first is 0.56, indistinguishable from the data in Figure 4.

I wish to emphasize that the numbers in Figure 4 represent the combined effect of all the batters in an inning, simply separated by lineup slot of the first batter. The actual performance of batters in the individual slots is shown in Figure 5. The performance of each lineup position in isolation follows the expected pattern and is quite different from the batting order analysis above.

Figure 5. Batting Performance by Lineup Slot, All Games, 1957–2005

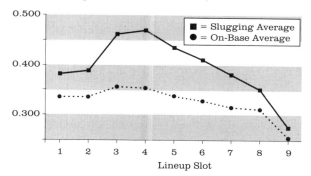

The next variable I looked at was the effect of the DH. There are ample data from several sources that AL teams score more than NL teams since 1973, but it is very clear that the difference in totals is accounted for entirely by the DH (see, for example, Table 3 in http://www.retrosheet.org/Research/ SmithD/batlearn.pdf). Figure 6 presents the differences in run scoring between the two leagues. There is a striking effect of substituting the DH for the pitcher, with a major effect upon which lineup slot bats first. For the leadoff and number two slots, the leagues are the same, because innings that begin this way are very unlikely to have the pitcher bat. Differences appear through the rest of the batting order, with the widest discrepancy being found when the men in the sixth and seventh slots bat first and the pitcher will very likely come to the plate in NL games and thereby decrease scoring in those innings. The overall level of scoring is slightly higher since the advent of the DH (data not shown).

Figure 6. Average Runs per Inning with and without the DH in Relation to Lineup Slot Batting First in an Inning, 1973–2005

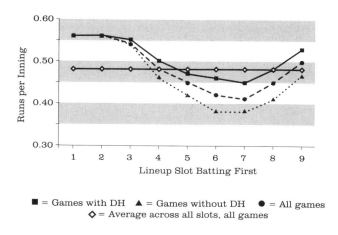

I then investigated how the scoring difference arose by looking at on-base and slugging averages for the teams as a function of which lineup slot bats first. Figure 7 has the on-base data, which show even fewer differences for first five slots than the scoring average did. However, there are wide differences for innings that begin with lineup spots six through nine, with the seventh slot showing the biggest difference.

Figure 7. On-base Average in Each Inning When Indicated Lineup Slot Bats First with and without DH, 1973–2005

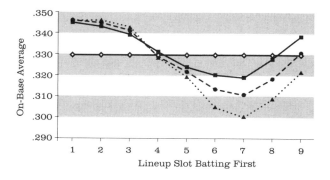

As noted above, almost all production differences between the leagues since 1973 are due to pitcher batting. I therefore recalculated the data of Figure 7 by omitting all plate appearances by pitchers. The results are in Figure 8, where we see that there is now some separation for innings that start with the second and third slots, but that the differences have almost completely disappeared from the fourth slot to the ninth.

Figure 8. On-Base Average in Each Inning When Indicated Lineup Slot Bats First with and without DH, 1973–2005, Pitcher Appearances Removed

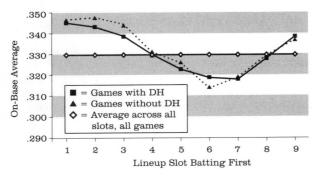

To finish the study of the DH, I prepared the parallel two figures for slugging average. These are Figures 9 and 10.

Figure 9. Slugging Average in Each Inning When Indicated Lineup Slot Bats First with and without DH, 1973–2005

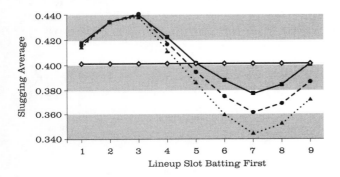

■ = Games with DH   ▲ = Games without DH   ● = All games
◇ = Average across all slots, all games

Figure 10. Slugging Average in Each Inning when Indicated Batter Bats First with and without DH, 1973–2005, Pitcher Appearances Removed

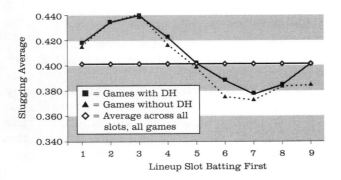

Once again, the removal of pitcher appearances brings the two leagues very close together, even closer than was seen for on-base average. The largest difference is found for the ninth slot, with the low National League value representing a large number of pinch-hitters who have a collective slugging average of .329 over these seasons.

There is one more topic I wish to discuss, and that is related to some work I did previously on batter learning. I made a presentation on this at the SABR meeting in Kansas City in 1996 and published an expanded version in the *Baseball Research Journal* in 2006. Briefly, what I discovered is that there is a dramatic improvement for starting batters against starting pitchers in batting average, on-base average, and slugging average between their first, second, and third times at bat. Figure 11 is a summary of these results:

Figure 11. Batting Performance by Starters in Different Times at Bat, 1960–2005

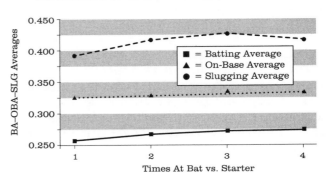

At first glance it appears that the scoring and batting order results I presented today do not agree with the batter learning study. As shown above in Figure 1, there is much more scoring in the first inning than in any other, followed by a great decline in the second inning. How can this be if batters are producing at a much lower rate their first time up, especially in terms of slugging average? The answer turns out to be simple and perhaps obvious. There is no disagreement and the apparent differences can be explained entirely by which batters typically bat in the first. Table 4 presents the percentage of plate appearances for each lineup position in each inning.

The numbers in Table 4 differ quite a bit from those in Table 3, which showed the percentage of times that each batting order slot batted first. The bulk of appearances (84.5%) in the first inning are by the best batters (see Figure 5), and in the second inning the weaker batters predominate (74.7% of total). In no other inning besides the first two is there such a disproportion in plate appearances between the different lineup slots. So, even though

Table 4. Percentage of Plate Appearances by Starting Batters in Each Lineup Slot in Each Inning

Slot	1	2	3	4	5	6	7	8	9	Extra
1	23.4	6.1	19.0	6.4	16.0	9.5	12.1	15.7	8.8	14.7
2	22.9	3.3	18.2	7.9	14.2	11.9	9.5	16.2	10.1	13.2
3	23.3	1.6	15.4	11.1	11.5	14.2	8.3	15.2	12.7	12.7
4	15.0	10.1	11.7	14.3	9.1	15.2	9.0	12.6	14.7	11.2
5	8.5	16.9	8.0	16.0	8.2	14.7	11.1	10.0	15.6	11.0
6	4.3	21.4	4.8	15.9	9.2	12.9	13.8	8.5	14.9	11.1
7	1.9	20.4	6.3	14.1	11.7	10.3	15.6	8.6	12.4	11.9
8	0.7	16.0	10.7	11.1	14.3	8.3	15.3	9.3	8.6	11.1
9	0.1	4.1	5.9	3.1	5.9	3.0	5.3	3.9	2.1	3.2

batters in all lineup positions do better the second and third times they bat, the absolute level of the most common batters in the second inning is very low. Since the numbers here represent starting batters, the percentage of batters from the ninth slot is low as the game progresses and starting pitchers are removed.

Conclusions

1. The lineup slot of the first batter in an inning matters a great deal in a team's average scoring.
2. Lineups appear to be well designed in that the best scoring results are seen when the man in the leadoff slot bats first in any inning.
3. The lowest scoring per inning occurs when the seventh slot leads off the inning.
4. There is a DH effect, but it affects only the detailed rates, not the basic patterns.

# # #

DAVID W. SMITH *received SABR's highest honor, the Bob Davids Award, in 2005. He is the founder and president of Retrosheet. This paper was presented in July 2006 a SABR36 in Seattle.*

More Interesting Statistical Combinations

In *Baseball Research Journal* 33 Fred Worth presented an intriguing article titled "Interesting Statistical Combinations," analyzing combinations like high batting average and low walks or lots of losses but a low ERA. He concluded the article, "Obviously there are many more comparisons that could be considered." I took this as a challenge and investigated a number of other statistical combinations I consider interesting. All data is taken from Sean Lahman's database (www.baseball1.com) and includes results from the 2004 season.

The Walking Men

Inspired by Barry Bonds' historic 2004 season, we'll look at the individual seasons for which a player had more walks than hits (minimum 100 at-bats). The top of the list ordered by maximum difference of (walks minus hits) looks like this:

Player	Year	AB	BB	H	BB-H	Age
Barry Bonds	2004	373	232	135	97	40
Barry Bonds	2002	403	198	149	49	38
Jack Crooks	1892	445	136	95	41	27
Jimmy Wynn	1976	449	127	93	34	34
Roy Cullenbine	1947	464	137	104	33	34
Eddie Yost	1956	515	151	119	32	30
Yank Robinson	1890	306	101	70	31	31
Ferris Fain	1955	258	94	67	27	34
Wes Westrum	1951	361	104	79	25	29
Yank Robinson	1889	452	118	94	24	30
Gene Tenace	1977	437	125	102	23	31
Denis Menke	1973	241	69	46	23	33
Jack Clark	1989	455	132	110	22	34
Gene Tenace	1980	316	92	70	22	34
Willie McGill	1891	107	37	16	21	18
Barry Bonds	2001	476	177	156	21	37

As expected, the list is headed by Barry Bonds, circa 2004. He had almost 100 more walks than hits, by far the highest margin in history. Next up is also Bonds with his impressive 2002 season, which at that point broke the MLB record for walks in a season. Of course, we're looking here at results only, not discussing whether they were achieved in a natural way or not. The above list shows all seasons with a (walks/hits) differential of 20 or more. There are four pre-1900 seasons in there as well as three third-millenium entries, all by Bonds. Note the absence of any entries for almost the entire first half of the 20th century. Roy Cullenbine's 1947 season is the first in the 20th century. Also quite as expected is that most players on the list are veterans, the majority being in their thirties while gaining entry. The obvious exception is Willie McGill in 1891 at just 18 years old, his second year in the league. He is the only pitcher on the list

Looking at totals, the following number of seasons is listed in which a player accumulated a positive differential (BBH), showing all players who achieved the feat at least twice: first season indicates the first season of more walks than hits for the player, not his debut season in the majors. We see two players with an impressive six seasons of more walks than hits, followed by five players with four seasons each, including modern sluggers Barry Bonds, Mark McGwire, and Jack Clark. Of course, Barry Bonds may climb up the ladder before his career is finished. Noteworthy is the relative absence of pre-1900 players on this list with only three entries, although this includes Yank Robinson with four seasons. Half of the players (14 out of 28) had their first (BB>H) season after 1960.

	# seasons	First Season
Max Bishop	6	1926
Gene Tenace	6	1974
Jack Clark	4	1987
Yank Robinson	4	1888
Barry Bonds	4	2001
Mark McGwire	4	1994
Eddie Yost	4	1955
Eddie Lake	3	1943
Mickey Tettleton	3	1990
Eddie Joost	3	1947
Don Mincher	3	1961
Jimmy Wynn	3	1969
Frank Fernandez	2	1968
Red Faber	2	1920
Ken Phelps	2	1986
Lee Mazzilli	2	1986
Jim French	2	1969
Marty Hopkins	2	1934
Aaron Robinson	2	1950
Merv Shea	2	1935
Mickey Mantle	2	1962
Jack Crooks	2	1892
Oscar Gamble	2	1984
Eddie Stanky	2	1945
Wes Westrum	2	1951
Charlie Bennett	2	1890

Roy Cullenbine	2	1940	
Willie McCovey	2	1973	

Primary Targets

After looking at players with exceptionally high walk totals, let's now look at another kind of feat involving walks: having been hit by pitches more than having walked in a season. What follows is a table of player seasons (100 at-bats minimum) achieving this with a differential of at least three: The list is dominated by players of the 1800s and the early years of the 20th century, led by Hughie Jennings in 1896 with a mind-blowing differential of 32 more HBP than walks. Of course, most seasons are ones with very low walk totals for the player in question. An exception is Hughie Jennings' 1897 season with 42 walks but even more hit-by-pitches. Jennings makes the list three times. These guys sure had a painful way of making up for their meager walk totals!

Player	Year	AB	BB	HBP	HBP-BB
Hughie Jennings	1896	521	19	51	32
Boileryard Clarke	1898	285	4	15	11
John Reilly	1884	448	5	14	9
Jay Faatz	1888	470	12	21	9
Art Fletcher	1915	562	6	14	8
Whitey Alperman	1906	441	6	14	8
Hughie Jennings	1895	529	24	32	8
Dan McGann	1901	423	16	23	7
Sal Fasano	1998	216	10	16	6
John Warner	1901	291	3	8	5
Felix Escalona	2002	157	3	7	4
Whitey Alperman	1909	420	2	6	4
Hughie Jennings	1897	439	42	46	4
Finners Quinlan	1915	114	4	8	4
Jay Faatz	1884	112	1	4	3
Shawon Dunston	1999	243	2	5	3
Jack O'Neill	1905	172	8	11	3
Ollie O'Mara	1918	450	7	10	3
Mike Kinkade	2003	162	13	16	3
Vance Wilson	2002	163	5	8	3
Deacon Phillippe	1900	105	1	4	3
Barney Pelty	1904	118	0	3	3

Hit Spectrum Inversions

Typically, the number of the different types of hits a player has in a season goes in the sequence singles-doubles-home runs-triples in descending order of frequency. Let's call this the "hit spectrum." Of course, as is often the case for one-dimensional sluggers, the order of doubles and home runs may be inversed. Here, we'll look at player seasons for which the order mentioned above doesn't hold. We

start with players having more home runs than singles in a season (50 at-bats minimum):

Player	Year	AB	H	1B	HR	HR-1B
Barry Bonds	2001	476	156	49	73	24
Mark McGwire	1998	509	152	61	70	9
Mark McGwire	1999	521	145	58	65	7
Mark McGwire	2001	299	56	23	29	6
Mark McGwire	1995	317	87	35	39	4
Milt Pappas	1962	69	6	1	4	3
J.R. Phillips	1996	104	17	5	7	2
Ben Wade	1952	60	7	1	3	2
Roric Harrison	1973	54	3	0	2	2
Rob Deer	1996	50	9	2	4	2
Richie Sexson	2004	90	21	8	9	1
Greg Pirkl	1994	53	14	5	6	1
Dick Williams	1964	69	11	4	5	1
Shane Spencer	1998	67	25	9	10	1
Jack Harshman	1956	71	12	5	6	1
Bobby Estalella	2002	112	23	7	8	1
Don Drysdale	1958	66	15	6	7	1
Neil Chrisley	1959	106	14	5	6	1

Once again, we have Barry Bonds heading the list. In 2001, on his way to breaking the single-season home run record, almost 47% of his hits were home runs while only 31% were singles. The differential (HR1B) of 24 is by far the biggest in history. Next up is Mark McGwire with four (!) seasons of his own with a differential of between four and nine. Obviously, all seasons are post-1950 with a predominance of the 1990s/2000s era. This indicates an increasing trend of all or nothing swings at the plate, at least for sluggers like McGwire. But even then, hitting more home runs than singles is very hard to achieve over a full season. Bonds and McGwire are the only ones who did it in what amounts to the equivalent of at least half a season. Some list entries with low at-bat totals are pitcher seasons like Don Drysdale's 1958 and Milt Pappas' 1962 campaigns.

Another example of an anomalous hit spectrum is players who hit more triples than doubles. This happened about 750 times in MLB history (100 at-bats minimum). Following is a table of all player seasons with a differential (triples/doubles) of at least seven:

Player	Year	AB	H	2B	3B	3B-2B	SB
Harry Davis	1897	429	131	10	28	18	21
Chief Wilson	1912	583	175	19	36	17	16
Duff Cooley	1895	563	191	9	20	11	27
Bill Kuehne	1885	411	93	9	19	10	0
Hughie Jennings	1899	224	67	3	12	9	18
Heinie Reitz	1894	446	135	22	31	9	18
Deion Sanders	1992	303	92	6	14	8	26
Edd Roush	1916	341	91	7	15	8	19
Tommy Leach	1902	514	143	14	22	8	25
Dale Mitchell	1949	640	203	16	23	7	10

Jake Daubert	1922	610	205	15	22	7	14
Les Mann	1915	470	144	12	19	7	18
Braggo Roth	1915	384	103	10	17	7	26
Joe Cassidy	1904	581	140	12	19	7	17
Dave Brain	1903	464	107	8	15	7	21
Perry Werden	1893	500	138	22	29	7	11
Scott Stratton	1892	219	56	2	9	7	9
Joe Visner	1890	521	139	15	22	7	18
Dick Johnston	1887	507	131	13	20	7	52
John Kerins	1885	456	111	9	16	7	0

The list is dominated by seasons from the early stages of professional ball up to and including the Deadball Era. Deion Sanders' 1992 season is the only one in the last half-century. Noticeable is the rather high number of at-bats, i.e., these players achieved the feat of tripling more often than doubling typically in a full season's worth of plate appearances. I suspect a number of reasons being responsible for the predominance of the Deadball Era on this list, including bigger parks, worse field conditions than today, smaller fielder's gloves, and various others. Possibly one would expect players with more triples than doubles to be very fast and therefore to also steal a lot of bases, too. However, as the number of stolen bases is also displayed in the table, this seems not to be the case. SB totals are moderate for most player seasons, Dick Johnston's 1887 campaign with 52 SB being the exception. The two entries with zero stolen bases (Kuehne and Kerins) are due to the fact that no stolen base records were kept for the league at that time.

Looking at total seasons with more triples than doubles for each player (not shown as a table), we have Sam Crawford and Tommy Leach with five seasons each and Bill Kuehne, George Van Haltren, Silver King, John Hummel, and Adonis Terry with four each as well as 16 players with three each. Therefore, hitting more triples than doubles in a season is not a total fluke but, at least to some extent, a persistent skill of a few dozen players, mainly from the 19th century.

So far, we've looked at a reverse differential of hit types two positions apart in the hit spectrum 1B–2B–HR–3B, i.e., more home runs than singles (positions 3 and 1) and more triples than doubles (positions 4 and 2). Of course, reverse differentials for adjacent positions, e.g., more home runs than doubles, are typically more common than for greater positional differences. So what has yet to be considered is the only possible reverse differential of three positions, i.e., hitting more triples than singles. This never happened in 100+ at-bats, but it happened once in MLB history in 50+ at-bats. In 1991, pitcher Charlie Leibrand posted this line:

Year	AB	H	1B	3B	3B-1B
1991	70	3	0	1	1

Of course, this is just a fluctuation because of the extremely small numbers involved (no singles, one triple). So basically hitting more triples than singles in any meaningful number of at-bats has never happened so far. If we lower our minimum requirement for at-bats even more (to 25 AB minimum), we have two players who hit at least two more triples than singles in a season. Obviously, these small numbers of at-bats render the accomplishments statistically completely meaningless; there's no persistent capability involved.

	Year	AB	H	1B	3B	3B-1B
Ron Fairly	1960	37	4	0	3	3
Mike O'Neill	1907	29	2	0	2	2

Before leaving the topic of hit spectrums, we will look at totals for relationships between the different types of hits. In the analyzed data set, there are 32,661 player seasons with at least 100 at-bats. The following table shows for the six possible combinations of hit types (single vs. double, single vs. triple, double vs. home run...) and the three possible relationships (hit type 1 greater than hit type 2, . . . smaller than . . . , . . . equal to . . .) the counts and percentages of the total 32,661 seasons (see Table X1).

Table [X1] tells us, in addition to the eight seasons of more home runs than doubles and the fact that a season with more triples than singles never

Table 1. Counts and Percentages

		Relationship					
		>		=		<	
Hit 1	Hit 2						
1B	2B	32653	99.98%	4	0.01%	4	0.01%
1B	3B	32661	100.00%	0	0.00%	0	0.00%
1B	HR	32652	99.97%	1	0.00%	8	0.02%
2B	3B	31251	95.68%	659	2.02%	751	2.30%
2B	HR	28722	87.94%	926	2.84%	3013	9.23%
3B	HR	12033	36.84%	3569	10.93%	17059	52.23%

happened, several interesting facts. First of all, a reverse differential between positions 1 and 2 in the hit spectrum (singles vs. doubles) is very rare; it happened only four times in history. Another four times the totals for the two types of hits matched exactly:

Table X2. Needs title

Player	Year	AB	H	1B	2B	2B-1B
John Kroner	1938	117	29	12	16	4
Adam Piatt	2003	132	30	11	13	2
Bobby Estalella	2002	112	23	7	8	1
Bill Duggleby	1905	101	11	4	5	1
J.R. Phillips	1996	104	17	5	5	0
Brian Hunter	1998	112	23	9	9	0
Lefty Grove	1933	105	9	4	4	0
Joe Bush	1925	102	26	12	12	0

Besides four seasons from the last ten years we have another four seasons from the first half of the 20th century. All seasons have relatively low at-bats totals, just making the cut of 100 at-bats. The results shown above regarding the counts/fractions of the hit spectrum relationships also indicate that the sequence triples/home runs is quite often reversed: more than one in three seasons is finished with more triples than home runs. However, this number drops to 22% if we consider only seasons after 1920, i.e., in the Lively ball era.

And now to something completely different.

Masters of the Three True Outcomes

The Three True Outcomes (TTO) as usual are defined as the three results from a batter's plate appearance which are (almost) solely in the responsibility of the pitcher: the walk, strikeout, and home run. Sometimes players whose plate appearances often result in one of the TTO are referred to as Three True Outcome Players, e.g., second baseman Mark Bellhorn in Boston's 2004 championship season. These types of players are considered valuable in a performance analysis, sabermetrics point of view, e.g., the Moneyball approach. Traditional scouting and evaluation often rate these players rather lower because of typically high strikeout totals. Table 3 shows the top TTO percentages in history (100 at-bats minimum). Column TTO is the sum of columns BB, SO, and HR. TTO percentage is TTO divided by the sum of at-bats plus walks (ignoring HBP, sac flies, and sac hits).

The list is headed by a few players with over 60% of their plate appearances resulting in one of the three true outcomes. Up front is a pitcher, Vida Blue, without a home run. He's solely on the list because of his impressive strikeout total (63 in 102 at-bats). The players on this list with a number of plate appearances equivalent to at least half a season are Mark McGwire in 1998, 2000 and 2001, Jack Clark in 1987, and Dave Nicholson in 1964.

Table 3. All-time Top TTO Percentages (min. 100 AB)

Player	Year	AB	BB	SO	HR	TTO	TTO perc
Vida Blue	1971	102	4	63	0	67	0.632
Dave Nicholson	1960	113	20	55	5	80	0.602
J.R. Phillips	1996	104	11	51	7	69	0.600
Mark McGwire	2000	236	76	78	32	186	0.596
Mark McGwire	1998	509	162	155	70	387	0.577
Dave McNally	1970	105	15	53	1	69	0.575
Mark McGwire	2001	299	56	118	29	203	0.572
Billy Ashley	1996	110	21	44	9	74	0.565
Dave Duncan	1967	101	4	50	5	59	0.562
Dave Nicholson	1962	173	27	76	9	112	0.560
Jack Clark	1987	419	136	139	35	310	0.559
Bob Purkey	1962	107	4	56	2	62	0.559
Russ Branyan	2004	158	20	68	11	99	0.556
Dave Nicholson	1964	294	52	126	13	191	0.552
Earl Moseley	1914	109	7	57	0	64	0.552
Rob Deer	1985	162	23	71	8	102	0.551

Again, almost all seasons in the table are from the second half of the last century. When these guys are at bat, there's not much to do for the fielders most of the time! Of course, we're not so much interested in players who are on the list solely because of their high strikeout totals, like Vida Blue in 1971 or Dave McNally in 1970, but in players who also achieve significant totals in the other legs of TTO, walks and especially home runs. Table 4 gives the top TTO percentages for player seasons with at least 20 home runs.

Here we have the usual suspects: modern sluggers like Bonds, McGwire, and Jim Thome as well as strikeout kings like Rob Deer. Mark McGwire has six seasons of at least a 50% TTO percentage.

The other end of the Three True Outcome spectrum are players who rarely walk or strike out and have little power. For these, the opposite defenders are involved in most of their at-bats. As expected, this was most often the case in the 19th century. In the list of lowest TTO percentages in history over at least 100 at-bats, the first modern entry (post 1900) is at position 166, Doc Powers in 1905. Restricting ourselves to the post-1900 era, Table 5 contains the top of the list.

Please note the extremely low TTO percentages here. These are guys that had absolutely no power, very rarely walked, and almost never struck out. When they were at bat, a good defense behind him was surely the pitcher's best friend (besides the double play). But even in the last few decades, there have been players with very low TTO percentages, as Table 6 shows, which has only seasons after 1970.

Three True Outcome Pitchers

So far we've looked at the Three True Outcomes for batters. But of course, this is also an interesting statistic to analyze for pitchers. I include hit-by-pitch as one of the true outcomes for pitchers because it's also solely in the control of the pitchers (never mind that now we should

Table 4. Top TTO Percentages for Player Seasons with at least 20 Home Runs

Player	Year	AB	BB	SO	HR	TTO	TTO%
Mark McGwire	2000	236	76	78	32	186	0.596
Mark McGwire	1998	509	162	155	70	387	0.577
Mark McGwire	2001	299	56	118	29	203	0.572
Jack Clark	1987	419	136	139	35	310	0.559
Melvin Nieves	1997	359	39	157	20	216	0.543
Jim Thome	2001	526	111	185	49	345	0.542
Dave Kingman	1973	305	41	122	24	187	0.540
Russ Branyan	2001	315	38	132	20	190	0.538
Rob Deer	1991	448	89	175	25	289	0.538
Rob Deer	1987	474	86	186	28	300	0.536
Jim Thome	1999	494	127	171	33	331	0.533
Ray Lankford	2000	392	70	148	26	244	0.528
Rob Deer	1986	466	72	179	33	284	0.528
Russ Branyan	2002	378	51	151	24	226	0.527
Barry Bonds	2004	373	232	41	45	318	0.526
Barry Bonds	2001	476	177	93	73	343	0.525
Jim Thome	2002	480	122	139	52	313	0.520
Mark McGwire	1996	423	116	112	52	280	0.519
Mark McGwire	1999	521	133	141	65	339	0.518
Fred McGriff	1987	295	60	104	20	184	0.518
Adam Dunn	2004	568	108	195	46	349	0.516
Jack Clark	1989	455	132	145	26	303	0.516
Dave Nicholson	1963	449	63	175	22	260	0.508
Jay Buhner	1997	540	119	175	40	334	0.507
Mark McGwire	1995	317	88	77	39	204	0.504
Jimmy Wynn	1969	495	148	142	33	323	0.502
Jack Clark	1990	334	104	91	25	220	0.502

Table 5. Lowest TTO Percentages, Post-1900

Player	Year	AB	H	BB	SO	HR	TTO	TTO%
Doc Powers	1905	154	24	4	0	0	4	0.025
Sport McAllister	1902	240	49	6	0	1	7	0.028
Emil Verban	1949	343	99	8	2	0	10	0.028
Tommy Thevenow	1933	253	79	3	5	0	8	0.031
Woody Jensen	1938	125	25	1	3	0	4	0.032
Johnny Sain	1948	115	25	1	3	0	4	0.034
Johnny Sain	1947	107	37	3	1	0	4	0.036
Stuffy McInnis	1924	581	169	15	6	1	22	0.037
Stuffy McInnis	1922	537	164	15	5	1	21	0.038
Walter Schmidt	1922	152	50	1	5	0	6	0.039

Table X6. Lowest TTO Percentages, Post-1970

Player	Year	AB	H	BB	SO	HR	TTO	TTO%
Felix Fermin	1995	200	39	6	6	0	12	0.058
Bob Bailor	1984	131	36	8	1	0	9	0.065
Bob Bailor	1985	118	29	3	5	0	8	0.066
Larry Milbourne	1978	234	53	9	6	2	17	0.070
Jesus Alou	1974	220	59	5	9	2	16	0.071
Jeff Torborg	1971	123	25	3	6	0	9	0.071
Jesus Alou	1971	433	121	13	17	2	32	0.072
Lenny Harris	1999	187	58	6	7	1	14	0.073
Mario Guerrero	1976	268	76	7	12	1	20	0.073
Tim Foli	1983	330	83	5	18	2	25	0.075

Table 7. Top TTO Percentages for Pitchers (min. 50 IP/Season)

Player	Year	IP	H	BB	HBP	SO	HR	TTO	TTO%
ByungHyun Kim	2000	70.2	52	46	9	111	9	175	0.634
Armando Benitez	1999	78.0	40	41	0	128	4	173	0.620
John Rocker	2000	53.0	42	48	2	77	5	132	0.617
Brad Lidge	2004	94.2	57	30	6	157	8	201	0.613
Matt Mantei	1999	65.1	44	44	5	99	5	153	0.612
Billy Wagner	1997	66.1	49	30	3	106	5	144	0.608
Billy Wagner	1998	60.0	46	25	0	97	6	128	0.607
Billy Wagner	1999	74.2	35	23	1	124	5	153	0.605
Eric Gagne	2003	82.1	37	20	3	137	2	162	0.596
Rob Dibble	1992	70.1	48	31	2	110	3	146	0.591
Bryan Harvey	1989	55.0	36	41	0	78	6	125	0.590
Armando Benitez	1997	73.1	49	43	1	106	7	157	0.579

correctly call it four true outcomes). We define pitchers' TTO as:

$$(BB+HBP+SO+HR)/(BB+HBP+HR+Outs)$$

Outs is innings pitched times three. Table 7 is a list of highest TTO percentages for pitchers with at least 50 innings pitched in a season.

This list, which shows all TTO percentages above .570, exclusively comprises modern relief pitchers, especially closers. There are only two entries more than 10 years old, Bryan Harvey in 1989 and Rob Dibble in 1992, and even those are not really from ancient baseball times. Note that for the top TTO guys, more than 60% of their batters faced result in one of the Three True Outcomes, including the hit-by-pitch. If we elevate our minimum requirement for innings pitched to 150, eliminating modern relievers, we arrive at the list of top TTO percentages for starting pitchers. Now, this should be called the Randy Johnson memorial list; the Big Unit has eight of the top 13 TTO percentages in history among starting pitchers. Kerry Wood makes the list three times, including the top spot in 1998, his rookie year. Johnson also has the highest total on the list for one of the Three True Outcomes in 2001 with 372 strikeouts (one of the highest SO totals in history), 85 walks, 11 hit-by-pitches and 14 home runs for a sum of 480. However, even these numbers pale in comparism to Nolan Ryan's 1974 season with 367 SO, 202 BB, 9 HBP, and 18 HR for a total of 596. Ryan also has totals of 570 and 566 in 1973 and 1977, respectively. Pitchers with a high TTO percentage don't depend heavily on the defenses behind them because the defense often isn't involved in the result from a batter's plate appearance. On the other end of the spectrum there are pitchers with very low TTO percentages who rely heavily on their defenses. In the post-1900 era, the table on the next page shows the lowest TTO percentages with at least 50 innings pitched:

Player	Year	IP	H	BB	HBP	SO	HR	TTO	TTO%
Kerry Wood	1998	166.2	117	85	11	233	14	343	0.562
Randy Johnson	2001	249.2	181	71	18	372	19	480	0.560
Randy Johnson	1997	213.0	147	77	10	291	20	398	0.534
Randy Johnson	2000	248.2	202	76	6	347	23	452	0.531
Bobby Witt	1986	157.2	130	143	3	174	18	338	0.531
Pedro Martinez	1999	213.1	160	37	9	313	9	368	0.529
Kerry Wood	2003	211.0	152	100	21	266	24	411	0.528
Randy Johnson	1998	244.1	203	86	14	329	23	452	0.528
Kerry Wood	2001	174.1	127	92	10	217	16	335	0.523
Randy Johnson	1991	201.1	151	152	12	228	15	407	0.520
Randy Johnson	1995	214.1	159	65	6	294	12	377	0.519
Randy Johnson	1992	210.1	154	144	18	241	13	416	0.516
Randy Johnson	1999	271.2	207	70	9	364	30	473	0.512

Player	Year	IP	H	BB	HBP	SO	HR	TTO	TTO%
Slim Sallee	1919	227.2	221	20	1	24	4	49	0.069
Eppa Rixey	1933	94.1	118	12	0	10	1	23	0.078
Bob Harmon	1918	82.1	76	12	0	7	3	22	0.084
Slim Sallee	1920	133.0	145	16	2	15	4	37	0.088
Benny Frey	1933	132.0	144	21	0	12	4	37	0.088
Nick Altrock	1908	136.0	127	18	2	21	2	43	0.100
Eppa Rixey	1932	111.2	108	16	4	14	3	37	0.103
Red Lucas	1933	219.2	248	18	2	40	13	73	0.105
Arnie Stone	1924	64.0	57	15	0	7	0	22	0.106
Huck Betts	1932	221.2	229	35	0	32	9	76	0.107

All entries are from the first 35 years of the 20th century. We see several pitchers whose batters' plate appearances result in one of the Three True Outcomes in less than 10% of the cases, i.e., the defense is involved in more than 90% of the plate appearances. This obviously puts a huge emphasis on the fielders' capabilities. In addition, following Voros McCracken's insight that pitchers have little or no control over batting average on balls in play, one may conclude that any success these types of pitchers have is largely thanks to the fielders behind them. From the data presented above it seems that Three True Outcomes percentages have risen throughout MLB history. To analyze this in some detail, Table 8 shows the average TTO percentage for pitchers weighted with innings pitched and broken down per decade.

Table 8. Average TTO Percentage for Pitchers by Decade, Weighted with IP

Decade	Total IP	TTO%
1876-1880	22,352.0	0.1209
1881-1890	168,591.2	0.2139
1891-1900	139,357.0	0.2041
1901-1910	202,594.2	0.2210
1911-1920	223,708.0	0.2280
1921-1930	207,473.0	0.2116
1931-1940	206,552.2	0.2354
1941-1950	206,353.0	0.2494
1951-1960	205,979.1	0.2850
1961-1970	279,079.2	0.3176
1971-1980	334,712.1	0.2937
1981-1990	331,941.1	0.3089
1991-2000	343,098.0	0.3438
2001-2004	148,752.0	0.3522

This table tells us several interesting facts. First of all, average TTO percentages started out very low in the 1870s but quickly rose to a level of about 21.23% and stayed there for over 50 years. In the middle of the 20th century they started to rise again and established a new level of about 30% for the 1960s through 1980. From the 1990s on, we have another hike up to about 35%, which still holds on. Reasons for this may probably be found in the increasing trend of almost all players swinging for the fences today, leading to higher strike out totals as well as an increased importance of walks as a tactical weapon for batters as taught by several teams today (as part of the often falsely abbreviated Moneyball approach). Please note that innings-pitched totals per decade reflect the expansions (starting in 1961) as well as the brief existence of the Federal League in the 1910s.

# # #

PETER UELKES *got a Ph.D. in particle physics from the University of Technology at Aachen, Germany. He is currently working as a senior project manager for the Vodafone group. A SABR member since 2001, this is his second publication in the BRJ.*

DAVID VINCENT

Fenway Park's Hand-Operated Scoreboard

On the evening of August 15, 2006, Nate Moulter and Mike Gavin arrived for work at Boston's Fenway Park and started their evening by making a list of that day's major league games with the uniform numbers of the starting pitchers. Then they turned to the main task of their job—posting information on the hand-operated scoreboard at Fenway Park. Nate and Mike are two of a three-man staff who work in the scoreboard during games. The 16-year veteran of the squad, Chris Elias, was away on business that night, but the board was ably manned by Mike, in his second year, and Nate, in his first season on the squad.

The left-field wall is one of the most recognizable features in any ballpark and has been a part of Fenway Park since it opened on April 20, 1912. The original wall was a 37-foot-tall wooden structure, but that was replaced by a sheet metal wall in 1934 as part of renovations made by the new Red Sox owner, Tom Yawkey. A 23½-foot screen was built on the top of the wall in 1936 to prevent home run balls from damaging buildings across Lansdowne Street, which runs behind the wall. Commercial advertisements covered the wall as late as 1946, but they were painted over before the 1947 season by the distinctive green paint, which has led many people to refer to the wall in the last few decades as the Green Monster.

When the park was built in 1912, hand-operated scoreboards were the norm. Fenway Park, the oldest ballpark in the majors, still operates as it did in 1912, with a person posting numbers on the board as the game progresses. Now there are new fields that feature retro-effects, such as hand-operated scoreboards. Among these parks are Minute Maid Park in Houston and Coors Field in Denver. Chicago's Wrigley Field, the oldest park in the National League, has a hand-operated scoreboard that was built in 1937, 23 years after it opened.

The Fenway scoreboard had sections for various purposes in the 1950s. In addition to an inning-by-inning section for the Sox game, there were sections showing the current score in all other major league games in progress. The National League section of the board was removed as part of a 1975 renovation, during which time the board was moved farther away from the left-field line toward left-center field. As part of that renovation, the sheet metal surface of the entire wall, which had been damaged by hundreds of baseballs striking it in four decades of use, was replaced. The 1976 covering is still in place on the wall in 2006, with its own collection of dents from baseballs. In July 2002, commercial signs were added atop the wall, and before the 2003 season major changes were made. Those included removal of the screen and replacing it with a new section of seating called the "Monster Seats." Those 274 tickets on the wall typically are the most sought after in Boston during the summer and provide a great view of the action and an occasional souvenir. Changes to the scoreboard in 2003 included the addition of a National League section, addition of the AL East division standings, and increased signage at either end of the scoreboard. Almost the entire 231-foot width of the wall is now covered with signs and the scoreboard.

Another feature on the scoreboard are the Morse Code initials of Tom Yawkey (TAY: dash, dot-dash, dash-dot-dash-dash) and his wife, Jean (JRY: dot-dash-dash-dash, dot-dash-dot, dash-dot-dash-dash). These vertical stripes appear just to the right of the Sox game section on the board.

Behind the scoreboard is a small room that runs most of the length of the scoreboard. This is the "office" of Chris, Mike, and Nate, three guys with second jobs that many people in New England would love to have. This room has a concrete wall along the back with beams that run out toward the back of the metal scoreboard. The concrete wall is covered with names of people who have come into the room through the years. Players, team officials, and others have memorialized their visit to this little room by writing their name somewhere on the concrete. Before the game this night, Nate pointed out the names of Wade Boggs, Trot Nixon, and model Leeann Tweeden to a visitor. Also on the wall are the names of Yankees GM Brian Cashman and Rockies Vice President of Communications, Jay Alves, among others. During batting practice, Magglio Ordonez of the Tigers visits the room with his son, Magglio, Jr. The younger Ordonez writes his name onto the concrete as his dad watches. The Tigers training staff also toured the small area behind the scoreboard, looking at names on the wall.

From this room the operators place metal number panels into slots for the Red Sox contest and the American League games. Since their room does not run as far toward the center-field end of the wall as the scoreboard, the National League scores must be put up from the front of the board. One of the workers runs out onto the warning track between innings with a ladder and places the numbers in the appropriate place on the scoreboard. Inside, there is a wooden step up to a small concrete wall just behind the scoreboard. Standing on the concrete, one can reach up to the slots to place numbers for each inning as the Sox game progresses.

The number panels used to indicate runs and hits are 16 by 16 inches and weigh three pounds each. The panels used for the pitcher's numbers, innings, and errors are 12 by 16 inches and weigh two pounds. Each panel has a different number front and reverse; they are consecutive, such as 2 and 3. There are small slits into which the numbers are inserted from behind the board. The slots for the number panels are similar to taking an inbox from a desk and placing it vertically against the scoreboard. Some of these are loaded from the top and some from the bottom. Each time the score changes in the Red Sox game, one team collects a hit or is charged with an error, one of the operators pulls the appropriate number out of its position on the board and either flips and reinserts it or takes a new number panel off the back wall and inserts that into the board. While an inning is in progress, the number of runs scored (greater than zero) are represented for that inning with a yellow digit, which is replaced with a white number at the end of the inning.

As the Red Sox game progresses through the first three innings, Mike watches an Internet site from a laptop computer for updates on scores from other big league games in progress. Occasionally, he yells out an American League score. Then one of the operators grabs a number panel off the back wall and moves to the correct slot in the scoreboard and updates that game's score and inning. Once the eight o'clock hour passes, many more games start and must be monitored. This means that there is more activity in the room as runs are scored in the Central Time Zone as well as Eastern. The current board display is kept on a notepad for comparison with the Internet scoreboard. The operators talk in their own code for out-of-town game scores. For each of those contests, there are two numbers for the pitchers, one for the inning and two more for the runs scored by the teams. When the score changes, someone might call out "3–0–1" for a game, meaning third inning with the home team ahead 1–0.

Keeping track of the Red Sox game requires looking through one of about eight slots in the scoreboard. These holes are approximately ten inches wide and one inch tall. From here, the operators can see the progress of the game as if standing in left field with Manny Ramirez. However, the view is restricted by the size of the slot; high fly balls can disappear from view and watching the fielder gives a better idea of what is going on. There is also a window in the wall between the words "Ball" and "Strike" that is used often by a television camera person. This vantage point offers a unique look as it is perfectly lined up with the baseline between first and second bases. Thus, one gets a great angle on a double play, in which the view is behind the throw to first base.

Fly balls that strike the metal scoreboard reverberate loudly in the room behind the wall. There is no running water, and therefore no toilet, thus left fielders who disappear into the room during a pitching change are not going in to relieve themselves, contrary to public belief. There is also no heat or air conditioning in the room, and it can get very warm during the hottest part of the summer as the sun beats off the metal facing of the scoreboard and heats the air in the room. No breeze relieves that heat as there is no possibility of cross-ventilation and little space in the wall for the breeze to enter. However, the board operators know that the temperature and lack of facilities is a small price to pay to work one of the coolest jobs in Boston.

Carlton Fisk hit one of the most famous homers ever at Fenway Park in Game Six of the 1975 World Series. As the ball flew down the left-field line, Fisk stood near home plate applying body English and waving with his hands, willing the ball to be fair as it reached the wall, and then leaped into the air when it hit the pole for a game-ending home run. This scene was captured accidentally by the television cameraman stationed in the scoreboard, as he had been instructed to follow the path of the ball but did not pay attention to that instruction since he was watching a rat at his feet, and kept the camera trained on Fisk and his gyrations, thus providing one of the most famous moments in World Series history.

In June 2006, board operator Nate Moulter's face looking out the camera window appeared on ESPN and other television outlets. During a three-game series with the Washington Nationals, Alfonso Soriano, Washington's left fielder and leading home run hitter, spent a few minutes during a pitching change talking with Nate at the window while leaning on the scoreboard. As Soriano started to leave, he said something and laughed, then swatted Nate with his glove and returned to his defensive position. Many left fielders have ducked into the room behind the wall during games. According to Moulter, Manny Ramirez

1. The room behind the scoreboard. Light enters through the window for the TV camera. Beneath it are casings that hold the lights used to indicate balls, strikes, and outs.

2. A viewing slot in the interior of the scoreboard wall (center), and slots in which number panels are placed.

3. Scoreboard number panels.

4. Outfielder Manny Ramirez, as seen from the scoreboard.

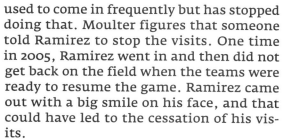

used to come in frequently but has stopped doing that. Moulter figures that someone told Ramirez to stop the visits. One time in 2005, Ramirez went in and then did not get back on the field when the teams were ready to resume the game. Ramirez came out with a big smile on his face, and that could have led to the cessation of his visits.

The next time you visit Fenway Park, take a look at the scoreboard and watch the changes in the display as the game progresses. Maybe you can help others understand how that information area is updated.

# # #

DAVID VINCENT *added his name to the scoreboard wall during his evening as rookie board operator.*

All Saves Are Not Created Equal

When the Fireman of the Year award was created in 1960, the term "fireman" had already been in use for more than 20 years, referring to a relief pitcher who entered the game to stop a rally. The connotation was that some emergency existed, requiring the rescue of one pitcher by another. It didn't matter what inning it was; with a small lead and runners on base, the manager would bring in his best reliever to put out the fire.

After saves became an official statistic in 1969, a generation of relievers built their reputations as firemen who doused rallies as early as the sixth inning and pitched the rest of the way to record saves. More recently, a new breed of relief ace has emerged, one of many specialized bullpen roles. These save-gatherers are spared the hazardous duty of putting out fires in the seventh or even the eighth inning. Instead, their sole assignment is to saunter in at the start of the ninth inning, with a lead of three runs or less, and record the final three outs. They are called "closers" ("fireman" has become obsolete), a business term for the person who irons out the final details of a deal after others have done the legwork. In essence, the game is already won when the closer enters; it is only a matter of what the final score will be.

On the rare occasions when a closer is brought in with no save possible, announcers feel compelled to account for the aberration. Most likely he hasn't pitched in a few days and needs the work. Some closers have admitted to pitching poorly with a four-run lead because they aren't sufficiently motivated. It's as if the manager gears his game strategy toward providing his closer with the chance to accumulate a lot of saves, compared to the earlier generations when the manager identified his best reliever and sought to get as many innings as possible from him, with victories and saves the by-product of quality work. For instance, when Mike Marshall set the record in 1974 with 208.1 innings pitched in relief, 93 of those innings came when he entered with his team losing or tied, and he became the winning pitcher in 15 of those 47 appearances.

Table 1. Career Save and Blown Save Totals

	G in Relief	SV Opps	SV	BS
Fingers	907	479	341	110
Gossage	965	463	310	112
Sutter	661	412	300	101
L. Smith	1016	616	478	103
Eckersley	710	484	390	71
Hoffman	821	556	482	56
Rivera	720	501	413	55
TOTALS	5800	3511	2714	608

Dennis Eckersley has said that "you can't blame a pitcher for the way a manager uses him." That is true, but we *can* assess the relative difficulty of their assigned tasks and their relative success in similar situations. Thanks to a wealth of data supplied by Dave Smith of Retrosheet, I've conducted numerous studies of seven relievers most prominently mentioned in debates about electing relievers to the Hall of Fame. Three are already enshrined: two firemen (Rollie Fingers and Bruce Sutter) and one closer (Eckersley). Two others were the top vote-getters among relievers on the 2007 ballot who were not elected: Rich Gossage and Lee Smith. The final two are the active pitchers regarded as the most likely to make the Hall of Fame someday: Mariano Rivera and Trevor Hoffman.

Table 2. Innings Pitched in Saves

	1/3	2/3	1	1 1/3	1 2/3	2	2 1/3	2 2/3	3+
Fingers	39	20	81	30	36	61	20	18	36
Gossage	24	23	70	33	35	73	16	12	24
Sutter	18	12	82	25	33	84	21	10	15
L.Smith	26	23	260	46	29	79	5	2	8
Eckersley	25	28	231	44	34	23	2	2	1
Hoffman	26	12	389	39	9	5	1	1	0
Rivera	16	11	299	49	27	10	1	0	0
TOTALS	174	129	1412	266	203	335	66	45	84

As a group, these seven standouts provide a vivid cross-section of the evolution from firemen to closers during the "saves era".

Did the elite relievers of the 1970s work that much harder than today's elite, and do they deserve more respect for doing so? A reliever's workload—his contribution to the team's winning effort—is easily measured in innings pitched. One argument in favor of enshrining Bruce Sutter was that even though he ranks just 18th in career saves, he worked harder for his saves, often pitching two or three innings to do so. So in Table 2 I tallied exactly how many outs were recorded in every one of these pitchers' saves.

The numbers tell us quite a bit. Sutter pitched at least two innings in 43.3% of his career saves, more than any of the others. Gossage and Fingers weren't far behind, and Fingers pitched at least three innings in more than 10% of his saves. It is impossible to pick any member of this trio over the other two in terms of how hard they worked for saves.

Contrast their innings with those pitched by Eckersley, Rivera, and Hoffman. The great majority of their saves involved pitching one inning or less, with few appearances earlier than the ninth inning. Consider this: from May 27 through July 4, 1984 (39 days), Sutter had more saves (nine) where he pitched at least two innings than Hoffman has in his whole career. Gossage did the same thing from August 15, 1980, through the end of that season, and Fingers accomplished it in a 53-day stretch in 1978. The earlier pitchers acted as their own setup men. These firemen put out the fire and cleaned up after themselves.

Rivera's work in post-season play proves that he is quite capable of shouldering a heavier burden. Manager Joe Torre has not hesitated to bring him in early. In 27 of his 34 post-season saves (79.4%), Rivera has entered in the eighth inning. A dozen times (35.3%), he has worked two full innings for a save. Throw in a career ERA of 0.81 in the post-season, and it's no wonder that he is considered a shoo-in for the Hall of Fame.

The change from multiple-inning to one-inning closers is seen most dramatically in the career of Lee Smith. From 1981 to 1990, he carried a load similar to the earlier trio. From 1991 through the end of his career, he was used much the same way that Hoffman has been. The statistical breakdown reflects the shifting trend. From 1981 to 1990, 44.2% of Smith's saves lasted one inning or less, a little more than Fingers & Co.; from 1991 on, that figure is a whopping 90.1%. His saves of 2+ innings went from 34% all the way down to 1.9%. Smith recorded his top four seasonal totals for saves after 1990, thanks to his managers lightening his work-

load as he grew older.

The biggest difference between the "old-style" firemen and the current crop of closers is the number of times they enter the game to start the ninth (or extra) inning, with no runners on base, the easiest situation for a reliever to face even with just a one-run lead. Figures supplied by Tom Ruane of Retrosheet indicate that if the home team starts the ninth inning with a one-run lead, it will win roughly 85% of the time. Put the leadoff runner on first, and the percentage drops to 75%, the same likelihood as having runners on first and second with nobody out and a two-run lead, or the bases loaded and nobody out with a three-run lead. Start the ninth inning with a two-run lead, and you'll win about 93% of the time; with a three-run lead, it jumps to a 97% win rate. Current managers love to put in their big-time closer with that three-run lead in the ninth inning because victory is a near-sure thing, but it would be a near-sure thing no matter who pitched the final inning.

Trevor Hoffman has been used in this situation 124 times in his career, compared to 11 for Fingers, 14 for Gossage, and 16 for Sutter. When Fingers recorded three outs for a save, he started the ninth inning only 65.4% of the time; Gossage got to start the ninth in 72.9% of his three-out saves. That is, about a third of the time they got the call only when the previous pitchers put runners on base. In 1975, Gossage pitched in 62 games and only twice entered without runners on base. By contrast, Hoffman faced only one inherited runner the entire 2006 season (recording the easiest save imaginable, retiring one batter with a runner on first base and a three-run lead).

Table 3. Performance When Entering to Start the Ninth Inning

	One-Run SV/BS	Two-Run SV/BS	Three-Run SV/BS
Fingers	25/12	17/2	11/0
Gossage	21/6	17/2	13/1
Sutter	28/10	22/4	16/0
L. Smith	96/30	87/9	61/0
Eckersley	78/22	78/8	65/1
Hoffman	139/26	121/9	117/7
Rivera	94/20	102/3	94/2
TOTALS	481/126	444/37	377/11

Table 3 breaks down the performance according to the size of the lead. As a group, the seven relievers have gotten the save 97.2% of the time with a three-run lead and 92.3% of the time with a two-run lead, very close to Tom Ruane's figures. The most striking thing is the high percentage of the time that the modern closers start the ninth inning, especially with more than a one-run lead.

Fingers and Gossage enjoyed this relatively care-free entrance in only one-sixth of their saves. It happened a little more often for Sutter, but still only 22% of the time. For Smith, it was 27.2% in the first part of his career, but 78.9% in the second part. Hoffman has had it very easy by this standard, with more than three-fourths of his career saves (78.2%).

Dan Quisenberry, the unjustly overlooked relief ace of the 1980s Kansas City Royals, advocated measuring saves by "degree of difficulty." I have attempted to do just that in my studies, examining the various "save situations" in which a reliever enters the game. First, I looked at the most difficult jam, with not only the tying run(s) on base but the (potential) winning run as well.

Table 4. Performance When Entering with the Winning Run on Base

	WROB	SV	BS
Fingers	50	24	25
Gossage	45	22	21
Sutter	26	11	15
L. Smith	27	14	13
Eckersley	15	7	8
Hoffman	17	11	5
Rivera	10	3	7
TOTALS	190	92	94

The finding that jumps off Table 4 is that even the best relievers blow the save in this situation more often than not. Hoffman has done the best and Rivera the worst, though the more significant point is that their opportunities are so few compared to Fingers and the earlier relievers. Give Rivera as many appearances as Fingers with the winning run on base and, using his "success" rate, we'd be adding 28 blown saves to his career total. Conversely, putting Fingers in that spot as seldom as Rivera has faced it would lop off 20 blown saves from his total. This doesn't even take into consideration what inning it is or how many outs there are.

The folks at Rolaids, who hand out the annual award for relief pitching, have tallied "tough" saves since 2000, defined as having the tying run on base when the reliever enters. In the past seven seasons, Rivera has more "tough" saves than any other reliever, 20, which happens to be only one more than John Hiller had just in 1973. The saves in Table 4 are "tough" by this definition. Here's the data from entries with the tying run(s) on base but not the go-ahead run.

Table 5. Performance When Entering with Tying Run(s) On Base

	TROB	SV	BS
Fingers	118	77	35
Gossage	102	59	36
Sutter	80	47	31
L. Smith	59	37	20
Eckersley	42	28	11
Hoffman	36	25	8
Rivera	41	26	13
TOTALS	478	299	154

As in the previous table, Fingers has as many of these dangerous outings as Rivera, Hoffman, and Eckersley put together. As a group, these seven stalwarts recorded the save less than twice as often as they blew it, a measure of the difficulty of handling inherited runners. Taking these two tables together, the career "tough" saves add up to: Fingers 101, Gossage 81, Sutter 58, Smith 51, Eckersley 35, Hoffman 36, and Rivera 29. For Fingers and Gossage, more than half of their career blown saves came in these spots, and in nearly half of those blown saves, they entered the game in the sixth or seventh inning. For Rivera and Hoffman, most of their blown "tough" saves come in the eighth inning, virtually the only time they enter with inherited runners.

Table 6. Performance When Entering With Tying Run at Bat

	TRAB	SV	BS
Fingers	175	126	37
Gossage	174	116	42
Sutter	161	117	41
L. Smith	259	189	54
Eckersley	168	128	37
Hoffman	188	158	27
Rivera	164	129	26
TOTALS	1289	963	264

This data is, on the surface, more comparable, since all seven relievers faced this situation roughly the same percentage of the time, 36–39% of their save opportunities for the earlier guys and 32–35% for the later group, with Lee Smith at 42%. The career figures for Fingers and Eckersley are almost identical, as are those for Sutter and Gossage. Hoffman and Rivera have significantly higher ratios of saves to blown saves when facing the tying run at the plate, but a breakdown of the situations reveals why. For Fingers, Gossage, and Sutter, more than two-thirds of their blown saves came when they entered no later than the eighth inning, meaning they not only had to get out of their first jam, they also pitched multiple innings and therefore had extra chances to blow the lead. Of Hoffman's 27 blown saves in this category, only one came when he entered before the ninth inning; similarly, for Rivera it was only five out of 26. For them, this situation usually occurs when they enter to start the ninth inning with a one-run lead.

Add up the evidence and it's clear that all saves are not created equal. Some save "opportunities" are gift-wrapped while others are booby-trapped. A whopping 59.8% of Hoffman's career saves have come when he entered the game with no more peril than having the tying run in the on-deck circle. It's even higher for Rivera at 61.7%. The percentage goes down as we look further back: Eckersley 58.2%, Smith 49.8%, Sutter 41.7%, Gossage 36.5%, and Fingers 33.4%. Compare the stats of the seven studs for these "easy saves" compared to the "tough saves" in which the tying run is on base.

Table 7. Tough Saves vs. Easy Saves

	Tough SV/BS	Tough Ratio	Easy SV/BS	Easy Ratio
Fingers	101/60	1.68	114/13	8.8
Gossage	81/57	1.42	113/13	8.7
Sutter	58/46	1.26	125/14	8.9
L. Smith	51/33	1.55	238/16	14.9
Eckersley	35/19	1.84	227/15	15.1
Hoffman	36/13	2.77	288/16	18.0
Rivera	29/20	1.45	255/9	28.3
TOTALS	391/248	1.58	1360/96	14.2

Fingers, with almost as many tough saves as easy saves, had a better success rate in those dangerous situations than Rivera, the most revered of current closers. Gossage's success rate was virtually the same. Why is Hoffman's ratio of tough saves to blown tough saves so much higher? Of the 102 career saves he has recorded in which he inherited runners, 65 came when he entered with two outs, and 26 of those were in the ninth inning. Only two of Hoffman's 482 saves saw him enter before the eighth inning, compared to 75 for Fingers.

This perspective suggests the difficulty of devising a unifying formula to evaluate all save performances in their situational context. Such a formula must take into account the immediate danger when the pitcher enters, where the runners are, how many outs, the size of the lead, how far he is from the end of the game, and run support. For instance, the fire is blazing when you enter in the seventh inning, but your team gives you a six-run cushion for the last two innings. How much easier is your save than the one where you have to nurse a one-run lead after the seventh inning, and how much tougher than facing the winning run when you enter in the ninth inning?

I believe it's possible to devise a formula which will satisfy Dan Quisenberry's wish for a "degree of difficulty" for saves, and which can be calculated by any fan watching the game. Until that time, Table 8 contains a final look at how our seven elites measure up in the separate parameters when entering the game.

# # #

GABRIEL SCHECHTER *has been a research associate at the National Baseball Hall of Fame's library since 2002, and is the author of three baseball books.*

Table 8. Performance In Game-entering Parameters

	Fingers	Gossage	Sutter	L.Smith	Eckersley	Hoffman	Rivera	TOTALS
1-run lead	117-77	116-69	97-71	162-76	120-43	167-34	127-37	906-407
2-run lead	114-23	101-34	103-23	169-20	130-21	136-15	132-13	885-149
3-run lead	80-6	67-7	84-6	120-7	109-5	141-7	120-2	721-40
4+-run lead	30-4	26-2	16-1	27-0	31-2	38-0	34-3	202-12
0 runners	138-38	128-38	152-45	320-64	265-43	380-43	314-28	1697-299
1 runner	88-28	96-35	79-28	83-19	68-12	31-3	46-13	491-138
2 runners	104-39	69-29	59-27	67-17	48-12	59-8	43-12	449-144
3 runners	11-5	17-10	10-1	8-3	9-4	12-2	10-2	77-27
0 outs	171-59	160-58	180-61	347-74	257-42	394-47	309-34	1818-374
1 out	79-27	73-40	56-24	53-14	62-16	22-4	38-10	383-135
2 outs	91-24	77-14	64-16	78-15	71-13	66-6	66-11	513-99
6th or 7th	75-50	52-36	46-22	15-12	5-4	2-2	1-3	196-129
8th	125-27	129-37	142-56	153-48	101-30	53-10	87-23	790-231
9th	141-33	129-39	112-23	310-43	284-37	427-44	325-29	1728-248

ALAN I. ABRAMOWITZ

Does Money Buy Success?

The Relationship Between Payrolls and Victories
in Major League Baseball, 1996–2005

Unlike every other major professional sport in the United States, Major League Baseball has no cap on team payrolls. As a result, there are vast disparities in the size of these payrolls. Teams from large markets with lucrative local television and radio contracts can vastly outspend teams from small markets that lack such contracts. In the 2005 season, team payrolls ranged from 29.7 million dollars for the Tampa Bay Devil Rays to 208.3 million dollars for the New York Yankees. And the gap between baseball's haves and have-nots has been growing. Between 1996 and 2005, the difference between baseball's largest payroll and smallest payroll increased from 36.8 million dollars to 178.6 million dollars.

Teams with larger payrolls should enjoy a substantial competitive advantage over teams with smaller payrolls. And this appears to be the case. In 2005, for example, the seven teams with payrolls larger than 90 million dollars won an average of 55.6% of their games while the seven teams with payrolls smaller than 50 million dollars won an average of only 45.1% of their games.

Still, there are many exceptions to the rule that a larger payroll means greater success on the playing field. In 2005, the San Francisco Giants with a payroll of 90.2 million dollars won only 46.3% of their games while the Cleveland Indians with a payroll of only 41.5 million dollars won 57.4% of their games. And such anomalies are not rare. In recent years teams with very modest payrolls, like the Minnesota Twins and the Oakland A's, have enjoyed considerable success while teams with much larger payrolls, like the New York Mets and Texas Rangers, have performed poorly.

So overall, how much difference does money make in team success? To answer this question, I calculated the correlations between team payrolls and won-lost percentages for the last 10 baseball seasons. The results are displayed in Table 1. A correlation coefficient measures the strength of the relationship between two variables. It can range from zero (no relationship) to one (a perfect relationship). The squared correlation coefficient measures the proportion of variation in one variable that is explained by the other variable.

The results in Table 1 show that the strength of the relationship between team payrolls and won-lost percentages varied considerably over these ten years. In some years the relationship was fairly strong while in other years it was quite weak. On average, however, the relationship between team payrolls and won-lost percentages was fairly mod-est—spending explained an average of only 26.3% of the variation in success on the playing field over these 10 seasons.

Despite the growing disparity in the size of team payrolls between 1996 and 2005, there is no evidence here that the impact of spending increased over time. In fact, the average correlation between team payrolls and won-lost percentages was somewhat larger during the first half of this time period than during the second half: the proportion of variation in team success explained by spending declined from an average of 32.5% between 1996 and 2000 to an average of only 20.1% between 2001 and 2005.

These correlations actually overstate the influence of spending on won-lost records. That is because the correlation between spending and

Table 1. Correlations Between Won–Lost Percentage and Payroll, 1996–2005

Year	Proportion of Correlation Coefficient	Variance Explained
1996	.582	.339
1997	.470	.221
1998	.684	.468
1999	.704	.496
2000	.321	.103
2001	.320	.102
2002	.444	.197
2003	.418	.175
2004	.538	.289
2005	.494	.244
10-Year Avg.	.499	.263
1996-2000 Avg.	.552	.325
2001-2005 Avg.	.443	.201

Note: Correlation coefficient is Pearson's r. Payroll data from *USA Today*. Won-lost percentages from Major League Baseball.

success reflects the influence of success on spending as well as the influence of spending on success. Teams that enjoy success on the playing field tend to increase their payrolls the next season because of increased revenues and increased salary demands from players. To control for the influence of success on payrolls, I calculated partial correlations between team payrolls and won-lost percentages while controlling for the previous season's won-lost percentages. As expected, these partial correlations were considerably smaller than the original correlation coefficients. They ranged from -.038 to .603. The average partial correlation between payroll and won-lost percentage, controlling for last season's won-lost percentage, was a very modest .203.

The general conclusion that can be drawn from these data is that team payrolls have only a limited influence on what happens on the playing field. Further evidence for this proposition can be seen by comparing actual team performance with what would be expected based solely on the size of team payrolls. Along these lines, Table 2 displays the difference between actual and expected wins per season for every major league team between 1996 and 2005.

The results in Table 2 show that over these 10 seasons, some teams consistently exceeded what would be expected based on their payrolls while other teams consistently fell short of what would be expected. The most successful teams in baseball during this period were the Oakland A's and Atlanta Braves. The A's won an average of 12.6 more games than expected per season based on their payroll while the Braves won an average of 10.3 more games than expected per season. At the other end of the spectrum, the least successful teams in baseball during this period were the Detroit Tigers and Tampa Bay Devil Rays. The Tigers won an average of 11.3 fewer games than expected per season based on their payroll while the Devil Rays won an average of 10.0 fewer games than expected per season.

These results demonstrate that while money matters in baseball, it matters considerably less than many people assume. A team's success on the playing field depends as much on leadership, organization, and baseball knowledge as it does on the size of its payroll.

#

ALAN I. ABRAMOWITZ *is an Alben W. Barkley Professor of Political Science at Emory University.*

Table 2. Difference Between Actual and Expected Wins per Season, 1996–2005

Team	Difference
Oakland A's	+ 12.6
Atlanta Braves	+ 10.3
Houston Astros	+ 7.4
San Francisco Giants	+ 6.3
St. Louis Cardinals	+ 5.8
Chicago White Sox	+ 4.9
Minnesota Twins	+ 4.4
New York Yankees	+ 3.3
Cleveland Indians	+ 3.0
Seattle Mariners	+ 2.2
Los Angeles Angels	+ 1.9
Boston Red Sox	+ 1.7
Washington Nationals	+ 1.6
Florida Marlins	+ 1.6
San Diego Padres	+ 0.6
Cincinnati Reds	- 0.8
Los Angeles Dodgers	- 1.0
Toronto Blue Jays	- 1.0
Arizona Diamondbacks	- 1.8
Philadelphia Phillies	- 2.0
Pittsburgh Pirates	- 2.1
Milwaukee Brewers	- 3.8
New York Mets	- 4.0
Chicago Cubs	- 5.1
Texas Rangers	- 5.2
Colorado Rockies	- 6.2
Kansas City Royals	- 7.0
Baltimore Orioles	- 8.3
Tampa Bay Devil Rays	- 10.0
Detroit Tigers	- 11.3

GARY GILLETTE & PETE PALMER

Interleague Attendance Boost Mostly a Mirage

Over the past 10 years, interleague play has become one of the rites of summer for baseball fans. Interleague play arrives with a lot of fanfare, as so-called "natural rivals" square off while new teams from the other league come to town for the first or second time, theoretically creating a set of unusual and attractive matchups that get the fans excited and boost attendance.

Interleague play is also typically one of the accomplishments cited as part of MLB's PR campaign to persuade people that the sport has come all the way back from the devastating strike of the mid-1990s. Along with the Division Series and the wild card, interleague play is given credit by many pundits for reviving interest in the national pastime and pumping up attendance.

Without detailed information from a marketing survey, it's impossible to quantify just how much extra interest interleague play generates among fans. Regardless, it certainly generates a spate of predictable stories each summer in the media, many of them focused on how much interleague play boosts attendance. Most of these stories are fueled by the annual press releases from MLB touting the increased attendance in interleague games as compared to intraleague games.

The Pitch

A July 3, 2006, press release published on MLB.com boasted that the 252 interleague games in 2006 set records for total fans (8,592,482) as well as average attendance (34,097). It added that interleague play had boosted attendance 13.2% from 1997 to 2006. On the surface, that seems an impressive endorsement of what was viewed as a radical policy back in the 1990s.

These numbers are very misleading, however, mostly because they fail to account for two scheduling factors that pump up interleague attendance and make interleague/intraleague comparison artificially positive. A closer look at this sunny spin on interleague play tells a different story.

Interleague Attendance Analysis

From 1997 through 2006, there have been 2,439 interleague games with an average attendance of 32,838, compared to 20,368 intraleague games with an average attendance of 29,099. On the surface, that would show an apparent increase of 13.2% in attendance for interleague games.

Except in the first year of interleague play in 1997, when some games were played in August and September, about 80% of all interleague games have been played in June, with most of the rest being played in July. Because of that favorable treatment, interleague play starts with a built-in attendance advantage: they aren't played in the cold weather months and are mostly played after school gets out for the summer.

Taking into account the time of the season when interleague games were played (i.e., normalizing by the day of the year), the weighted average of intraleague attendance becomes 29,763, reducing the apparent attendance increase to only 10%. (The weighted average is calculated by taking the intraleague average for days of interleague play multiplied by the number of interleague games on that date.)

That's not the only important advantage the schedulers bestow on interleague games, however. Previous analyses of the positive effect interleague play has on attendance have ignored the fact that more than 61% of interleague games have been played on the weekend, compared to only 46% of intraleague games. Scheduling the bulk of interleague games on weekends provides a hidden favoritism and represents an overlooked factor that dramatically changes any attendance assessment.

Taking into account the effects of the days of the week when interleague games have been played, the average of intraleague games on those days is 29,910, making the apparent attendance increase for interleague play also about 10%. When both special factors are considered, we add 664 to the average intraleague attendance to compensate for the day of the year and a further 811 to compensate for day of the week. These adjustments raise the weighted intraleague average to 30,574, which reduces the overall attendance gain for interleague play to only seven percent.

As one might expect, most of the interleague attendance gain was in 1997, its first year, where the apparent (i.e., unadjusted) attendance increase was 33,421/27,727 or 21%. The apparent increase for subsequent seasons (1998–2006) was much smaller: 32,783/29,249 or 12%. *The true gain provided by interleague play, then, is reduced to only five percent after the first year* (the 32,782 interleague average divided by the 29,248 intraleague average plus adjustments of 970 for days of the month and 904 for days of the week).

Figures Sometimes Lie

All "attendance" figures announced by Major League Baseball and its 30 clubs are actually the number of tickets sold, not the number of people *at the game* or even the number of people *at the game* who paid to get into the park. Because MLB no longer announces what used to be called "the turnstile count," it's easy to jigger these modern "attendance" figures. Moreover, both individual clubs as well as MLB itself can engage in various maneuvers to pad reported attendance.

One typical way that MLB has spun its attendance numbers in the past few years is by publicizing total attendance instead of per-game attendance. Since baseball expanded by adding four teams in the 1990s, thus adding more than 15% to the number of games played in the past 13 years, these "all-time" records really aren't that impressive. MLB *should* be setting records for total attendance because it has more teams than ever before. MLB reported per-game attendance of 31,423 in 2006, a tiny bit higher than 1993's 31,337 and second only to the strike-shortened 1994 season's all-time peak of 31,612.

Another, more blatant attendance-padding fiction was engaged in by Florida in 2002. Apparently in order to avoid the embarrassment of having new owner Jeffrey Loria's Marlins draw fewer fans than his former club—the forlorn, MLB-owned Expos—someone supposedly bought more than 10,000 tickets to the last Florida home game in late September. The club acknowledged the bulk purchase but refused to provide any information about who bought the ducats or why.

A September 30, 2002, story by respected veteran Associated Press sports business reporter Ron Blum, reported:

> Florida drew 813,118, an average of 10,038. On Sunday the Marlins announced a crowd of 28,599—its second largest at home this year—but only about 8,000 fans appeared to be in the ballpark.

Marlins president David Samson said a long-time fan of the team who lives in south Florida bought more than 15,000 tickets that went unused—which enabled the Marlins to surpass the Expos. Samson said the fan wasn't affiliated with the organization but declined to identify him.

On a much bigger scale, MLB organized a "charitable" ticket donation in 2004 and 2005 called the "Commissioner's Initiative for Kids." This program distributed one million tickets each season to Boys & Girls Clubs and other charities *after* Ameriquest—one of MLB's official sponsors—paid one dollar each for those tickets. Because these "charitable" tickets were actually paid for, they were counted in the attendance totals.

How many of those tickets actually put a kid in a ballpark is unknown, but it's likely that many went unused given that the initiative wasn't even announced until August 9 in 2004 and until July 27 in 2005. No explanation was given for announcing the initiative about two months after school got out in most cities, especially in the second year of the program, when it could have been announced before the season started.

MLB did not announce any new Commissioner's Initiative for Kids for the 2006 season. With 2006 MLB attendance headed for another all-time high, perhaps the padding was deemed unnecessary. Or perhaps the lateness of the announcement each season meant the benefit was limited. Or maybe no one cared anymore about the short-lived "initiative" since it clearly wasn't designed with the primary goal of benefiting children.

Conclusions

Interleague play is only one of the recent innovations that have continued to change the face and the pace of the national pastime. Scheduling interleague play in large blocks only during the summer months interrupts the flow of the great baseball tradition that Jim Brosnan simply but eloquently dubbed *The Long Season* in his 1959 diary. In a similar way, the wild card has depleted the excitement of old-fashioned pennant races: the Detroit Tigers celebrated—complete with champagne sprays—clinching a post-season berth in 2006 a week before they *lost* the AL Central title to the Twins on the last day of play.

Both innovations have positive and negative effects. With the wild card, more teams appear to be in contention for a longer period of time, boosting attendance in cities where interest would suffer late in the season. That's a real and obvious gain. Yet the wild card also has its less visible costs. It has pretty much made the classic barnburner–kind of pennant race obsolete; after all, if both teams get to advance to the post-season, the pressure and excitement is greatly diminished. Bobby Thomson's home run surely would never have been dubbed the "Shot Heard 'Round the World" by New York's ink-stained wretches if there was a wild card berth in 1951.

In the same way, the extra layer of post-season series simultaneously creates a visible benefit along with a longer, subtler kind of corrosive effect. Clubs that haven't played in October for years are thrilled to see any kind of post-season action, but teams that perennially make the post-season quickly find that many fans eschew the Division Series, viewing it merely as an extension of the regular season or as a tune-up for the LCS and World Series. The thousands of empty seats seen at so many Division Series games—not to mention TV ratings in the low single digits—testify to the blasé attitude so many baseball fans display toward the first round of MLB's "playoffs."

Notwithstanding the measurable benefit, there are very real—if yet unmeasured—costs associated with interleague play that profoundly affect baseball's popularity and financial health. The dramatic drop in interest in the All-Star game appears to be directly related to interleague play, and the almost yearly setting of all-time lows seen in post-season TV ratings in the past five years—even as announced regular-season attendance was setting records—is also related.

Historically, one of baseball's core strengths compared to other sports was the attractiveness of its midsummer classic. With interleague play showcasing the stars of one league against the other league during the regular season, the All-Star game naturally loses much of its luster. Thus, the decline in ratings is part of the hidden but very real cost of interleague play.

The same is true of the World Series, where game one in 2006 garnered an unbelievably low 8.0 rating—meaning that less than one TV set in 12 was tuned to the first game of the fall classic. The five-game match between the Tigers and Cardinals—a Cinderella team versus an underdog team, both led by famous managers, both of whom had defied the odds—managed to garner only a record-low 10.1 rating and 17 share. Games three, four, and five of the World Series were not even ranked among Nielsen's top 10 most-watched prime-time programs for the week, drawing fewer viewers than NBC's *Sunday Night Football*, ABC's *Desperate Housewives* and *Dancing with the Stars*, and several different *CSI* series on CBS.

Now that interleague play has taken the bloom off the All-Star rose, baseball is faced with the Hobson's choice of cutting out interleague play or changing its traditional All-Star format. Since the former seems unlikely to happen in the near future, MLB has to figure out how to avoid having its midsummer classic become merely an afterthought to its home run-hitting contest, somewhat like the NBA's slam-and-jam all-star game, or an afterthought to the season like the NFL's Pro Bowl.

One factor that could not be measured with the available attendance data is the real possibility that fans who plan on attending a certain number of games per season might be more likely to choose an attractive or unique interleague matchup, thus reducing attendance at other games. The extent to which this happens is unknown, but whatever effect it has would create an incorrect appearance of a net gain when it is really just shifting attendance from intraleague games to interleague ones. And it would further reduce the real boost given by interleague play below the current five percent.

While it provides some tangible benefit, interleague play's effect on attendance is mostly a mirage. When one considers that interleague schedules are engineered to be as attractive as possible, more than half of the apparent attendance gain that MLB boasts melts away. When one considers the double scheduling of "natural rivals" and the rotation of divisions in interleague play, the average five percent advantage realized since 1998 is extremely modest.

# # #

NOTES

Per-game attendance figures quoted in this analysis are technically per-opening numbers. In baseball parlance, an opening is defined as a single game or a doubleheader with a single admission price. Day/night doubleheaders with separate admissions are considered the same as single games. Because of the fact that doubleheaders have rarely been played in the past decade, per-game and per-opening figures are virtually identical.

Unofficial attendance figures as reported in the media were used for this analysis. These attendance figures originate with MLB or with its clubs. There may be some small differences between those figures and the final, official figures released by MLB after the season ends, but they would be very minor.

GARY GILLETTE *and* PETE PALMER *are co-editors of both the* ESPN Baseball Encyclopedia, *now in its fourth edition, and the* ESPN Pro Football Encyclopedia, *the second edition of which will be published in 2007.*

Revisiting Bill Veeck and the 1943 Phillies

Few pieces published in a SABR journal have had a greater impact than "A Baseball Myth Exploded: The Truth About Bill Veeck and the '43 Phillies," the cover story in the 1998 edition of *The National Pastime*.[1] The article, authored by David Jordan, Larry Gerlach, and John Rossi, challenged legendary baseball executive Bill Veeck's claim that in 1943 he had attempted to buy the Philadelphia Phillies with plans to stock the team with Negro League stars, only to be thwarted by the machinations of Commissioner Kennesaw Mountain Landis and National League president Ford Frick. "The major difficulty with this oft-told story," read a quote on the cover of *The National Pastime*, "is that it is not true. Veeck did not have a deal to buy the Phillies. He did not work to stock any team with Negro League stars. No such deal was quashed by Landis or Frick."[2]

Veeck, the authors charged, had, at the very least misrepresented his actions, and more likely, lied to enhance his image as an integrationist. This contention, aggressively argued and persuasively supported by diligent research, became the new conventional wisdom. However, now the "major difficulty" is that recently uncovered evidence, while not definitively absolving Veeck, raises questions about the conclusions of the Jordan/Gerlach/Rossi article and lends greater credence to Veeck's original story.

The saga of Bill Veeck and the 1943 Phillies gained wide circulation with the publication of Veeck's celebrated autobiography, *Veeck As in Wreck*, in 1962. In a relatively brief two-page aside to his discussion of his 1946 signing of Larry Doby, Veeck revealed that during World War II he had approached beleaguered Phillies owner Gerry Nugent and made arrangements to purchase the club. Unbeknownst to Nugent, Veeck, working with Negro League booking agent Abe Saperstein and *Chicago Defender* sports editor Doc Young, planned to field a virtual Negro League all-star team that he believed would win the 1944 National League pennant. Veeck said that he had arranged financing with the Congress of Industrial Organizations (CIO), and when that fell through, he had Phillies Cigars as another potential backer lined up. But, added Veeck, "Out of a long respect for Judge Landis I felt he was entitled to prior notification of what I intended to do." Suddenly, the National League seized control of the Phillies, and Ford Frick sold the team to lumber magnate William Cox "for about half of what I was willing to pay." According to Veeck, he soon heard that "Frick was bragging all over the baseball world . . . about how he had stopped me from contaminating the league."[3]

Veeck's story adhered to the historical record in some respects but also contained key inaccuracies. The National League had indeed taken the Phillies from Nugent when he could not find an acceptable buyer and subsequently arranged a sale to Cox (who would be barred from baseball the following year for betting on his own team.) But Veeck's scenario had the date wrong, placing these events in 1944 rather than 1943, misnamed one of his co-conspirators, confusing *Chicago Defender* editor Fay Young, with A. S. "Doc" Young, whom he would know in Cleveland, and identifying among the Negro Leaguers he planned to sign Luke Easter, who would not make his debut until 1946.[4] There was also another reason to be skeptical of Veeck's claims. Veeck already possessed substantial credentials as a key figure in baseball's historic integration. In 1947 he had signed Larry Doby to become the first African American player in the American League, becoming only the second major league owner to add a black athlete to his squad, after Branch Rickey of the Brooklyn Dodgers. Now Veeck was saying that if not for the intervention of baseball officials, he, not Rickey, would have won the accolades lavished on baseball's "Great Emancipator."

Nonetheless Veeck's account, as Jordan et al write, had become "an article of historical faith, found in virtually every general history of black and white professional baseball as well as studies of racial integration."[5] Robert Peterson included it in *Only the Ball Was White*. Donn Rogosin and I, both of whom also interviewed Veeck on the subject, presented the story uncritically in our 1983 books, *Invisible Men* and *Baseball's Great Experiment*.[6] All of us took Veeck at his word; none of us sought to corroborate the tale.

The 1998 *National Pastime* article thus came as a bombshell. Indeed, the journal presented it as such. In addition to the splashy cover and provoca-

tive title, *The National Pastime* presented the revelations as its lead story and, in a periodical in which the typical article ran two to five pages, devoted 11 pages to its exposition. Editor Mark Alvarez in his preamble comments to the issue wrote, "Our lead article...definitively debunks a baseball myth created by Bill Veeck, one of the few owners who would probably get a favorable rating by SABR's membership."[7] The prominence of the three authors lent even more credibility to the exposé. David Jordan, the author of three biographies, including one of pitcher Hal Newhouser, is one of the foremost authorities on Philadelphia baseball history. John Rossi is a professor of history at LaSalle University in Philadelphia. Larry Gerlach, a professor of history at the University of Utah, had published the pioneering volume of oral histories, *The Men in Blue: Conversations With Umpires*, and more significantly, was the president of SABR at the time.[8]

Jordan, Gerlach, and Rossi noted that Veeck's account "has never been corroborated by anyone else...the source always turns out to be the two pages in the autobiography or an interview with Veeck himself."[9] Despite dogged digging in newspapers, document collections, and autobiographies they could uncover no evidence to support his tale. Abe Saperstein had never discussed Veeck's plan, nor had Fay Young. No Negro League player had ever mentioned being recruited by Saperstein, Young, or Veeck to play for the Phillies. Contemporary newspaper reports and an interview with Rudie Schaffer, Veeck's top assistant during these years, confirmed that Veeck had met with Phillies owner Gerry Nugent in October 1942. But according to Schaffer and other accounts, nothing had come of this meeting. No firm offer had been made or accepted. During the critical months leading up to the sale of the team in February 1943. Veeck's name never came up as a potential buyer.

The three scholars searched not only the mainstream press and *The Sporting News* for corroboration of Veeck's claims, but the African American weeklies as well. The *Philadelphia Tribune* never picked up on the story. Fay Young's *Chicago Defender*, which supposedly had an inside track, never mentioned Veeck's plan; nor did any of the other major African American periodicals. "The silence of the black press," concluded Jordan et al, "is deafening."[10] *The Communist Daily Worker* had addressed the sale of the Phillies and even advised the new owner to "look for first rate players...among those Negro League players who have never been given a major league chance." But the *Worker* never mentioned Veeck's name in connection with this story.[11] With regard to CIO involvement, the authors note, "a bankrupt baseball team seems an odd investment for the CIO to make during the war." Research into the CIO archives uncovered "no mention of Bill Veeck or the possible financing of his purchase of the Phillies."[12]

Jordan et al also searched the black and white press at key moments of Veeck's career when the story might have surfaced. Veeck purchased the Cleveland Indians in 1946, the year when Jackie Robinson debuted in Montreal and speculation existed about which other teams might follow the Brooklyn Dodger lead. The only mention of Veeck's attempt to buy the Phillies appeared in a column by Red Smith. Smith wrote, "Hardly anyone knows how close Veeck came to buying the Phillies when the National League was forcing Gerry Nugent to sell. He had the financial backing and the inside track, but at the last minute, he decided the risk was too great to take with his friend's money."[13] Smith had worked for the *Philadelphia Record* in 1942–43, but, as Jordan et al point out, this story likely came not from any firsthand knowledge, but from Veeck himself and the reason that the deal fell through offered here differs from later accounts. More significantly, neither Smith nor any newspaper in 1946, black or white, not even the *Chicago Defender* or *Cleveland Call and Post*, displayed an inkling of awareness of Veeck's plan to field a team of Negro Leaguers. Similarly, in 1947 when Veeck signed Doby, and 1948 when, amidst great publicity he recruited Satchel Paige, no one brought up the Phillies precedent.[14]

Moreover, the three authors found numerous inaccuracies, inconsistencies, and improbabilities in Veeck's version of events. Why would the cash-strapped Nugent have accepted an offer for his team that would have netted him half as much as the Veeck bid? Since Veeck owned the minor league Milwaukee franchise and Landis had no jurisdiction over the minors, why hadn't Veeck assigned the players he had recruited to play for the Brewers? How, if Frick had "bragged all over the baseball world" about his actions, had the story never leaked out? As Jordan et al observed, Veeck had "a singularly cavalier attitude toward the details of the story."[15] Interviews with Rogosin, Wendell Smith, Shirley Povich, and me differed in the names of the players involved, the sportswriter he had worked with, and the timing of his offer, sometimes placing it before Nugent had turned the team over to the National League and at others implying that he had dealt directly with Frick after the takeover.

Indeed, these inconsistencies led Jordan et al to conclude that Veeck's integration saga was an "ex post facto . . . latter-day construction,"[16] a tale concocted by Veeck in the early 1960s. Veeck, they argue, might have thought about buying the Phillies and might have been influenced by 1942 articles in the *People's Voice* and *The Sporting News*

that speculated about how successful an all-black team would be in the National League, but he had never seriously attempted to bring this scenario to fruition.[17]

The first published version of the story discovered by Jordan et al appeared in 1960. Veeck told a writer for *Ebony* magazine that he "wanted to buy the Philadelphia ballclub to put in an all-Negro team." Shortly before the publication of *Veeck As in Wreck*, *Pittsburgh Courier* sportswriter Wendell Smith, who had covered the integration beat since the 1930s, described Veeck's efforts to buy the Phillies, but his account came not from first-hand knowledge, but from a recent interview with Veeck. Jordan et al imply that Veeck's fabrication dated from this time. In commenting on the *Ebony* piece, they state, "Clearly the story was embellished and changed for the autobiography a couple of years later."[18] At another point they suggest that "this story may have resulted from Bill Veeck's ill health at the time he sat down with Ed Linn to

Above: Danny Litwhiler, the Phillies' best player in 1942.

Left: Bill Veeck

do his book." Fearing that he might soon die, "he probably felt this book was to be the last chance to poke the baseball powers in the eye, to steal some credit from Rickey, and to polish his own place in baseball history."[19]

The arguments presented in "A Baseball Myth Exploded" fell into two categories. As in the case of "Sherlock Holmes's nonbarking dog," their inability to discover any corroboration for Veeck's claims, they believed, spoke volumes about the validity of the story.[20] Furthermore, many of the elements of Veeck's tale lacked even a modicum of common sense. Jordan et al, using the strongest possible language, speculated on how people would have acted if confronted by various situations. It is, they assert, "*inconceivable* that Veeck's Phillies project would not have become a matter of public currency, at least within the world of Negro baseball." That the black press would not have reacted to Veeck's betrayal "with great vehemence" is "simply not believable." Nugent's acquiescence in Frick's chicanery "defies economic logic." [21] Thus, they concluded, "we must face the fact that Bill Veeck falsified the historical record."[22]

Given the revisionist nature of the article and its open attack on Veeck's character, "A Baseball Myth Debunked,' triggered surprisingly few challenges. Gerlach had sent me an earlier draft in June 1997 and requested a critique. In an e-mail response I raised several objections.[23] I pointed out that he, Jordan and Rossi, were trying to prove a negative, a virtually impossible task. Gerlach responded, "That is why we read so far and wide in every conceivable source. In the end we concluded that the absence of evidence is ipso facto negative; it would not be reasonable to conclude otherwise." I also argued that I found the press silence on this matter less unusual than they did and could think of other reasons why they might not have pursued this. I did not agree with the proposition that had Veeck been serious about integration in 1942, he could simply have added black players to the Brewers.

I also made two other criticisms. In the article Jordan et al had indicated that sportswriters had not commented on the Phillies revelation, indicating that they did not believe Veeck. I noted that the episode occupied on two pages in a 377-page book and that sportswriters had probably overlooked it, rather than rejected it. More pointedly, I wondered about Frick's response, or lack of one, to Veeck's charges. In 1962 Frick was the commissioner of baseball. Veeck had charged him with being a duplicitous racist. Yet Frick had never denied the tale. "Why did Frick allow this blot on his record to stand if it were not true?" I asked.

In the published version of the article, Jordan

et al addressed this point, noting that Veeck had taken many "potshots" at Frick in the book, but argued that since "the baseball press generally gave the volume short shrift . . . there was little pressure on Frick to respond to any of Veeck's charges." Frick had decided "that his best course would be to ignore Veeck's work altogether."[24] Indeed, when Frick published his own autobiography in 1973, he made no mention of Veeck at all.[25] The assertion that the press, baseball or otherwise, gave *Veeck As in Wreck* "short shrift" seemed odd. The book, after all, was a sensation. It was widely reviewed and within twelve days of publication had gone into four printings. It rose as high as ninth place among *New York Times* bestsellers and remained on the list at least eight weeks.[26] Nonetheless, while reviewers and other commentators remarked on his sending a midget to the plate and other promotional stunts and described his running battles with the baseball establishment, none had addressed the Phillies integration saga. Jordan et al were probably correct in their assessment of Frick's response.

Despite my reservations about particular arguments, I generally accepted the overall thrust of *The National Pastime* article. Not so Mike Gimbel. He was a SABR member who published annual player ratings manuals and had worked as a statistics analyst for the Montreal Expos and Boston Red Sox. He wrote to SABR executive director Morris Eckhouse, protesting the Veeck article.[27] "It is with great sadness and outrage that I must request that my name be removed from the membership list of SABR," wrote Gimbel. "Shame on SABR for printing this scurrilous article. Shame on SABR for putting it on the cover." Gimbel raised some of the same points I had: the negative nature of the evidence, the failure of Frick to rebut the charges, the popularity of Veeck's book. But in far more pungent prose he attacked the authors as "mean spirited" and protested the tone of the article. He criticized their overreliance on newspapers. "For Veeck to have gone to even a single reporter to tell anyone of his plans would have been suicidal of the time," wrote Gimbel, given the "absolute and total racism in the US, both North and South," at the time. He noted that the inconsistency in Veeck's retelling could be construed as a point in his favor. "If it were totally consistent then I would really be suspicious about the story," countered Gimbel. He had hoped that SABR would publish his response in a subsequent publication, but the organization failed to do so.[28]

Gimbel's angry missive notwithstanding, the article in *The National Pastime* convinced most SABR members and those in the baseball world who became aware of it that Veeck, a master storyteller often prone to exaggeration, had largely invented the tale of his attempt to integrate the 1943 Phillies. However, their considerable exertions notwithstanding, Jordan et al had not, indeed could not possibly have, examined all of the available newspapers that might have mentioned this scheme. They had, in effect, rounded up all of the usual suspects, looking for coverage at times it seemed most likely the story might be referenced. But in recent years researchers perusing the African American press have found earlier references to Veeck's plans that at least partially debunk the new myth that the 1998 exposé created.

In a footnote in his path breaking 2004 study, *Negro League Baseball: The Rise and Ruin of a Black Institution*, Neil Lanctot wrote, "there is scattered evidence to suggest [Veeck's] involvement with Saperstein and Fay Young." Lanctot references an article in the *Chicago Defender* on February 26, 1949, in which Young had described an address by Veeck to the Chicago Urban League. The Indians owner stated he had spoken with Young "for several hours about integrating Negroes in major league baseball. At that time I was planning to buy the Philadelphia Nationals." Lanctot also noted a 1954 report from the Associated Negro Press in which Abe Saperstein talked about the matter.[29]

In 2005, while thumbing through *Great Negro Baseball Stars,* a long out-of-print book written by A. S. "Doc" Young in 1953, I found a passage about Veeck when he bought the Indians in 1946: "Negro writers soon recognized Veeck as a person likely to give an ear to the proposition of Negroes playing in the American League. Perhaps they had heard the unsubstantiated story that Veeck once shocked baseball's late commissioner Kennesaw Mountain Landis, with a proposal to buy a major league club and transform it into an all-colored aggregation."[30]

These citations clearly disproved one of the basic Jordan/Gerlach/Rossi assertions—that Veeck's story was a "latter-day creation" that he had begun to tell widely only in the early 1960s. It also offered at least partial corroboration from three individuals whom the authors had deemed central to their 1998 exposé. Fay Young and Saperstein, Veeck's purported collaborators, had indeed both mentioned the plot. With regard to "Doc" Young, who as the sports editor of the *Cleveland Call and Post* had had extensive access to Veeck during the latter's years in Cleveland, Jordan et al had asserted, "Young's silence is significant."[31] But he too, like Fay Young and Saperstein, had not truly been silent on this matter.

Upon discovering the passage in *Great Negro Baseball Stars,* I sent a message to SABR-L, the dis-

cussion list for the Society of American Baseball Research.[32] I received several responses from people who had also found pre-1960 references to the Veeck-Phillies venture. Christopher Hauser fleshed out the Saperstein connection. He reported on the following item in the August 14, 1954 *Philadelphia Independent*:

> Abe Saperstein of the fabulous Harlem Globetrotters stated this week in a press interview that baseball magnate Bill Veeck had intended to use a baseball trick back in 1942 which would have upset the thinking in the major league, had it materialized. "I'll tell you one thing about Veeck," said Saperstein, "something that few people know. In 1942 the Phillies were for sale and Veeck attempted to buy them. But Bill Cox raised more money and got the club. Do you know what Veeck planned to do? He was going to take the Phils to spring training in Florida and then—on the day the season opened—dispose of the entire team. Meanwhile, with a team composed entirely of Negroes, who would have trained separately, he could have opened the National League season. I don't think there was a team in either league, back in 1943, that could have stopped the team he was going to assemble."[33]

Saperstein's account bore striking similarities to that offered by Veeck confidant Rudie Schaffer in *The National Pastime* article. Jordan et al had interviewed Schaffer, the only participant still alive when they were conducting research. Schaffer had told them that Veeck "even had the idea of holding two separate spring training camps, one as a blind, for the white players he was not going to use, the other for the blacks who would constitute his team when the season started."[34] Jordan et al had summarily dismissed this recollection in a footnote, exclaiming, "One wonders how eager Veeck's backers would have been to finance *two* training camps instead of the usual one!"[35]

Hauser had also uncovered a relatively detailed account of Veeck's plans in an article by Randy Dixon in the *Philadelphia Independent* on September 9, 1956. Dixon's rendition adhered closely to Veeck's later versions. Veeck and Saperstein had dreamt up the scheme and had proposed it to Landis, who referred them to Frick. Landis had expressed his displeasure to Frick, who "wouldn't talk business" with Veeck and sold the franchise to Cox. The article offered a longer list of proposed players, including Oscar Charleston and Cool Papa Bell, whose careers had more or less ended by 1943.[36] Another SABR-L participant, David Kaiser, produced a reference to a column by Shirley Povich on May 10,

1953.[37] Veeck told Povich the same story reported by Dixon: "Landis stopped me, I think. It was after Gerry Nugent had tossed in the towel with the Philadelphia Phillies and the franchise was back in the lap of the league. Abe Saperstein, an owner in the Negro National League, and I had plans." Frick refused to deal with Veeck. "I don't blame the other club owners," Veeck allowed. "We'd have walked away with the pennant."[38]

Taken together, these references loosen the underpinnings of some, though not all, of the Jordan/Gerlach/Rossi exposé. In all of these accounts the only voice telling the story remains Veeck's. Saperstein repeats the tale but never acknowledges his own role, does not indicate that this is a firsthand account, and fails to confirm the details of a meeting with Landis. Doc Young's knowledge of the rumors most likely came from Veeck. Fay Young reports Veeck's account that describes his role and does not contradict it. In this case the Holmesian dog does not bark in Veeck's favor. In particular, Young's role is reduced to several hours of consultation rather than active participation. Nonetheless, if Veeck's story was a "latter-day construction," he created it not in the early 1960s but sometime in the 1940s, shortly after the events purportedly took place. He told one variation to Red Smith no later than 1946. Three years later he described his plan in greater detail to the Chicago Urban League. Over the next decade he retold the story frequently. Certain elements varied—whether he made his offer to Cox or to Frick, the lineup of Negro League stars—but the basic framework of Veeck's contentions is remarkably consistent.

The overall assessment of Jordan et al—that Veeck's notion of buying the Phillies and fielding a team of Negro League stars never quite moved as far from the drawing board as Veeck claimed—may still be true. We still lack any solid evidence that confirms that Veeck had not only conceptualized this action, but made a firm offer to buy the Phillies and met a rebuff by Landis and Frick. But Jordan et al's blanket dismissal of Veeck's assertions and confident branding of Veeck as a liar no longer stand uncontested. In their *National Pastime* article they had correctly chastised earlier historians for accepting Veeck's narrative at face value and injected a dose of skepticism, replacing unwarranted certainty with healthy debate. Their own rush to judgment, however, offers yet another cautionary tale of relying on an absence of evidence and overreaching one's resources in drawing conclusions.

# # #

JULES TYGIEL *is a Professor of History at San Francisco State University. He is the author of* Baseball's Great Experiment: Jackie Robinson and His Legacy.

NOTES

1. David M. Jordan, Larry R. Gerlach, and John P. Rossi. "A Baseball Myth Exploded: The Truth About Bill Veeck and the '43 Phillies," *The National Pastime* (1998), 3–13.
2. *The National Pastime* (1998), cover.
3. Bill Veeck, with Ed Linn. *Veeck—As in Wreck* (New York: G.P. Putnam's Sons, 1962), 171–72.
4. Jordan et al also fault Veeck for including Monte Irvin on his list, since Irvin was in the military. However, Irvin had played in the Negro Leagues in 1942, and in the fall of 1942 Veeck might not have been aware that Irvin had entered the military.
5. Jordan et al, 3.
6. Robert W. Peterson. *Only the Ball Was White* (Englewood Cliffs, NJ: Prentice Hall, 1970); Donn Rogosin, *Invisible Men: Life in Baseball's Negro Leagues* (New York: Atheneum, 1983); Jules Tygiel, *Baseball's Great Experiment: Jackie Robinson and His Legacy* (New York: Oxford University Press, 1983). Jordan et al list 15 additional books that uncritically accepted Veeck's recollections.
7. *The National Pastime* (1998), 1.
8. David Jordan. *A Tiger in His Time: Hal Newhouser and the Burden of Wartime Ball* (Diamond Communications, 1991); Larry M. Gerlach, *The Men in Blue: Conversations With Umpires* (New York: Viking, 1980). In subsequent years Jordan has also written *The Athletics of Philadelphia: Connie Mack's White Elephants, 1901–1954*, (Jefferson, NC: McFarland, 1999) and *Occasional Glory: The History of the Philadelphia Phillies*, (Jefferson, NC: McFarland, 2003). Rossi is author of *A Whole New Game: Off the Field Changes in Baseball, 1946–1960*, (Jefferson, NC: McFarland, 1999); *The National Game: Baseball and American Culture* (New York: Ivan R. Dee, 2000); and *The 1964 Phillies: The Story of Baseball's Most Memorable Collapse* (Jefferson, NC: McFarland, 2005).
9. Jordan et al, 5.
10. Jordan et al, 6.
11. Jordan et al, 6.
12. Jordan et al, 9.
13. Jordan et al, 6.
14. Jordan et al, 7.
15. Jordan et al, 8–9.
16. Jordan et al, 8, 11.
17. Jordan et al, 9.
18. Jordan et al, 9.
19. Jordan et al, 11.
20. Jordan et al, 3.
21. Jordan et al, 6, 5. Italics added.
22. Jordan et al, 12.
23. The following references all come from an e-mail, Larry R. Gerlach to Jules Tygiel, July 9, 1997. I do not have a copy of the original critique I sent to Gerlach, but excerpts from that message were included in Gerlach's response.
24. Jordan et al, 9–10. In his e-mail to me Gerlach indicated that this issue had been addressed at greater length in a fuller version of the article that I had not seen.
25. Ford C. Frick. *Games, Asterisks, and People: Memoirs of a Lucky Fan* (New York, Crown, 1973).
26. See *New York Times Book Review*, August 5–September 16, 1962, and *New York Times*, August 1, 1962.
27. Mike Gimbel to Morris Eckhouse, July 11, 1998 (author copy). For a brief portrait of Gimbel, see Alan Schwarz, *The Numbers Game: Baseball's Lifelong Fascination With Statistics* (New York: St. Martin's Press, 2004).
28. E-mail Mike Gimbel to Jules Tygiel, March 19, 2005. Gimbel did later rejoin SABR.
29. Neil Lanctot. *Negro League Baseball: The Rise and Ruin of a Black Institution* (Philadelphia: University of Pennsylvania Press, 2004), 236–41.
30. A. S. "Doc" Young. *Great Negro Baseball Stars and How They Made the Major Leagues* (New York: A.S. Barnes, 1953), 52.
31. Jordan et al, 8.
32. E-mail Jules Tygiel to SABR-L, March 12, 2005.
33. E-mail Christopher Hauser to SABR-L, March 14, 2005.
34. Jordan et al, 11.
35. Jordan et al, 13–39.
36. E-mail Christopher Hauser to SABR-L, March 23, 2005.
37. E-mail David Kaiser to SABR-L, September 18, 2005.
38. *Washington Post*, May 10, 1953.

STEW THORNLEY

The Demise of the Reserve Clause

The Players' Path to Freedom

Amoment that marked a dramatic shift in the power structure between major league baseball players and owners occurred on December 23, 1975, when an arbitrator's decision brought an end to the primary effects of the reserve clause. Prior to the decision, the pendulum of power had been firmly with the owners. The players had made some gains, particularly with the formation of a viable union, but the owners were still in control. However, once the owners lost the ability to bind players to their teams indefinitely, which had been the result of the reserve clause for nearly 100 years, the pendulum swung greatly toward the players. The owners have spent the ensuing 30 years trying to reverse its direction.

The reserve clause bound a player to his team for as long as the team, not the player, desired. Even after the contract itself expired, a player remained tied to the team. He could be traded, sold, or released, but the player himself could not initiate any moves on his own.

The reserve clause had its origin at the end of the 1879 National League season and soon evolved into the form it would keep well into the second half of the 20th century.[1]

The reserve clause kept a player from choosing where to work for whatever reason, fiduciary or otherwise. And simple economics demonstrate how this inhibited the player's salary with regard to what he could have received in a free market.

A Definition

Although it was widely accepted that players had no freedom in determining their fates and destinations, it appears that few people from either side, players or owners, gave much thought to the mechanics of the reserve clause.

The clause was codified into the Uniform Player's Contract, eventually becoming Paragraph 10A of the document:

> On or before December 20 (or if a Sunday, then the next preceding business day) in the year of the last playing season covered by the contract, the Club may tender to the Player a contract for the term of that year by mailing the same to the Player at his address following his signature hereto, or if none be given, then at his last address of record with the Club. If prior to the March 1 next succeeding said December 20, the Player and the Club have not agreed upon the terms of such contract, then on or before 10 days after said March 1, the Club shall have the right by written notice to the Player at said address to renew this contract for the period of one year on the same terms, except that the amount payable to the Player shall be such as the Club shall fix in said notice; provided, however, that said amount, if fixed by a Major League Club, shall be an amount payable at a rate not less than 80 percent of the rate stipulated for the next preceding year and at a rate not less than 70 percent of the rate stipulated for the year immediately prior to the next preceding game.[2]

More than 200 words, much of it devoted to explanations of timing and salary-reduction limits, the clause has its essence in the 64 words bolded in the above paragraph. If a player and team could not come to terms, the team could unilaterally renew the player's contract for one year.

While teams had this option, it wasn't one they had to exercise. Just having the ability to unilaterally renew a contract meant they never had to. If a player didn't like the contract being offered, his only option, hardly a good one, was to hold out. Thus, for many years the reserve clause served its function as owners and players routinely accepted the effect of the clause without serious scrutiny as to how it worked.

Open to Interpretation

The reserve clause was an iron cable that bound a player to his team, or so everyone thought until the mid-1960s, when growing awareness of the clause's wording brought about a realization that it was actually a thin thread.

Although long considered unambiguous in its power, the reserve clause included a phrase that was open to interpretation. "To renew this contract for the period of one year" left hanging the question of what would happen after one year. Could a team renew the contract again (and again and again, into perpetuity, if necessary), or could it exercise the contract renewal only once?

The question was significant because if the answer was ruled to be the latter, it created not just a window but a wide-open door to free agency for a player. All he would have to do was report for duty without putting his signature to a contract, thereby forcing the team to unilaterally renew the contract for a year if it wanted to retain control of the player. After a year, if a team didn't have the ability to renew the contract again, the player would be a free agent.

If this was so simple, why weren't players doing it? Because it was still a question whether a team could renew a contract only one time. Through the 1960s, the arbitrator of this issue would be the commissioner of baseball, an employee of the owners who surely would not answer the question in this manner.

A Route to Free Agency

Meanwhile, Marvin Miller was envisioning a different approach. The 48-year-old Miller had experience as an economist in the United Steelworkers of America when he became the first full-time executive director of the Players Association in 1966. Miller said he discovered the potential in Paragraph 10A even before he officially took office. "I did a double take the first time I saw it," Miller said. "I couldn't believe the whole reserve system rested on this." Miller said he knew then that two elements were necessary for a challenge: a grievance system with an impartial arbitrator and a player who felt strongly enough about challenging Paragraph 10A to withstand the "brick bats" that would be thrown at him.[3]

The formula Miller had for challenging the reserve clause did not emerge right away. Although the players sought a revision of the reserve clause as well as an impartial arbitrator to supersede the commissioner and resolve disputes, they initially had to settle for simpler gains. However, in 1968 they did achieve a collective bargaining agreement (CBA, also known as the Basic Agreement), the first in professional baseball history, which included a procedure for handling grievances.[4]

Although the commissioner would act as the arbitrator of the grievances, Miller said it was still significant. "Nineteen-sixty-six and 1967 there was no grievance procedure—and no grievances," he explained. "First came the procedure, and then the players had to be taught about the procedure and that they had the right to grieve. The owners claimed that there was a procedure in the past, but they were unable to produce a record of a single grievance having ever been filed."[5]

Miller said the first grievance filed by the Players Association after the CBA was reached was on behalf of Curt Blefary, who had been fined by his team, the Baltimore Orioles, for taking part in an organized basketball league in the offseason. Although Commissioner William Eckert's ruling went against Blefary, Miller characterized it as a "great thing" since it outraged the players and helped to solidify them.[6]

The players demonstrated solidarity again, over the 1968–69 offseason, by collectively refusing to sign their individual contracts until negotiations over their pension fund were settled. It was new commissioner Bowie Kuhn who helped end the dispute just prior to the March 1969 opening of spring-training camps.[7]

The players had another cause that brought them together in 1969, when they backed Curt Flood's lawsuit against baseball, which challenged the sport's exemption from antitrust laws and in turn the reserve clause. Flood, an outfielder who decided to fight baseball after being traded from the St. Louis Cardinals to the Philadelphia Phillies in October 1969, ultimately lost his case; however, the battle produced additional solidarity among the players.[8]

The players stood together again in 1972 in another dispute over the pension, one that resulted in a strike that delayed the beginning of the regular season. (Within a year, the pension was incorporated into the CBA.) Charles Korr, in *The End of Baseball As We Knew It: The Players Union, 1960–1981*, called the 1972 strike one of the union's defining moments, writing that it "established the credibility of the union and showed the players that a solid union could prevail in a battle against the owners."[9]

Potential Challenges to the Reserve Clause

Barely noticed amid all this activity was that in the 1970 CBA negotiations the players got an impartial arbitrator to hear their grievances. (It was actually a three-member arbitration panel, which contained one representative from labor, one representative from management, and an impartial arbitrator agreed upon by both sides.) The commissioner would no longer decide all disputes, only those concerning the integrity of the game.[10]

The first piece was in place for the players. Next they would need someone to challenge the interpretation of Paragraph 10A.

Although Al Downing had had his contract unilaterally renewed by the New York Yankees during spring training in 1969, he had no thoughts of becoming the test case for the players. First, the commissioner would still adjudicate such questions; in addition, Downing had little leverage. Coming off an injury-plagued season that left him with little value on the open market, Downing was actually fearful of being cut loose by the Yankees, and he ended up signing a new contract before the regular season opened.

It wasn't until 1972 that anyone played into the regular season on a renewed contract. Catcher Ted Simmons had had a solid season in his first full year in the majors, playing for the St. Louis Cardinals in 1971. He rejected his club's contract offer the following spring. Rather than follow the usual, but internecine, path of holding out, Simmons wanted to get in shape and play while continuing to negotiate with the Cardinals. He reported to spring training, forcing the Cardinals to renew his contract.

"Simmons refused to be bluffed into signing a new unsatisfactory contract in order to be 'allowed' into uniform," said Marvin Miller. "The union advised [him] that once his contract was renewed, he was under contract and could not be barred from spring training or from the regular season, even if he refused to sign that contract."[11]

Miller also said he never made recommendations to the players, that the initiative had to come from them. He simply advised the players as to what their rights were.[12]

Although Simmons, as had been the case with Downing three years earlier, was only trying to negotiate a better deal for himself, some of the more astute sports columnists around the country were picking up on the potential significance of his situation.[13] What if he went the entire season without signing a new contract? Would he become a free agent?

The question never came before the arbitration panel as Simmons signed a new contract with St. Louis on July 24. The Cardinals said the signing—reportedly for two years at $35,000 per year—was made possible by the Federal Pay Board's decision to exempt athletes from wage controls then in effect.[14]

However, it's possible that the Cardinals might have also been feeling pressure to sign Simmons, lest he become the test case for the players. Simmons later said the Cardinals had "buckled under" and given him exactly what he had been requesting.[15] Simmons reportedly had considered challenging the renewal clause, possibly in the courts as opposed to through a grievance to baseball's arbitration panel, but he had been adamant

at the time that he would rather settle his contract situation with the Cardinals. "I don't think I ever seriously considered that," he said of a court challenge. "If I had gone to court and won, I don't think I could do anybody in the future in baseball that much good, if you know what I mean."[16]

The owners' fear of a test case might have benefited players who followed Simmons's lead and went into the 1973 season on renewed contracts. According to The Sporting News Official Baseball Guide 1974, seven players opened the 1973 season without having signed new contracts and were playing on renewed contracts: Stan Bahnsen, Rick Reichardt, and Mike Andrews of the Chicago White Sox; Jim Kaat of Minnesota; Dick Billings of Texas; Fritz Peterson of the New York Yankees; and Jerry Kenney of Cleveland.[17] (Kaat had actually signed a contract with the Twins the day before the regular season began.)[18]

Bahnsen, Billings, and Peterson signed new contracts with their teams during the 1973 season while Kenney, Reichardt, and Andrews were released from their teams. "The Chisox probably could have easily sold Reichardt and Andrews for the $20,000 waiver price but instead asked for and received waivers on both players for the purpose of giving them their unconditional releases, a process in which the Sox, in exchange, received $1 for each player," according to Jerome Holtzman in the "Review of 1973" in The Sporting News Official Baseball Guide 1974. "It was believed that the Sox chose this route essentially in fear of a subsequent grievance by the Players Association, which may be eager to test the validity of the renewal clause in a courtroom."[19]

In addition to the leverage individual players might have been getting because of the owners' fear of a challenge to the reserve clause, collectively the players were making gains as the owners were refusing to budge on modifying the reserve clause in collective bargaining.

In negotiations for a new CBA, to replace the one that expired at the end of 1972, the players sought a loosening of the shackles, reportedly in the form of a proposal for a player to become a free agent if not offered a certain salary, depending upon the player's length of service.

The new agreement contained no such provision. However, veteran players—those with more than 10 years in the same league and five years with the same team—would have the right to veto a trade. In addition, the owners agreed to salary arbitration for players with more than two straight years of service in the majors or three years of noncontinuous service. Although this wouldn't allow a player to choose the club he wanted to play for, it at least meant players could ensure that their salaries were in line with others of their caliber.[20] "Salary arbitration has been a major factor in eliminating gross inequities in the salary structures from club to club (and sometimes on the same club)," wrote Miller in his 1991 autobiography.[21]

These were significant gains for the players, particularly the salary arbitration, which remains today and continues to vex the owners. Not only that, the players kept the owners nervous regarding the interpretation of the reserve clause as two more, Sparky Lyle of the New York Yankees and Bobby Tolan of the San Diego Padres, started the 1974 season on renewed contracts. (One of the reasons for the decline of players going unsigned into the regular season in 1974 was because of salary arbitration, which started that year. Many players resolved their salary disputes in this manner rather than refusing to sign contracts.)

On the final day of the regular season, Lyle signed a two-year deal with the Yankees, one that covered the nearly completed season and the 1975 season, but Tolan finished the 1974 season on a renewed contract. On October 17, the Players Association filed two grievances. One was specifically on Tolan's behalf, requesting free agency for him; the other, more significant, requested clarification of the renewal clause, which could mean free agency for any player who played out his option in this manner.[22]

Tolan's case reached the arbitration panel, but on December 9 he signed a new contract with the Padres. He received the salary increase he had been seeking for 1974 along with another increase for his 1975 contract. The following month the Players Association dropped the grievances that had been filed on Tolan's behalf.[23]

If it was the intent of the owners to continue to postpone a test case, they were succeeding—in a sense. The question was how expensive was it becoming for them to do so. Would Tolan have received what he wanted if not for the fear by the owners that he could become a free agent—and take everyone else along with him? Were owners more likely to accede to the requests of players on renewed contracts? Marvin Miller contends that this was the case, that "players were picking up gradually that they had leverage by the threat of being a test case."[24]

Catfish Hunter Grabs the Headlines

As Tolan was signing his contract, another player was in the process of getting his freedom, and it was this case that dominated the news. Oakland A's pitcher Jim "Catfish" Hunter was claiming to be a free agent on the grounds that his owner, Charles Finley, had reneged on his contract by not making payments for deferred compensation as scheduled during the 1974 season. Hunter would be the biggest free agent ever to hit the market, coming off a season in which he had won 25 games and the Cy Young Award, if he was successful. And he was.

After deliberating two weeks, Peter Seitz, the impartial member of the arbitration panel, ruled in Hunter's favor in mid-December. The circus scene that developed later in the month—team representatives lining up at the office of Hunter's attorney in the small town of Ahoskie, North Carolina—was a story no media outlet could resist, particularly when Hunter finally signed a five-year deal with the New York Yankees worth more than $3 million, a then unheard-of amount (although reportedly not the highest offered).

While the story was surely an attention grabber, Hunter became a free agent in a way that set no precedent for any other player (except, of course, for anyone fortunate enough to play for an owner foolish enough to be as remiss as Finley). Mostly ignored in this frenzy was what could have happened had Tolan been granted his free agency, which would have opened the door to everyone else. So little attention was paid to Tolan's signing that it was mentioned in a one-paragraph item a "Sports News Briefs" section of the *New York Times*.[25]

Still, the Hunter case was significant in that it provided an indication of how restrained player salaries were because of the reserve clause. The owners used the situation as an example of how salaries would escalate out of control with rich teams (such as the Yankees) snapping up the biggest stars if others were allowed to sell their talents in an open market. Emil "Buzzie" Bavasi, president of the San Diego Padres, reported to have been one of the highest bidders for Hunter, said, "What we saw happen here fully demonstrates the importance of the reserve clause. This manifests why we can't afford to change the reserve rule. The richest clubs would offer the top players the biggest salaries and the biggest bonuses."

Marvin Miller countered by saying, "The Hunter case established zero about what would happen in a free market. Here we had a supply of one and a demand of 24 [clubs in the major leagues at that time]. Obviously, when the supply is one and the demand is great, prices will go up dramatically."[26]

Privately, however, Miller made sure the players realized how much free agency could be worth to them. The Hunter experience, he contended, displayed "concrete evidence" of how much salaries were held down by the lack of freedom players had. He added that freedom, not just money, was a significant issue to the players, although the media never touched on this, focusing only on the money issue. Beyond the dollars, players wanted the opportunity to choose where to play; for some players the motivation was to get to a team that was thin in talent at their position, thereby providing a greater opportunity for playing time. In Hunter's case, getting out of Finley's clutches was more important than the money. "There were many valuable things in freedom that had nothing to do with money—but money was there, too."[27]

The Hunter case increased Miller's hopes that some freedom could be gained through collective bargaining (which would take place in the next year as the Basic Agreement was expiring at the end of 1975). Before the Hunter decision, Miller said he would never have recommended a strike as a means of challenging the reserve clause. After the Hunter decision, a strike became a viable strategy should they need it.[28]

The Final Beginning of the End

Beyond negotiations, the opportunity to end the reserve clause through a grievance remained. The 1975 season began with three players on renewed contracts, Andy Messersmith of the Los Angeles Dodgers, Richie Zisk of the Pittsburgh Pirates, and Dave McNally of the Montreal Expos. Zisk played through the regular season on the renewed contract but signed a new contract before the playoffs began that fall.[29]

That left Messersmith and McNally as the potential challengers to Paragraph 10A. Messersmith wanted a no-trade clause in his contract, a provision the Dodgers were reluctant to agree to. It's possible that they would have given in, however, if not for the presence of McNally.

McNally was significant because he had retired during the season. Following an outstanding pitching career with the Baltimore Orioles (in which he had four consecutive seasons with at least 20 wins), McNally had been traded to Montreal after the 1974 season. However, after a good start with the Expos, he struggled and, after losing six straight games, retired in June 1975, and eventually returned to his hometown of Billings, Montana, where he operated a car dealership with his brother.

Even though he was no longer pitching, McNally, because he had begun the season on a renewed contract, would be eligible to claim free agency after one year. While it wouldn't benefit him, it would mean much to the current and future players. Since he was retired, there wasn't any way he could be tempted to sign a new contract. Or was there?

Marvin Miller says McNally called him in November to report that Expos president John McHale had come to Billings and tried to get him to sign a contract. The reported offer was for $125,000 for the 1976 season along with a $25,000 signing bonus, which McNally could keep even if he didn't pitch again.

However, McHale says his trip to Billings occurred soon after McNally left the Expos, and he was trying to persuade the pitcher to return to the team immediately. McHale said he was trying to salvage something from the trade with Baltimore to take the pressure off Expos general manager Jim Fanning, who was on the hot seat as a result of the trade. (The other major league player the Expos got in the deal was Richie Coggins, who barely played for Montreal because of a thyroid infection. In June, at about the same time McNally retired, the Expos put Coggins on waivers. Meanwhile, the players the Expos gave up in the deal, Ken Singleton and Mike Torrez, were having good seasons for the Orioles.)

McHale denies offering McNally a bonus that could be kept even if he didn't pitch again but says he "may have offered him [McNally] more money to come back."

McHale's offer was viewed by some as a sham, nothing more than a bribe to remove McNally from the test case. If McNally signed a new contract with Montreal, the Dodgers could then renew their efforts to sign Messersmith, removing the final possibility for a challenge in 1975. McHale maintains that wasn't the case. "I had never even given a thought that it had anything to do with the player relations problem. That was not the motivating factor for me to go to Billings. . . . I was pulling out all the stops [to get McNally to return to the Expos]. I couldn't have been more serious about wanting him to come back."[30]

Regardless of McHale's intent, McNally did not sign a new contract. With a grievance now assured because of McNally, it meant that the long-awaited challenge to the reserve clause would finally happen. As a result, the Dodgers didn't bother to try and sign Messersmith. They had to resign themselves to having his, and others', fate in the hands of the arbitration panel.

The Players Association filed grievances on behalf of Messersmith and then McNally in early October.

The Decision

At the heart of the Players Association's case before the arbitration panel was the argument that the word "one," when used in Paragraph 10A, meant a single year rather than a rolling number of one-year renewals stretching into perpetuity. The owners' argument was that they had the right to renew the entirety of the contract, including the right to renew the renewal provision.

The hearing was held in the latter part of November and early December of 1975. Miller and owners' representative John Gaherin quickly ruled in favor of their respective employers.

Just before Christmas, reports came out that Peter Seitz, the impartial arbitrator, would rule for the players. Even so, Miller said he felt great trepidation when the decision was released on December 23. He immediately turned to the final page of the document containing the decision, then sighed with relief as he saw what Seitz had ruled, that Messersmith and McNally were free agents.[31]

McNally stayed retired, and Messersmith, free to deal with anyone, eventually chose the Atlanta Braves as his next employer, but the significance of the decision went well beyond either player. The door to free agency was open. A player could refuse to sign a new contract, forcing his team to unilaterally renew his contract for one year. After that year, since the team could not renew it again—the crux of the issue decided by Seitz—the player would then be a free agent.

While Seitz's decision resulted in freedom for the players, he made clear that it wasn't his job to decide on the merits of the reserve clause. He maintained that the issue before the arbitration panel was not "to determine what, if anything, is good or bad about the reserve system. The panel's sole duty is to interpret and apply the agreements and understanding of the parties."[32] In other words, the demise of the reserve clause was not created by Seitz but by the wording of the contract itself.

Nevertheless, Dick Young of the *New York Daily News*, in his column entitled "Young Ideas" (considered a misnomer by many), blasted Seitz with typical intemperance. Young's opening read, "Peter Seitz reminds me of a terrorist, a little man to whom nothing very important has happened in his lifetime, who suddenly decides to create some excitement by tossing a bomb into things."[33]

Other Options for the Owners

Were the owners really stuck in 1975 when there was no way to get Dave McNally to sign a new contract? What if the Expos had just released McNally, similar to what had been done in 1973 with the White Sox with Rick Reichardt and Mike Andrews and the Indians with Jerry Kenney? That would have made McNally a free agent but without setting a precedent that could affect others.

In a telephone conversation in February 2003, when this question was asked of Marvin Miller, he replied that he had never thought of the possibility. A follow-up letter to Miller the next month included the statement "McNally would have been a free agent without setting a precedent in the process" had the Expos released him. Miller replied, "Given the circumstances, I do not agree."[34]

Even if the owners could have indefinitely postponed a showdown before an arbitrator, the cost of heading off a challenge would probably have become increasingly expensive, as they would have had to continue to accede to the requests of players, no matter how extravagant they were seen by the owners, to keep them from becoming a test case.

It would appear that the owners had no good choices in hanging on to the reserve clause.

Of course, there had always been another way. All along, the owners could have superseded Paragraph 10A, the troublesome clause, by agreeing to modify the reserve clause through collective bargaining.

In fact, Seitz reportedly tipped his hand on his decision in the Messersmith-McNally case, urging the owners not to force a decision from him but to instead settle the matter in the negotiations then taking place for a new collective bargaining agreement. "That Seitz had urged negotiation was a tip-off of impending defeat [for the owners]," wrote Jerome Holtzman in the "Review of 1975" in *The Sporting News Official Baseball Guide*.[35] If true, it was tantamount to a jury letting a defendant know they were going to find him guilty, giving him the chance to instead cop a deal with the prosecutor. However, the owners pressed Seitz for a decision, even though they knew what it would be, opting instead to appeal his ruling in federal court.

What would the owners have been able to achieve had they bargained at this point rather than allow Seitz to rule on the matter? They probably could not have come out as well as owners in other sports, who did allow players to play out their options but with significant restrictions.

Since the early 1960s, the National Football League (NFL) had operated under a system in which a player could become free to sign with another team. However, the team signing the player would have to compensate the team losing the player with something of equal value (money, a draft choice, or another player or players). This meant that a player could only force his team to perform what was essentially a trade. In this sense, the freedom was limited, especially with regard to the monetary amount a player would be offered by a new team. Under such a system, salaries would still be severely restricted vis-à-vis what one could receive in a truly free market. (Because Commissioner Pete Rozelle would rule on the compensation one team would have to give the other if the teams themselves could not agree, the system became known as the "Rozelle Rule.")[36]

Marvin Miller said, "Once we had impartial arbitration, I would not have recommended anything except the most meaningful of reform," adding that he never would have settled for free agency that called for significant compensation, similar to the Rozelle Rule. But what if the owners had been willing to give something as early as 1968, during the negotiations for the first CBA? Would they have been able to have gotten a system similar to that of their brethren in the NFL? "The thing is," said Miller, "they never tried."[37]

Bowie Kuhn concurs that it was a mistake not to have been flexible on the issue while they had the upper hand and that he had urged the owners to negotiate.[38] But the executive contingent—particularly hard-liners such as Bob Howsam of Cincinnati, Paul Richards of Atlanta, August Busch of St. Louis, and later Allan "Bud" Selig of Milwaukee would not let this become a possibility.[39]

Even in 1975, with their own bargaining position significantly reduced as Seitz considered his ruling on McNally-Messersmith, the owners could have held on to some portion of player control through negotiation. Instead, once Seitz made his ruling, they had lost it all.

Aftermath

The first thing the owners did after the decision came down was fire Seitz, which was the right of either side to do at any time. Then, as expected, the owners appealed Seitz's decision to federal court. The appeal was based not on the decision itself but that the grievance procedure was not the proper forum for such a case.

"The owners had great confidence in their ability to prevail in the courts," said Miller, offering an explanation as to why the owners chose this route rather than accept Seitz's suggestion to work out their differences through negotiations.[40]

However, the owners were unsuccessful in their appeal, first in the U. S. District Court of the Western District of Missouri and then in the Eighth District Court of Appeals. They had the option of appealing to the U. S. Supreme Court, which they finally chose not to pursue.[41]

The legal challenges did not end until March 1976, which delayed negotiations on a new CBA, which had expired December 31, 1975. The new Basic Agreement would define the workings of free agency.

"Following the Seitz decision, all the owners could do was bargain with the players on the new Basic Agreement," said Miller. "This time, the players held all the cards, not that you could tell by the way the owners negotiated. They offered a reserve system that would allow players with nine years' experience to become a free agent after playing another season on a renewed contract. In other words, it would take 10 years—nine plus the option year—for a player to become a free agent." Miller added that the owners' proposal called for a player becoming a free agent only if his team did not offer him a certain salary. Other restrictions called for compensation to the team losing a free agent from the team that signed the player (along the lines of the NFL's Rozelle Rule) and a limit on the number of teams that would be eligible to sign a particular free agent. Miller was amazed at the chutzpah exhibited by the owners and said it was akin to Robert E. Lee showing up at Appomattox and trying to dictate terms to Ulysses Grant.[42]

With no agreement on a modified reserve system in sight, the owners ordered a lockout of spring training camps. In his negotiations, Miller faced pressure from the players in different ways. If he gave away too much, he could face litigation from players claiming that the rights gained by the Seitz decision had been abrogated by the new Basic Agreement. "I think the majority of players are willing to make a compromise on a retroactive reserve system," said Miller at the time. "But the arbitrator's ruling gave all the players certain legal contractual rights. Not every player would be willing to bargain these away."[43]

On the other hand, some players wanted the lockout ended, even at the cost of their newly gained freedom. Miller says he received a call from a member of the Houston Astros, telling him that something had to be done to end the lockout, even if it meant giving up the free-agent rights that the players had just received. Ken Forsch later called Miller to say that Houston general manager Tal Smith had coerced this player into making the call.[44]

Fearing a split in the players' ranks, Miller said the players would agree to a structured free agency along the general lines suggested by the owners. On March 17, Commissioner Bowie Kuhn ordered the training camps opened. The 1976 regular season started on schedule as negotiations continued.[45]

A new four-year Basic Agreement was reached in the summer of 1976, calling for free agency for players with six years of major league service after playing a year under a renewed contract. These players would go into a re-entry draft, in which a maximum of 12 teams, 13 starting after the 1977 season, would draft the rights to negotiate with the player. (The player's previous team would also retain negotiating rights to the player, and any player selected by fewer than two teams in the re-entry draft would be eligible to sign with any team.)

All players who had not yet signed a contract for the 1976 season would become free agents at the end of the 1976 season, and all players who had not yet signed a contract for the 1977 season would become a free agent at the end of the 1977 season, regardless of whether or not they had six years of service in the majors by that time. (This is how some short-term players, such as Lyman Bostock of the Minnesota Twins, were able to become free agents.)[46]

The new system called for compensation to a team losing a free agent, but it wasn't as significant as what the owners had hoped for. A team signing a free agent had to give the team losing the player one of its picks in the next amateur draft.[47] Dworkin notes that if the team acquiring a free agent was in the bottom half of the selecting clubs in the re-entry draft, it would have to give up its first pick in the upcoming amateur draft to the team that lost the player; if the acquiring team was in the top half of the re-entry draft, it would give up its second pick. Teams signing more than one free agent would give up draft choices in succeeding rounds. (Amateur draft choices in baseball are not as coveted as in some other sports, particularly football and basketball. Baseball players entering pro ball usually require time to develop in the minors and, in general, the prospects are more uncertain regarding how good the players will eventually be.)

The first re-entry draft was held November 2, 1976, and involved more than 20 players who had played on renewed contracts through the 1976 season. Two days later, Bill Campbell, a relief pitcher who had made $23,000 with the Minnesota Twins in 1976, signed a four-year deal for $1 million with the Boston Red Sox. Marvin Miller had expressed concern about the owners colluding to not draft and sign free agents, but his fears subsided as many other top players signed million-dollar deals with new teams over the next three weeks. Baltimore's Reggie Jackson was the last of the big-name free agents to sign and got $3 million for five years from the New York Yankees.[48]

This system of free agency lasted through the remainder of the CBA, which expired at the end of 1979. The owners were adamant in wanting more substantial compensation included in the free-agent system to be negotiated in the next Basic Agreement. The players were equally adamant in their opposition. A strike was averted in May 1980 only by deferring the issue of free agency for another year.

A strike did eventually come, wiping out the middle third of the 1981 season. It was finally settled with the agreement of a player pool to be used to compensate teams losing free agents. Teams could protect either 24 or 26 players in their organization (the number depending on whether or not they signed a Type A free agent, meaning one of the top players in the majors as established by a statistical formula). The rest of the players in a team's organization would be placed in the pool and could be drafted by a team losing a player to free agency. Up to five teams could exempt themselves from supplying players to the pool by forfeiting their right to sign a Type A free agent.[49]

The significance of the player pool was that it did not require direct compensation from a team signing a free agent to the team losing that player. The new agreement also ended the re-entry draft, and free agents were no longer restricted as to the number of teams they could negotiate with.

Owners' efforts to restrict player freedom and/or limit salaries continued, including some underhanded tactics. In the 1980s, teams operated in concert and adopted a hands-off policy with regard to signing free agents from other teams for the purpose of keeping salaries down. Arbitrators later determined that teams had conspired against free agents over the course of three offseasons, in violation of the collective bargaining agreement, and the owners had to agree to establish a $280 million fund to distribute to the players affected by the collusion.[50]

An attempt by the owners to impose a salary cap resulted in a strike that wiped out the final portion of the 1994 season, including the playoffs and World Series, and delayed the beginning of the 1995 season. The strike ended after the players lodged an unfair labor practices complaint with the National Labor Relations Board, which sought, and received, an injunction to restore the terms and conditions of the previous Basic Agreement.[51] Although the players fended off a salary cap this time, the owners were eventually able to create a "payroll tax" system, calling for a tax on salaries above a certain limit for each team.

Conclusion

The million-dollar contracts of the free-agent pioneers were significant, even if they look puny in comparison to ever rising salaries in the ensuing decades.

Salaries would have risen even without the abrupt demise of the reserve clause, in part simply because of inflation but also because, most likely, some freedom would have eventually been afforded the players through collective bargaining. Had the owners allowed modifications to the reserve system while they still controlled it, they no doubt would have held on to more than they have with their post-Seitz attempts to restrict salaries and player movement. Their attempt to gain substantial compensation in 1980-81 was doomed but might have been possible had it been offered earlier.

In his introduction to Marvin Miller's 1991 autobiography, Bill James summed up the futility of the owners: "From 1966 to this moment, the owners have been just behind the curve, always trying to get the players to accept today the offer that would have been acceptable yesterday and generous a couple weeks ago."[52]

ACKNOWLEDGMENTS

The author appreciates the help of Mark Armour and Bill Deane, who reviewed the content of this article for accuracy and made valuable suggestions. I am not a lawyer (although I have had the Miranda warning read to me more than once), so I am grateful for the input from SABR members Mitchell Nathanson and Larry Boes. Charles Korr also answered questions from me and contributed information. Special thanks to Marvin Miller, Bowie Kuhn, and John McHale, who consented to be interviewed.

NOTES

1. Al Kermisch. "First Reserve Clause Enacted 100 Years Ago" in "From a Researcher's Notebook," *Baseball Research Journal.* Cooperstown, NY: Society for American Baseball Research, 1979, pp. 9–10; Andrew Zimbalist, *Baseball and Billions: A Probing Look Inside the Big Business of Our National Pastime.* New York: Basic Books, 1992, p. 4. According to Zimbalist, the National League was "following the lead of the avaricious owner of the Boston club, Arthur Soden," who proposed baseball's first reserve clause. "His proposal secretly to reserve five players per team was adopted by the owners at a meeting in Buffalo, New York, on September 30, 1879. The number of reserved players was enlarged to eleven in 1883, twelve in 1885, fourteen in 1887; by the early 1890s the reserve clause had been extended to cover the contracts of all players."

2. James B. Dworkin. *Owners versus Players: Baseball and Collective Bargaining.* Boston: Auburn House, 1981, p. 63. Dworkin noted that although the clause had been amended slightly at times, the language presented is from the 1973 collective bargaining agreement, which Dworkin describes as "a fairly standard version of the pre-free-agency reserve clause." *The Sporting News Official Baseball Guide 1975*, p. 302, describes Section 10A of the Uniform Player's Contract: A club can automatically renew the contract of an unsigned player "for a period of one year" with the player entitled to at least 80 percent of his prior salary; *The Sporting News Official Baseball Guide 1976*, p. 285, Section 10A: "If, prior to March 1, the Player and the Club have not agreed upon the terms of the contract, then on or before 10 days after said March 1, the Club shall have the right by written notice to the Player to renew this contract for one year."

3. Interview with Marvin Miller, May 22, 2003.
4. *The Sporting News Official Baseball Guide 1968*, p. 168.
5. March 2003 correspondence with Marvin Miller.
6. Interview with Marvin Miller, May 22, 2003.
7. *The Sporting News Official Baseball Guide 1969*, pp. 174, 190.
8. Leonard Koppett. "Flood, Backed by Players, Plans Suit to Challenge Baseball Reserve Clause" by Leonard Koppett, *New York Times*, December 30, 1969, p. 42; Leonard Koppett, "Baseball Is Sued Under Trust Law," *New York Times*, January 17, 1970, p. 1; *The Sporting News Official Baseball Guide 1970*, pp. 302-307; *The Sporting News Official Baseball Guide 1971*, pp.272-278; *The Sporting News Official Baseball Guide 1972*, p. 296; *The Sporting News Official Baseball Guide*

1973, pp. 281-282; U. S. Supreme Court decision of *Flood v. Kuhn*, 407 U. S. 258 (1972), available online at http://laws.findlaw.com/us/407/258.html.
9. Korr, *The End of Baseball As We Knew It*, p. 246.
10. *The Sporting News Official Baseball Guide 1971*, p. 291.
11. Correspondence with Marvin Miller, March 2003.
12. Interview with Marvin Miller, May 22, 2003.
13. Bob Broeg. "The Simmons Case—A Touchy Issue," *The Sporting News*, July 8, 1972, p. 4.
14. "Cards Sign Simmons," *New York Times*, July 25, 1972, p. 29; Dick Kaegel, "Simmons Is 'Relieved' with 2 Year Contract," *St. Louis Post-Dispatch*, July 25, 1972, p. 1C.
15. *The Sporting News Official Baseball Guide 1975*, p. 303.
16. "Simmons Is 'Relieved,'" p. 1C.
17. *The Sporting News Official Baseball Guide 1974*, pp. 266–267.
18. Sid Hartman. "Kaat Signs," *Minneapolis Tribune*, April 6, 1973, p. 2C; Interview with Jim Kaat, April 19, 2003.
19. *The Sporting News Official Baseball Guide 1974*, p. 267.
20. "New Contract Assures Baseball 3 Years' Peace," *Los Angeles Times*, February 26, 1973, p. E1; 1974 *The Sporting News Official Baseball Guide 1974*, pp. 259–263.
21. Marvin Miller. *A Whole Different Ball Game: The Sport and Business of Baseball.* Secaucus, NJ: Birch Lane Press, 1991, p. 109.
22. "Lyle Signs with Yanks for 1975—and 1974," *Chicago Tribune*, October 3, 1974; *The Sporting News Official Baseball Guide 1975*, pp. 302–303.
23. "Baseball Avoids Showdown Over Reserve Clause," *Los Angeles Times*, January 14, 1975, p. D1.
24. Interview with Marvin Miller, May 22, 2003.
25. "Sports News Briefs: Tolan and Padres Agree on '74 Pay," *New York Times*, December 10, 1974, p. 62; Leonard Koppett, "A's Hunter Ruled Free Agent," *New York Times*, December 16, 1974, p. 51; "Catfish a Free Agent—His Price: Million Plus," *Los Angeles Times*, December 17, 1947, p. F1.
26. *The Sporting News Official Baseball Guide 1975*, p. 300.
27. Interview with Marvin Miller, May 22, 2003.
28. Interview with Marvin Miller, May 22, 2003.
29. *The Sporting News Official Baseball Guide 1976*, p. 285; Oscar Kahan, "Messersmith, McNally Attack Reserve System," *The Sporting News*, November 1, 1975, p. 8.
30. Telephone interviews with John McHale, October 31 and November 1, 2006; Miller, *A Whole Different Ball Game*, pp. 244–245; Korr, *The End of Baseball As We Knew It*, p. 152; "Dejected McNally Tells Montreal He's Retiring," *The Sporting News*, June 21, 1975, p. 30; Bob Dunn, "McNally Declares His Decision to Retire Is Firm," *The Sporting News*, June 28, 1975, p. 17.
31. Interview with Marvin Miller, May 22, 2003; Miller, *A Whole Different Ball Game*, p. 250.
32. "Baseball's Future Was Not Issue—Seitz," *Chicago Tribune*, December 24, 1975, p. A3.
33. Dick Young. "Baseball's Reserve Clause Is Dead . . . Maybe," *New York Daily News*, December 24, 1975, p. 38.
34. Telephone conversation, February 15, 2003, and correspondence, March 2003, with Marvin Miller.
35. *The Sporting News Official Baseball Guide 1976*, p. 290.
36. Paul D. Staudohar. *Playing for Dollars: Labor Relations and the Sports Business.* Ithaca, NY: ILR Press, 1996, pp. 65-83; Dworkin, *Owners Versus Players*, pp. 249–250.
37. Interview with Marvin Miller, May 22, 2003.
38. Interview with Bowie Kuhn, February 26, 2003.
39. Correspondence with Marvin Miller, August 2006.
40. Telephone conversation with Marvin Miller, February 15, 2003.
41. *The Sporting News Official Baseball Guide 1977*, p. 286.
42. Telephone interview with Marvin Miller, February 15, 2003; *The Sporting News Official Baseball Guide 1977*, p. 287; Miller, *A Whole Different Ball Game*, p. 255.
43. *The Sporting News Official Baseball Guide 1977*, pp. 287-288.
44. Interview with Marvin Miller, May 22, 2003; Miller, *A Whole Different Ball Game*, pp. 269-270.
45. *The Sporting News Official Baseball Guide 1977*, p. 291.
46. *The Sporting News Official Baseball Guide 1977*, p. 291.
47. Korr, *The End of Baseball As We Knew It*, p. 193; Dworkin, *Owners Versus Players*, pp. 86–87.
48. *The Sporting News Official Baseball Guide 1977*, p. 283.
49. *The Sporting News Official Baseball Guide 1982*, p. 11.
50. *The Sporting News Official Baseball Guide 1990*, pp. 20-21; *The Sporting News Official Baseball Guide 1991*, p. 25.
51. Murray Chass. "Labor Board to Seek Injunction against Baseball Club Owners; Action May Open the Way for Players' Return," *New York Times*, March 27, 1995, p. A1; "Backed by Court, Baseball Players Call Strike Over," *New York Times*, April 1, 1995, p. 1.
52. Miller, *A Whole Different Ball Game*, pp. xiv-xv.

Still Searching for Clutch Pitchers

More than two decades ago, Pete Palmer contributed what I think is one of the best baseball statistical analysis efforts ever done. The results were published in *The National Pastime* in 1985, in article entitled "Do Clutch Pitchers Exist?"

Palmer examined pitchers with at least 150 decisions between 1900 and 1983, accounting for how many runs each pitcher allowed, how many were scored on his behalf, and what his career won-lost record "should" have been based on that data. He was searching for "clutch" pitchers: men who won significantly more games than expected because of some unusual ability to pitch to the score and emerge victorious in the close games. With 23 years of additional data, and newly available research tools, now seems a good time to revisit this project.

The overwhelming majority of the time, a team's won–lost record correlates to the number of runs it scores and the number it gives up. It follows that the same is true about pitchers: if a pitcher has a winning record, most likely it is because he allowed fewer runs than average (reflected in his ERA), or his team scored more runs than average, or both.

There is another factor involved in statistical results: luck, or what statisticians call random chance. For example, if you flip a coin 100 times, you'd expect to get heads about 50 times, but you might get a little more or a little fewer than 50 just by luck. In fact, based on the laws of random chance, there is a 68% chance you'd get within one standard deviation of that total (between 45 and 55 heads), and a 95% chance you'd get within two standard deviations (between 40 and 60 heads).[1]

What Palmer found is that most pitchers wound up with about as many wins as they should have, with variations within those rules of random chance. In other words, if you win more games than expected, you're lucky, and if you win fewer, you're unlucky. His conclusion: "Clutch pitchers do not exist."

Palmer has updated and fine-tuned his research since then. For one thing, he essentially eliminated modern relievers, because their inclusion skewed the data. Many had much lower winning percentages than expected because of their usage patterns: entering almost exclusively with their teams ahead, they are more likely to suffer a loss than earn a win. Thus, Palmer's current study includes only pitchers (501 in all) with at least 200 starts and 200 decisions between 1876 and 2006.

In the original study, Palmer used a complex method to estimate a pitcher's run support, based on his innings pitched, his team's offense, his own batting performance, and the Linear Weights formula. Thanks to Retrosheet, he is now able to use actual run-support figures (though the figures are not broken down to show runs scored while the pitcher is actually in the game).

Nevertheless, the results of the updated study are very similar to those of the original, and produce the same conclusions.

According to Palmer's formulas, the number of runs needed to produce an extra win over the course of a season is equal to ten times the square root of the number of runs scored by inning by both teams. Using this theory, it is possible to project a pitcher's won-lost record based on the number of runs scored and allowed. For example, Johnny Allen made 241 starts in his career, during which his teams scored 1,393 runs, an average of 5.78 per game. Since Allen pitched a total of 1,950.1 innings (the equivalent of 216.7 nine-inning games) in his career, we estimate that his teams scored 1,253 runs (216.7 times 5.78) on his behalf. Meanwhile, Allen allowed a total of 924 runs, an average of 4.26 per nine innings. He thus projects to have had 329 more runs scored on his behalf than he gave up.

To figure out Allen's expected won-lost record, we need to determine the number of runs per win in his era. In this case, that number is ten times the square root of (5.78 plus 4.26 divided by nine), or 10.56 runs per win. We divide the 329 by 10.56, determining that Allen should have been 31.2 wins above .500. Since he had 217 decisions in his career, his projected wins are 31.2 plus half of 217, or 139.7. So Allen should have gone about 140–77 based on his runs scored–runs allowed patterns. In fact, his career record was 142–75.

Incidentally, Palmer has expanded his study to determine how many of a pitcher's "extra" wins (wins over .500) can be attributed to his pitching, and how many to his offensive support. For example, Whitey Ford, an excellent pitcher on a great team, finished with a 236–106 record, or 65 games over .500 (171–171). Palmer finds that 38 of those wins were attributable to Ford's pitching, 22 were courtesy of the Yankees' bats, and the other five were due to luck.

In a sampling of 501 pitchers, we would expect to find about 160 (32%) who finished more than one standard deviation above or below projection, 25

(5%) who finished more than two, and one (0.25%) who finished more than three. The actual totals are 161, 16, and zero (with Red Ruffing just missing, at 2.98), respectively. Thus, the results are about what we would expect from random chance, and there is no evidence of clutch pitchers.

Here are some highlights of the new study:

- Of 501 qualifying pitchers, 100 (20%) came within *one win* of projection (rounding off to the nearest integer). Only four pitchers were more than 15 wins off projection.

- Of the 161 pitchers who were at least one standard deviation off projection, 102 were over projection and 59 were under. Of the 16 who were at least two standard deviations off, 14 were over projection but only two were under. The average pitcher among the 501 was one win over projection. This could be because those who are "lucky" in the win column are more likely to get 200 decisions.

- Two of the three luckiest pitchers were named Welch: Mickey (+21) and Bob (+17). The unluckiest, by far, was Red Ruffing (-24). Table A shows the pitchers who exceeded projection by the greatest number of wins, while Table B shows those who came in under projection by the most. Table C shows the projected and actual records of some other pitchers of interest, including several commonly regarded as "clutch" pitchers.

- Several pitchers might have made the Hall of Fame, or at least become more serious candidates, had they only matched their projected records. They include Bert Blyleven (287–250 to 299–238; I think somehow he would have managed one more victory), Carl Mays (208–126 to 217–117), and Jim McCormick (265–214 to 280–199).

- On the other hand, Rube Marquard (201–177 to 195–183), Early Wynn (300–244 to 297–247), Happy Jack Chesbro (198–132 to 187–143), and Smiling Mickey Welch (307–210 to 286–231) might not be as Happy or Smiling anymore, on the outside of Cooperstown looking in.

NOTES

1. In this case—a binomial distribution—a standard deviation is the square root of $P \times Q \times N$, where P is the probability of success (50%), Q is the probability of failure (1 – P, or again 50%), and N is the number of tries (100). So the standard deviation here is 5. Finding the standard deviation (or sigma) for expected wins is a much more complex process, varying from pitcher to pitcher based on his number of decisions and his winning percentage. The average sigma in this group is 6.2 wins.

Table A: The Luckiest
(Most Wins over Projection, 1876–2006)

	W	L	Proj.W	DIFF	StdDEV
Mickey Welch	307	210	286.4	+20.6	+2.47
Greg Maddux	333	203	315.2	+17.8	+2.21
Bob Welch	211	146	194.2	+16.8	+2.52
Clark Griffith	237	146	221.8	+15.2	+2.17
Christy Mathewson	373	188	357.9	+15.1	+1.85
Roger Clemens	348	178	334.0	+14.0	+1.78
Harry Gumbert	143	113	129.0	+14.0	+2.43
Randy Johnson	280	247	266.4	+13.6	+1.97
Bill Hutchison	183	163	169.5	+13.5	+1.93
Ed Morris	171	122	157.9	+13.1	+2.12

Table B: The Unluckiest
(Most Wins under Projection, 1876–2006)

	W	L	Proj.W	DIFF	StdDEV
Red Ruffing	273	225	297.3	-24.3	-2.98
Jim McCormick	265	214	279.7	-14.7	-1.90
Dizzy Trout	170	161	183.7	-13.7	-2.12
Bob Shawkey	195	150	208.4	-13.4	-1.95
Walter Johnson	417	279	430.1	-13.1	-1.39
Bert Blyleven	287	250	299.1	-12.1	-1.43
Murry Dickson	172	181	182.9	-10.9	-1.61
Ned Garver	129	157	139.9	-10.9	-1.80
Sid Fernandez	114	96	125.5	-10.5	-1.91
Bob Friend	197	230	207.5	-10.5	-1.34

Table C: Others of Interest (Through 2006)

	W	L	Proj.W	DIFF	StdDEV
Grover Alexander	373	208	364.9	+8.1	+0.95
Bob Gibson	251	174	249.9	+1.1	+0.14
Sandy Koufax	165	87	160.8	+4.2	+0.73
Pedro Martinez	206	92	201.2	+4.8	+0.86
Nolan Ryan	324	292	318.5	+5.5	+0.67
Curt Schilling	207	138	210.4	-3.4	-0.45
Tom Seaver	311	205	305.0	+6.0	+0.74
John Smoltz	193	137	200.6	-7.6	-1.23
Warren Spahn	363	245	366.6	-3.6	-0.34
David Wells	230	148	222.6	+7.4	+1.02
Cy Young	511	316	511.9	+0.9	-0.10

In a clutch performance, BILL DEANE *pitched his team to the Cooperstown Co-Ed Softball League Playoff Championship in 2006.*

CORRECTIONS

RAIN CHECK

Clay Eals's article about Fred Hutchinson states that "In his last at-bat, in 1953, he homered." Bill Deane notes that Hutchinson hit the homer in the August 31, 1953 game in which he made his last pitching appearance, but that he played in another game at first base in late September, going 0-for-1.

THE NATIONAL PASTIME 2006

John Scott points out an error on page 99. It was not Eddie Collins scoring a run in 1917, it was Shano Collins.

In Frank Jackson's piece on spring training in Texas, he states that the Browns trained in Taylor, Alabama in 1920. This location has been published elsewhere as well, including *Total Baseball*. Following Jackson's article a project was started in Texas to put up plaques in all the towns that hosted spring training sites for major league teams. During the project research Steve Steinberg confirmed that the 1920 spring training location for the Browns was Taylor, Texas, northeast of Austin, and not Taylor, Alabama. This puts the Browns in Texas for 17 years, now just one behind the Giants, who were there 18 years.

Steinberg cites Sid Keener's column in the *St. Louis Times* of March 1, 1920:

BROWNS SHIVER IN COLD AT WINDY TAYLOR CAMP: TEMPERATURE IS TEXAS HEADQUARTERS IS COLDER THAN IN ST. LOUIS

"According to the natives, 'She's a-sho' going to be wahmah heah tuh-mawah'. . . . The folks who promised July and August weather to Bob Quinn . . . have been apologizing to [manager Jimmy] Burke, 'Havint nevah had nothin' like this befoah.'

"Taylor, Texas, on a Sunday night is located chiefly at the Blazilmar Hotel, where the folks, by heck, put on their dress togs and entertain with dinner parties. Outside of a Sunday dinner at the Blazilmar Hotel they say there isn't much stirring around here."

The Browns stayed at the Blazilmar Hotel in 1920. A link to an article on the hotel, which mentions the Browns' stay, can be found on the web.

The Rattlesnake Sacking Championships are held in Taylor, Texas each March.